A Lynched Black Wall Street

—Remembering 100 Years—

A Lynched Black Wall Street

A Womanist Perspective on Terrorism, Religion, and Black Resilience in the 1921 Tulsa Race Massacre

JERROLYN S. EULINBERG

Foreword by Lee H. Butler, Jr.

CASCADE Books • Eugene, Oregon

A LYNCHED BLACK WALL STREET
A Womanist Perspective on Terrorism, Religion, and Black Resilience in the 1921 Tulsa Race Massacre—Remembering 100 Years

Copyright © 2021 Jerrolyn S. Eulinberg. All rights reserved. Except for brief quotations in critical publications or reviews, no part of this book may be reproduced in any manner without prior written permission from the publisher. Write: Permissions, Wipf and Stock Publishers, 199 W. 8th Ave., Suite 3, Eugene, OR 97401.

Cascade Books
An Imprint of Wipf and Stock Publishers
199 W. 8th Ave., Suite 3
Eugene, OR 97401

www.wipfandstock.com

PAPERBACK ISBN: 978-1-7252-9603-9
HARDCOVER ISBN: 978-1-7252-9602-2
EBOOK ISBN: 978-1-7252-9604-6

Cataloguing-in-Publication data:

Names: Eulinberg, Jerrolyn S. | Butler, Lee H., Jr., foreword.

Title: A lynched Black Wall Street : a womanist perspective on terrorism, religion, and Black resilience in the 1921 Tulsa Race Massacre / Jerrolyn S. Eulinberg; foreword by Lee H. Butler, Jr.

Description: Eugene, OR: Cascade Books, 2021 |Includes bibliographical references.

Identifiers: ISBN 978-1-7252-9603-9 (paperback) | ISBN 978-1-7252-9602-2 (hardcover) | ISBN 978-1-7252-9604-6 (ebook)

Subjects: LCSH: Tulsa Race Massacre, Tulsa, Okla., 1921. | African Americans—Oklahoma—Tulsa—History—20th century. | Womanist theology. | Womanist ethics.

Classification: F704.T92 .E50 2021 (paperback) | F704 (ebook)

05/07/21

*I dedicate this book to
my precious mother, Mary V. Stephens,
whom I lost during the writing of this research.
Thank you for always being there and supporting me.*

*To my precious daughter, Meyon Ward;
granddaughter, Shatia Stephens;
sister, Wendy Fontenot;
and nephew, Jadon Fontenot,
who all supported me through this process.*

*To my God-given gift of a friend,
Rev. Dr. Teresa Smallwood,
who believed in me.*

Contents

List of Illustrations | ix
List of Tables | xi
Foreword by Lee H. Butler, Jr. | xiii
Acknowledgments | xvii

Introduction | 1

CHAPTER 1
The Making of a Promised Land: Native Americans, African-Americans, and the Black Migration | 14

CHAPTER 2
Agents of Resistance: The Black Migration Continues—Protest, Black Towns, and Race Theories | 31

CHAPTER 3
Black Wall Street and the Greenwood District | 55

CHAPTER 4
A Living Faith: Black Religion, Praxis, and Greenwood | 72

CHAPTER 5
The Hidden Secrets: Black Women's Resistance and Resilience | 92

CHAPTER 6
White Parties of Terror: Lynching Terror, Religion, and the Laws | 115

CHAPTER 7
White Parties of Terror Continue | 134

CHAPTER 8
A Lynched Black Wall Street: The 1921 Tulsa Massacre | 152

CHAPTER 9
Following the Massacre: Black Resilience | 181

Appendix | 201

Bibliography | 225

Illustrations

Trail of Tears Map | 17

Establishing All-Black Towns in Oklahoma | 36

Oklahoma State Map | 38

All-Black Towns in Twin Territories | 39

Langston City and Langston University | 40

The Williams Dreamland Theatre | 66

Laura Nelson and L. D. Nelson Lynching | 140

Newspaper Page in the Race Riot File | 153

Mt. Zion Baptist Church on Fire | 163

Race Riot Collection: Martial Law Declared | 173

Aftermath of Massacre | 174

Newspaper Headlines | 176

Tulsa's Black Businesses 1907–1923 | 201

Mabel Little House Greenwood Cultural Center Tulsa, Oklahoma | 202

Vernon African Methodist Episcopal Church (1 of 3 Historical Black Churches in Tulsa) | 203

Mt. Zion Baptist Church (2 of 3 Historical Black Churches in Tulsa) | 203

Mt. Zion Baptist Church (2 of 3 Historical Black Churches in Tulsa) | 204

First Baptist Church (3 of 3 Historical Black Churches in Tulsa) | 204

Mary Jones Parrish, The Events of the Tulsa Disaster: An Eye-witness Account of the 1921 Tulsa Race Riot | 205

Mabel Little Fire on Mount Zion | 206

Contrast of Black Tragedy and White Women | 207

KKK Brochures and Coin | 208

Article on Tulsa Bombing | 209

Aftermath Pictures | 210

Famous Historical Picture of Black Men Being Guarded After Massacre | 211

Historical Picture of Black Men Being Marched to Internment Camp | 211

Historical Picture Used Commercially for Postcards Mt. Zion Baptist Church | 211

Tents African-Americans Lived in After the Massacre | 212

Telegram from National Organization on Behalf of Black Tulsans | 213

Telegram from National Organization on Behalf of Black Tulsans | 214

Letter Written by the Governor Blaming W. E. B. Du Bois | 215

Monday, June 6, 1921—Sunday Sermon Referenced in Newspaper | 216

Actual Sermon by Bishop Mouzon, *Tulsa World* Newspaper | 217

Law Office Set-up in Tent to Fight Legally after the Massacre | 218

Freedmen and Freedwomen's Court Victory | 219

Yoruba Memorial and March Sample Flyer Advertisement for Remembrance | 220

1921 Black Wall Street Memorial (Located at the Greenwood Cultural Society) | 221

Unpaid Financial Claims | 221

Tulsa's Greenwood Street Today (OSU and Langston University's Tulsa Campus) | 222

Front Campus Entrance | 223

Tables

Table 1. Land Runs | 28
Table 2. Lynchings by Race and State | 120
Table 3. NAACP: Thirty years of Lynching in the United States | 126
Table 4. Ritual of Blood, 1882–1968 | 126
Table 5. Equal Justice Initiative, 1877–1950 Lynchings in the South | 127

Foreword

FROM THE DECLARATION OF Independence through the Continental Congress that developed the Constitution of the United States of America, freedom was the possession of any white American who staked a claim and owned land. The men that framed those founding documents regarded freedom to be embodied by white men and unfreedom to be colored bodies deemed less than human. As a result, whiteness represented privileged and defined white people as divinely blessed beings with dominion. This ideological embrace of freedom inspired the Revolutionary War and provoked the War Between the States. And although the Civil War ended in 1865, the dynamics of the postbellum period continued to challenge the meaning of freedom in the United States.

While there is a statement of progress undergirded by a social theory of change, I am more persuaded that there is a cyclical repeating of history being represented as new events that emerge from a forgotten or revisionist history. The State of Oklahoma and its City of Tulsa are a case studies on the meaning of freedom in the United States. First identified as a territory for Indian Nations through forced migration and redefined as a chosen destination for Whites and Blacks, Oklahoma became America's westward vision of the land of opportunity. The postbellum migrations from southern states in the east to Oklahoma, however, promoted a statehood grounded in segregationist ideas of freedom. The southern ideologies of separation and segregation became the national law of the land with the US Supreme Court decision on *Plessy v. Ferguson* (1896), the case that declared "separate but equal" to be constitutional. Yet, the case placed emphasis upon separation since equality is always determined by superior-inferior dynamics. The justices concluded that persons of African descent were never considered by the nation's founders to be equal with whites in America, neither in the Declaration of Independence nor the Constitution of the United States of America.

During the antebellum period, the "Black Codes" were experienced as an obligation among law-abiding white persons in America. Of course there were abolitionists and integrationists who opposed slavery in America, yet slavery, which was supported religiously and theologically, would not end without violent confrontation. Consequently, the postbellum period included the southerners' commitments to restore the South to its social hierarchy under slavery organized by a Christian theology of resurrection. The statement that "the South will rise again" was a religious declaration and a battle cry of a faithful adherence to segregation. Because southern culture includes Christian triumphalism, sacrifice is embedded in the southern psyche. This aspect of the southern socio-cultural experience of sacrifice was not a profession of self-sacrifice, rather it was a ritual of azazel sacrifice to petition God for their lifestyle to be restored. With crosses burning in the night, lynching emerged as the ritualized terrorism initiated during Reconstruction to restore the old South culture of slavery. As a ritual compulsion for petitioning god's favor, lynching declared a new era in American life to resolve issues of race and citizenship. An analysis of the 1921 Tulsa Race Massacre demonstrates that the United States has not always been as our pledge declares, "one nation, under God, indivisible, with liberty and justice for all." Rather, it has been a land that has wrestled with notions of separation, segregation, and equality throughout its young history.

Early twentieth-century Tulsa was an example of separate not being perceived as equal due to the racism that divided the city. Settled in 1828 by the Creek Indians in what was Indian Territory, Tulsa grew from being tribal land with a trading post, to a railroad stop for the cattle industry, to a site for urbanization during Reconstruction, to an oil town prior to statehood in 1907. Oklahoma culture blended Confederate ideology and Indian life mingled with an ideology of freedom that was articulated as self-determination. Because Oklahoma was inhabited by red, white, and Black bodies, freedom was color-coded. As a result, when freedom was defined on the color spectrum, it was enforced by acts of terrorism and ritual sacrifice as ways of preserving the white ideology of freedom that is deeply embedded in the national unconscious.

The City of Tulsa became an urban center of opportunity in Black and white as well as a prime example of living "separate but equal." With numerous Black towns populating Oklahoma, Blacks were quite content being equal in their communities separated from white culture. Unfortunately, when social equality is based upon "othering" and separation, the scales will always tip to declare inequality. This typically results in those seen as not "measuring up" being exterminated. It was the white Tulsans' inability to maintain separate but equal that provoked violence. The detailed descriptions of white Tulsan attitudes and actions suggests that white Tulsa could not live with the reality of Black Tulsa being equal. Because Black Tulsans were never seen as human beings able to measure up in the eyes of white Tulsans, Black Tulsa had to be utterly destroyed beyond restoration. The Tulsa Race Massacre, May 31–June 1, 1921, has been identified as the worst race riot in the history of the United States due to the extreme destructive behavior of the white citizenry.

The community of Greenwood, known across America as "Black Wall Street," was a bustling and economically thriving community. It was a self-determined all-Black community within Tulsa's city limits. Famed for having all the markers of any thriving metropolis—businesses, entertainment, professionals, health services, hotels, home ownership, and proud people—the Greenwood District was a shining example of African Americans living prosperously. The massacre began with a failed lynching of one young man that, in actuality, resulted in an entire cultural center being lynched. Popular descriptions of the massacre often misrepresent the context of the Greenwood District and the details of the violence.

Although separate but equal was the law of the land in Tulsa, separate and unequal was the unwritten law within the white Tulsan heart that participated in destroying the Greenwood District. Like a batterer justifying "his" assault by blaming "his" partner for provoking the violence, the white newspaper reporting and sermons that followed the massacre suggested that the destruction of Black Wall Street was actually instigated by Black residents and Black outside agitation. The outside agitator was identified as Dr. W. E. B. Du Bois, who visited Black Wall Street. Du Bois, who espoused racial uplift by a "talented tenth" and not armed revolution, was no doubt exalting Black Wall Street as a talented shining example of prosperity and self-determination. This description stood in stark contrast to the interpretation of events offered by Methodist Bishop Edwin Mouzon on the Sunday following the Race Massacre. He titled his sermon, "Tulsa's Race Riot and the Teachings of Jesus." His sermonic retelling of the Tulsa Race Massacre and the destruction of the Greenwood District concluded that peaceful whites needed to protect their community from immoral Blacks.

Mouzon was born in Spartanburg, South Carolina either just before or at the close of the Civil War. Although he was too young to know the institution of slavery firsthand, he was socialized to embrace the world slavery created, a Confederate world with deeply held beliefs on "nature and nature's God." His description of Tulsa reflected an imaginary paradise lost by the Confederacy. His description of the citizens of Tulsa having come from states in the North, South, and Midwest, who together created a new Western identity, was for him a shining example of an American city enjoying the fruits of its labor because it had embraced Jim Crow and not the integration proposed by Reconstruction.

Historically identified as the Tulsa Riot, the actions that decimated an entire community, which not only destroyed property but also resulted in mass murder, is more accurately identified as a massacre. Identifying the community violence as a riot, however, was more than a description of racial conflict. It was identified as a riot in order to prevent Black citizens from being able to make insurance claims on their losses. And just as the nature of the crimes against Black humanity were covered by descriptions of white innocence, the white Tulsans' assault on Black life have been largely hidden within American history. For instance, before Pearl Harbor was bombed by a Japanese aerial assault in 1941, Black Wall Street was bombed by a white Tulsan aerial assault in 1921. After Indian internment camps but before Japanese internment camps, African Americans who survived the assault in Tulsa were placed in a concentration camp like contraband during the Civil War.

As we now find ourselves at the centennial anniversary of the Tulsa Race Massacre, Jerrolyn Eulinberg takes a fresh look at the historical data surrounding the Massacre. Black Wall Street lives did not matter one hundred years ago. Using a womanist interpretive lens and the religious ritual of lynching, she reexamines the details of the massacre to offer new insights on the theology, morality, and hate that mediated the razing of Greenwood while never losing sight of the communalism and resiliency of the residents of Greenwood. She takes the reader on a journey to and through the 1921 Tulsa Race Massacre, pointing to the many lessons it has to teach America on race and citizenship, trauma and resiliency, violence and restoration, dignity and courage. May we all learn our lessons well!

Lee H. Butler, Jr., PhD
Vice-President of Academic Affairs and Academic Dean
William Tabbernee Professor of the History of Religions
Professor of Africana Pastoral Theology
Phillips Theological Seminary
Tulsa, Oklahoma

Acknowledgments

MY HEART IS OVERJOYED, and I am so thankful to the many people who supported me during my academic research. I would have never made it without your prayers, love, encouragement, and support.

This book is derived from my PhD research at Chicago Theological Seminary. Thank you to the many people in Tulsa who gave me interviews —Senator Maxine Horner; Senator Judy Eason McIntyre; Julius Pegues, Chairman of the Board for the John Hope Franklin Center; Bob Blackburn, Executive Director for the Oklahoma Historical Society; Hannibal Johnson, local author and attorney; Chief Ifalade Amusan of the Yoruba faith community; Ms. Hazel Smith, the last survivor in Tulsa at the time; Ian Swart at Tulsa Historical Society; Marc Carlson, Director of Special Collections and Archives at Tulsa University Library; Alicia Latimer, the African American Resource Coordinator at Tulsa Rudisill Library, Oklahoma State Tulsa Library; the Greenwood Cultural Center; and members from Vernon AME Church. All helped to make this book possible for the centennial celebration of Black Wall Street and the commemoration of the 1921 Tulsa Race Massacre. I also thank my mother, Mary Vernita Stephens, who clipped newspaper articles over the years and kept me abreast of Tulsa's events.

Thank you to my exceptional advisor, Dr. Lee H. Butler, Jr., who is now the Vice-President of Academic Affairs and Academic Dean at Phillips Theological Seminary in Tulsa, for his support and belief in me. Thank you for the many debates and your open door to me. I will be forever grateful for your academic excellence, time, pastoral quietness, and friendship.

I am thankful for the beautiful and outstanding womanist scholars who served on my committee: Dr. JoAnne Marie Terrell, thank you for demonstrating what it means to allow yourself to be vulnerable and to love so freely. Thank you for the special holiday celebrations at your home. Dr. Julia M. Speller, thank you for always being available to me. I appreciate your excellent guidance for the historical work and investigation of African-American women in religion and society.

Dr. Christophe Ringer, thank you for your enthusiasm, welcoming personality, and willingness to always engage me in the discussion of current events and cultural issues.

To the best colleagues anywhere—thank you, Dr. Teresa Smallwood, I will always thank God for you. Thank you for the years we shared with laughter, tears, and in prayer—being together with you made life worth living in Chicago. To Thomas Grinter, Malene Minor Johnson, Melanie Jones, Quincy James Rineheart, Benjamin Reynolds, and Howard Wiley: I would have been so lonely without your friendship. Thank you for good food, drinks, laughter, and prayers, not to mention the countless discussions on religion, theology, and domestic and international issues. Thank you to my many Korean colleagues, Song, Sunhee, and Giesok, with whom I spent intense hours of study over the years.

To the MDiv students who always made me smile as I watched their new commitments to the ministerial vocation: Thank you, Sherrie Phillips-Johnson, for supporting me and for your friendship, especially the semester after the passing of my mother. Thank you, Erica Weathers and Aris Simpson, for being wonderful, serious women of God. Tim Wright, I have never met anyone like you—thank you for your laughter and kindness.

I thank my wonderful church family at Greater Institutional African Methodist Episcopal Church. Thank you, pastor, Rev. Dr. Walter B. Johnson, for welcoming me and supporting me over the years in Chicago. Thank you, Dr. Sandra Womack-Johnson for your friendship as a kind first lady. To the beautiful women on the ministerial staff—Reverends Diane Bogues, Donna Anderson, Vickie Hayden-Lee, Anese Adams-Collier, Crystal Honesty-Wilson, and Loretta Reed—you are fabulous women of God.

To my family: I would not exist without your love; that is how much you all mean to me. Thank you, Meyon Ward, Shatia Stephens, Wendy Fontenot, and Jadon Fontenot for your understanding of the many years that I have spent away from you. I am a better person today because of you. To Rita Riley and Kevin Riley, thank you for encouraging me to pursue my desires.

Introduction

> Our objective is to use Walker's four-part definition as a critical, methodological framework of challenging inherited traditions for their collusion with androcentric patriarchy as well as a catalyst in overcoming oppressive situations through revolutionary acts of rebellion. Our overall goals in this project are to recast the very terms and terrain of religious scholarship.
> —KATIE G. CANNON
> *Katie's Canon: Womanism and the Soul of the Black Community*

> Being a Black woman in the academy necessitates that one knows who she is, whose she is, and how it is that she came to be if remaining sane, safe, and successful are her goals. Learning is not a luxury of Black women, nor is the academy an ivory tower. Our work is an endeavor of head and heart that is done for and with our communities in mind if not in tow.
> —STACEY FLOYD-THOMAS
> *Mining the Motherlode: Methods in Womanist Ethics*

OVERVIEW OF THE 1921 TULSA MASSACRE

THE TULSA MASSACRE OCCURRED over a two-day period in 1921, May 31, and June 1, against Black business owners, in the area known as Black Wall Street, and the residents of the Greenwood District. Tulsa had become a booming oil town, growing at the rate of seven and one-half times between 1890 and 1920, with the greatest expansion from oil in 1905. People were coming from the surrounding states and territories, both Black and white.[1] Although segregated from the white community due to the Jim and Jane Crow laws, the Black community had also grown rapidly and become quite prosperous. Oklahoma and the city of Tulsa were both known as the "Promise Land," or the place to get a new start. When Mary Jones-Parrish, author of the eyewitness account of Tulsa's tragedy, first visited Tulsa from Rochester, New York, she was impressed that there were so many Negro[2] businesses with such a harmony of spirit among them, and homes of splendor.[3]

Despite racism, this Black community of the Greenwood District was self-sufficient in providing goods and services for one another. In their Black community, they had nice homes, Black churches, schools, doctors, lawyers, dentists, movie theaters, clothing and grocery stores, beauty salons, and so on. White Tulsans, however, believed Black Tulsans had become too prosperous and that they were living too successfully. There are several theories regarding why the massacre occurred, but most agree on how it was ignited. On May 31, there was an attempt to lynch a young Black man, named Dick Rowland, being held in jail at the local courthouse for assaulting a white woman. As the white mob, totaling 1,500 to 2,000, gathered with their guns to take Rowland from the courthouse, Black World War I veterans assembled to protect Rowland and indicate there would be no lynching.

The massacre lasted about seventeen hours, killing countless people, burning down all the Black businesses and most of the African American residential community. It is reported the mob consisted of the Ku Klux Klan, local white residents who were not Klansmen, and other whites from surrounding communities, armed with guns and ammunition. An estimated 10,000 Blacks were left homeless, forcing them to spend the winter of 1921 to 1922 in tents. For years after the 1921 Tulsa Race Massacre, these two days were rarely spoken of. The Massacre was omitted from Oklahoma's approved history books, classrooms, and private conversations for decades.

I categorize this tragedy in Tulsa as a "massacre" rather than a "race riot" to emphasize the significance of what transpired on May 31 and June 1 in 1921. Race riots are uproars or incidents that occur between two opposing racial groups, usually resulting in some disagreements and conflict, or fighting. The magnitude of what occurred during these two days was certainly more devastating than a race riot. A massacre, on the other hand,

1. Ellsworth, *Death in a Promised Land*, 8.

2. The term *Negro* is used interchangeably with Black, African-American, and African American. I do not consider this term derogatory. Negro is being used in this dissertation as a historical racial category, the same as Black or African American is used today.

3. Jones Parrish, *Events of the Tulsa*, 7.

is undertaken with a deliberate and violent intent to kill, slaughter, or annihilate a large group of people based on racial hatred. This is what happened in Tulsa. Unfortunately, classifying or categorizing Tulsa's massacre as a race riot authorized the insurance companies to deny and reject all claims for the destruction of Black-owned property. Many Black Tulsans fled from the town, never to be seen again; others stayed and rebuilt, demonstrating the extraordinary presence of Black resilience.

REFLECTIONS

The year 2021 commemorates one hundred years since the 1921 Tulsa Race Massacre and historical legacy of Black Wall Street. One can imagine people everywhere are buzzing about the upcoming centennial celebrations. Tulsa had a groundbreaking ceremony in August of 2020 to celebrate the new museum—Greenwood Rising, which is under construction at the historical intersection of Greenwood and Archer. This exciting project will be completed in time for the centennial, but not open to the public until September 2021. Hip hop artists have already created an album entitled *Fire in Little Africa*, released February 2021. The title is a play on the pejorative phrase "Little Africa" used historically to describe the Black community of Greenwood, and the postcards sold by whites to show Tulsa on fire. There have been conversations of producing a movie, even as the television series *Watchmen* was released in 2019. The African American museum in Washington, DC also has an exhibit for Black Wall Street. However, I remember just a few years ago, only a limited number of people were talking about this historical place and tragedy in Tulsa because so many people had never heard about it.

The secrecy and silence surrounding Black Wall Street's lynching remained hushed for approximately seventy-five to eighty years. Although acknowledged by local survivors and longtime residents of Tulsa, the massacre was rarely spoken of. This historical narrative was referenced by some as a "conspiracy of silence." I grew up in Tulsa and I never heard or read about the massacre in those years. As a young girl, I attended Vernon African Methodist Episcopal Church, located right there on Greenwood. I often remember people saying Greenwood was once filled with thriving Black businesses. I simply thought, over time, they all eventually went out of business, but forty years ago people never explained the true destruction. Surprisingly enough, the history was not taught in high school. In fact, the high school I graduated from—Booker T. Washington—had served as the makeshift hospital for Tulsa's Black residents wounded during the two-day attack.

The first time I officially heard about the massacre I was sitting in one of my PhD courses, listening to my professor Lee Butler lecture, and reviewing the research results from the Race Riot Commission's report. I was devastated and I remember saying, "You cannot possibly be speaking about the city that I grew up in." Today, people of all races and backgrounds, from around the nation and even out of the country, have been intrigued and fascinated by the history of the 1921 Tulsa Race Massacre. Tulsa's public libraries and historical societies say they still receive calls daily—bringing questions about the disaster, and requesting research information regarding the tragedy.

As a womanist scholar, I embarked upon this research with a genuine need to interrogate the question: How should we understand the history of Black Americans and Black Tulsans in particular as we contextualize the future of Black life in America? As one investigates the socio-religious ethos that shaped America and the intrinsic racial dichotomy between white and Black America, this work has implications for interpreting the unethical and immoral sociological formation of America's cultural and racial bias, which not only dehumanized but criminalized the ontology of Blackness.

As a Black woman who personally experiences the injustices in American culture, I am continually forced to recognize the undeniable racial inequities operating against African-Americans in the social, political, and economic realms. I am outraged by the public lynching and police violence conducted on Black women and men over the last several years and certainly during the summer of 2020, against such people as Breonna Taylor, Ahmaud Arbery, George Floyd, and Jacob Blake. The Black minds, bodies, and African-American communities are constantly confronted with "post-traumatic stressors"[4] each time these public-square tragedies occur.

These tragic situations generate traumatic remembrances of historical realities such as slavery and lynching while living in a "protracted-traumatic world,"[5] which represents the evil in the world initiated through multiple forms of suffering such as incarceration and the killing of African Americans across the nation. This book seeks to present a way to better understand the ethical challenges of white supremacy and racism today by investigating a historical event through sociological analysis. I probe the horrific terrorism experienced by Blacks in the late nineteenth and early twentieth century and the unjust laws that gave it authorization. Yet, at the core of Black struggle is a Black theological praxis that subverts evil and perpetuates Black resilience.

4. Butler, "Lynching," 20.
5. Butler, "Lynching," 20–21.

My process explores through a womanist lens the moral dilemma of Black ontology and the existential crisis of living in America as human beings equal to white Americans. The interlocking systems of white hegemony continues to terrorize the life experiences of African Americans in our society. In Tulsa I examine race, gender, religion, and Black resilience at the intersection of terrorism, economics, and law, which legally sanctioned the violence against African Americans and historically helped to construct pejorative Black identities.

My purpose in writing this book is not just to tell about a one-hundred-year-old legacy of Black Wall Street, and the terrorism of white supremacy and racism that destroyed it, but to reveal for both the academic world and general public the opportunity to see the exceptional Black people who established the businesses on Black Wall Street, and the extraordinary citizens who lived in the Greenwood District during that time. Concomitantly, it is critical to see "traditional communalism" at work to construct Black resilience.

I am elevating this story from society's general gaze of telling some history to seeing the lived experiences of remarkable Black people, their brutal terrorism from racism, the agency of Black culture, and their determination not just to survive, but thrive. Trying to tell this deeply hidden secret with a few facts or blending fictional characters with some historical truths, we miss the whole story. I am repositioning reality into the theological, and ethical ethos, using a sociological analysis. I have investigated historical truths, while researching the social and legal components that frame this era in America history and trace the illumination of Black resilience. These components include race relations, economics, faith, religious praxis and its impact on American culture, Black survival and the unjust laws that have shaped this nation.

Moreover, interpreting the destruction of Black Wall Street through a womanist theo-ethical lens allows us to examine the socio-economic and political norms in Tulsa that operated to oppress and destroyed an entire Black community. I hope this research stimulates a consciousness for understanding how social injustice, and the ways in which it is so deeply entrenched into our American ethos through unjust laws and the cultural legality of white privilege, authorizes terrorism and freely discriminates against non-white races with impunity. The circumstances from the 1921 Race Massacre should not only make our nation ashamed of white supremacy, the racial hatred, and other discriminatory hierarchies, but create a new consciousness to work strategically toward eradicating these unresolved issues still at the center of our nation.

EXAMINING THE PROBLEM

This project examines the historical location known as Black Wall Street and the Greenwood District, which resulted in the "1921 Tulsa Race Massacre," to understand how acts of terrorism based upon race, gender, religion, and sexuality intersected with extreme violence leveled at the Black community in order to decimate its economic stability, disrupt its communal organization, and silence its religious expression. Whites in Tulsa, Oklahoma lynched Black Wall Street and the Greenwood District through mob action that resulted in bludgeoning, shooting, mutilating, and burning the bodies in the name of self-defense, yet always for pleasure. Whites used unjust laws and white supremacist domination to distort the motivations and responsible actors of the massacre. For years this historical tragedy was commonly referred to as the "1921 Tulsa Race Riot." However, Black Wall Street was the Black body that was lynched. The Tulsa Massacre also provokes questions regarding the ideology of freedom for African-Americans.

The Tulsa Massacre was the destruction of Black Wall Street, which was comprised of both a successful African-American business district and a residential community located in the Greenwood District of Tulsa. Recorded history references Tulsa as having one of the finest Black commercial districts and one of the wealthiest Black communities in the United States. The Black Wall Street area had 190 Black businesses, according to the Tulsa's Race Riot Commission's report. The community had two Black schools, two Black hospitals, and two Black newspapers—the *Tulsa Star* and the *Oklahoma Sun*. The area included more than thirteen churches, three fraternal lodges, two Black theaters, and a Black public library.[6] Other Black businesses included law offices, doctors, dentists, retail stores, grocery stores, drug stores, cleaners, and nightclubs.

Prior to this massacre, the nation experienced numerous race riots against African-Americans, dating back to the Cincinnati Riot of 1829, and possibly before, causing many to leave and relocate to Canada. It appears "race riots" were the modus operandi of white supremacy and hegemony toward Blacks in this country. America has a history and ethic of violence, which operates as terrorism to normalize power and control by the ruling class. In 1917, a terrible race riot occurred, called the "East St. Louis Riot." Whites attacked and killed Blacks over industrial labor opportunities in St. Louis, Missouri. Another series of well documented riots were known as the "Red Summer of 1919," consisting of more than three dozen race riots across the United States, but none quite as devastating as the Tulsa Massacre

---

6. Ellsworth, *Death in a Promised*, 14.

in 1921. The Tulsa tragedy has been recorded as one of the most racially violent acts of terrorism against African-Americans in American history.

Through a womanist lens I will examine the intricacies of the Tulsa Massacre as constructed by white supremacy, capitalism, patriarchy, sexism, and racism. This examination will reveal an interpretative parallel to the ways in which womanist ethics have elucidated the tri-dimensional oppressions from which black women have had to confront their oppressors historically. The examination will have a heavy emphasis upon the ways in which hegemonic power continues to reinforce the moral dilemma for African-Americans[7] to live and be treated as equal human beings with white Americans.

This book highlights the protracted trauma, the ideological tension in freedom and legal dilemmas created by the trauma, as well as the manipulation of the rule of law to circumvent punishment for the willful acts of violence and degradation by white against Black during the Tulsa Massacre. For example, when these violent acts of terrorism resulted in the destruction of property and loss of Black lives, victimized Black people were blamed for the malicious acts, jailed without due process, and unlawfully held against their will; when, in actuality, they were the targets and victims of the terrorism. White supremacy justified the Tulsa Massacre with the approval of state power, creating a dichotomy between Black bodies as innocent and Black bodies as always guilty, and therefore, punishable. This historical example adds to the discourse on the historical creation of pejorative Black identities as social constructs. Consequently, when the innocence of Blackness is juxtaposed against "blame" or the "accusation" of whiteness, the Black body is invariably found guilty. The Tulsa Massacre exemplifies this fact.

BLACK WOMEN'S LITERARY CONTRIBUTIONS TO HISTORY

According to the current literature and available resources, people began to write about the destruction of Black Wall Street and Greenwood District in the later twentieth century. However, Mary Jones Parrish, a Black woman and mother who lived in Tulsa at the time of the massacre, wrote the only eye-witness account in 1921, entitled *Events of the Tulsa Disaster*. In 2003 *Riot on Greenwood: The Total Destruction of Black Wall Street* was written by Eddie Faye Gates, a local high school history teacher, public school administrator, and curriculum writer. She also served on the Oklahoma Race Riot

---

7. When I use the hyphenated term *African-American* or *African-Americans*, I am referring to those who are further removed from the indigenous African homeland.

Commission in 2000/2001 and the Survivors Commission. Dorothy De-Witty wrote *Tulsa: Tale of Two Cities*. She was another educator who served as a principal and spent thirty years in Tulsa's public schools. DeWitty was a civil leader and member of Tulsa's first City Council. A few novels have also been written by women, but the other books about the Tulsa Massacre have all been written by men. My methodological approach is through a womanist lens, which is from a Black woman's perspective and experiences.

METHODOLOGY

I use a womanist interdisciplinary methodology of theology, ethics, pastoral psychology, and sociology to analyze the Tulsa Massacre. This combination helps me to interpret the ways discrimination and evil function to terrorize African-Americans and others. Defining *womanist* work and the tenets are important because they establish the collective and concise understanding when using the terms and identifying their impact on society. The term *womanist* was first coined by Alice Walker in her book *In Search of our Mother's Gardens: Womanist Prose*.[8] Ethicist Katie G. Cannon adopted a four-part definition (unpacked in the next section) and began to use it in the Christian Ethics discipline as a way to uniquely construct Black women's theological contributions to scholarship, by highlighting and expanding the voices of Black women's experiences, while simultaneously challenging the white normative narratives as not the only voices that have value in academic scholarship. Today the Womanist orientation is used across a wide variety of disciplines.

Katie Cannon's theory of the literary tradition and oral narratives are important components to my work because they offer insights into the Black communities. This is why Mary Jones Parrish's eye-witness account of the Tulsa tragedy is so important. "Most of the writing by Black women captures the values of the Black community within a specific location, time and historical context."[9] Cannon informs us that literature from Black women mirrors Black history. Cannon further states, "Black women writers convey the Black community's consciousness of values which enable them to find meaning, in spite of social degradation, economic exploitation and political oppression."[10]

The womanist lens is vital to interpreting the Tulsa Massacre for several reasons. First, womanism magnifies and appreciates the "traditional

8. Walker, *In Search of Our*, xi-xii.
9. Cannon, *Black Womanist Ethics*, 77.
10. Cannon, *Black Womanist Ethics*, 78.

communalism" praxis by African-Americans represented throughout this time in history. Second, womanism highlights the "critical engagement" of Black women and the "radical" ways in which they operated to effect societal transformation during a time when they had even less freedom and respect than today. Third, womanism focuses on "redemptive self-love" that it took to ignite a Black women's movement. Fourth, womanism and the Black woman's literary and oral traditions parallel Black history. Lastly, womanist sensibilities provide vital information regarding the Tulsa Massacre from a Black woman's perspective.

This book illuminates Black women and their contributions to the Black community and American society in the nineteenth and twentieth centuries. It further illuminates how phenomenal "womanist spirituality is a social witness,"[11] as defined by Emilie Townes. We can see how Black women accomplished their work through faith and the complete assurance that God was with them. I highlight Black women's contributions through religious efforts and social activism, beginning in the West and moving across the country. I exhibit Black women's activism through the women's club movement and the "politics of respectability." I also explore Black women's spiritual witness in society and across the nation. Finally, I examine the social, political, and literary work of women in Oklahoma, along with their commitment to preserve Black history with truth and power.

Womanist Four-Part Definition

The four-part womanist definition was expanded by ethicist Stacey Floyd-Thomas, a former student of Katie Cannon's, who created four new terms called "tenets." Each of these tenets corresponds to and represents each of the four parts of the original definition. The first tenet is "radical subjectivity"—which captures the intergenerational interaction found between mother and daughter, and agency of being outrageous, audacious, courageous, to be responsible, serious, and in charge.[12] Radical subjectivity speaks not only to my voice in desiring to pursue this project, but also to my belief that Black women's voices have been under-represented in the discourse of Black Wall Street and the Tulsa Massacre. I am convinced that the radical presence of Black women will contribute an important perspectival dimension to Black Wall Street, the massacre, the reconstruction of Greenwood, and the years that followed in Tulsa.

---

11. Townes, *In a Blaze*, 19.
12. Floyd-Thomas, *Mining the Motherlode*, 8.

The second tenet is "traditional communalism"—which encompasses not just writing about individual Black women's culture but the entire Black community, history, and culture:

> They render a better understanding of how black people collectively undo the historically constructed racist-sexist-classist-heterosexist ideologies that have homogenized them in ways that discount the variations of their humanity and that have deprived them of seeing themselves culturally as traditionally capable . . . even in the most oppressive circumstances.[13]

Traditional communalism is apropos for interpreting the massacre because the tenet speaks directly to the experience of the entire Black community of the Greenwood District before and after the massacre. I will investigate the role of African-American women to highlight distinctions regarding gender differences from a historical basis and for the Tulsa massacre.

The third womanist tenet is "redemptive self-love"—which calls women to love themselves regardless. Floyd-Thomas quotes: "Michele Jacques as saying 'the womanist call to love herself regardless is one of the most foundationally holistic and revolutionary political actions African-American women can take,' a call that is the hallmark of the womanist tradition."[14]

The fourth tenet is "critical engagement"—Womanist is to purple as feminist is to lavender, representing a deeper intensity of Black women's struggle. This tenet "obliges black women to critically engage their world at the intersection of their oppression since they have borne the brunt of social injustice throughout the history of the modern world."[15] Being critically engaged helps Black women move beyond the limitations of what is normative, seeking to expand resources and utilize all relevant components to explore and engage Black women's experience, while transforming their communities.

CHAPTER SUMMARIES

Chapter 1 explores how Native Americans and African Americans came to occupy the land that would later become known as the state of Oklahoma. I investigate the Trail of Tears, the Civil War, and the Emancipation Proclamation to understand the impact these historical events had on the Natives' and African Americans' relationships. I further explore the blood-mixing of

---

13. Floyd-Thomas, *Mining the Motherlode*, 9.
14. Jacques, "Testimony as Embodiment," 145.
15. Floyd-Thomas, *Mining the Motherlode*, 10.

the two cultures and the ethical challenges in America. Subsequent to the Trail of Tears, there were Black migration movements west to Oklahoma for freedom and dignity.

Chapter 2 continues to trace the Black migration movement west and social challenges associated with racism and survival. More specifically, I highlight the protest movement from Memphis to Oklahoma, initiated by three lynchings, and lead by Ida B. Wells-Barnett. The establishment of All-Black towns and Black Nationalism is sought to escape terrorism and create places of peace in Oklahoma Territory. Ultimately, the freedom of Black ontology, multiple Black migrations movements, and lynchings were the social antecedents to the ethical challenges and hegemonic conditions that existed leading to Tulsa's "two cities," one Black and one white. Finally, I use critical race theory to explore racial construction of social inequality and the interior world of Black life.

Chapter 3 presents the remarkable history of African-Americans in Tulsa and highlights some of the professional businesses. Tulsa had the most successful Black business district in America, called "Black Wall Street," which flourished from 1905 to 1921, and their residential community was called the Greenwood District. Black Wall Street was established during the epoch when African-Americans were lynched with impunity, and fighting not only against the hegemonic conditions of Jim and Jane Crow, but also white hatred, economic access, and jealousy of Black accomplishments.

Chapter 4 explores the multiple components that contributed to Black faith praxis in Tulsa and across the nation. I highlight some African American religious claims and philosophies, from their African God to Black Christianity, that influenced and helped to shape a broad African American religious culture. Tulsa currently has several historical churches from the Black Wall Street era still serving the Black community. I probe what impact Negro religion and theological understandings had, and how it sustained people in the community of Greenwood. One window into Black religious belief is to investigate specific denominations. In this chapter I trace the African Methodist Episcopal Church's historical religious philosophies to better understand the roots of Vernon AME Church in Tulsa and some faith claims of the denomination. Finally, I explicate womanist "traditional communalism" and the success of Black Wall Street.

Chapter 5 magnifies the role of African-American women in history, which is often overlooked or simply forgotten, particularly in the late nineteenth and early twentieth centuries. I highlight what roles and contributions Black women in religion and society made across the nation. I investigate the role of Black women in the West to understand how their agency, as a social witness, had significant impact on the flourishing of communal development and Black resilience, particularly in Tulsa. I examine African-American women in the women's club movement, as it found expression in Oklahoma and initiatives related to Tulsa. Finally, I highlight Black women's participation in the various businesses of Black Wall Street and illuminate the contributions they made to the Greenwood District community, with particular emphasis upon The Mabel L. Little House as an enduring contribution.

Chapter 6 investigates the heinous acts of terrorism through lynching for African-American women, men, and children in the late nineteenth and early twentieth centuries. I examine the laws, social characteristics of influence, and statistics that define or highlight the most intense span of the era. I further examine what the religious implications and rituals of lynching represented for white Americans. Remembering that the Tulsa Massacre was ignited by the white community's attempt to lynch young Dick Rowland is critical.

Chapter 7 continues to investigate the lynching terrors of human sacrifice and the controversial involvement of the KKK in Tulsa's massacre. A deeper plunge into the psychology of lynching reveals the ongoing trauma associated with "violence of death" for African Americans. I ask the question, how did lynching become such an acceptable practice in the white American psyche? Lastly, I explore some womanist perspectives on suffering and Black blood sacrifice, ending with comments from James Cone's *The Cross and the Lynching Tree*.

Chapter 8 outlines one of the worst racial tragedies of white violence in American history. I briefly present the social milieu and racial conflicts that existed around the nation prior to the massacre. The research shares the excuse that white Tulsans attempted to give about what spawned the massacre—the age-old claim of rape. The Black community presents a vastly different experience. The role from the newspaper media also assisted in helping to ignite this pogrom. The research reveals through pictures, newspaper headlines, and the aftermath how African-Americans in Tulsa were tortured by white supremacy and the moral evil found in racial hatred. I present the unspeakably detailed experiences of this two-day massacre, which remained quiet for almost eighty years, suffered by the Negro community.

Chapter 9 concentrates on the aftermath of the massacre. A sermon from a Methodist Bishop gives us insight into the white church, and a white religious perspective following the massacre. I also share the grand jury report and who was blamed for the tragedy. I illuminate the role of traditional communalism, as well as the Black resilience of African American people in the months and years that followed. The ongoing tragedy here requires a white American consciousness to understand that this deeply embedded racial hatred and continued lived practice of white supremacy and privilege is still alive and at work in structural racism and the social structures of oppression that it created.

CHAPTER 1

The Making of a Promised Land
Native Americans, African-Americans, and the Black Migration

> The colonized, underdeveloped man (sic) is a political creature in the most global sense of the term.
> —FRANTZ FANON
> *The Wretched of the Earth*

OKLAHOMA TERRITORY

OKLAHOMA CAME INTO EXISTENCE through the massive influx of many different Native American tribes as they were expelled over the years from their various homelands across the nation. Arthur Tolson investigates tribes that were moved from upper Louisiana across the Mississippi River from as early as the 1790s through the 1830s.[1] Yet many other Indian tribes came from the southeastern sector of the United States. Some of the first tribes in Oklahoma were Kickapoos, Delawares, Shawnees, Osages, and Cherokees. As time passed, another sixty-two Native American tribes would come. The

---

1. Tolson, *Black Oklahomans*, 20.

forcible and painful removal of Indians from their tribal and ancestral land is known as the Trail of Tears.[2]

The Trail of Tears was initiated by the Indian Removal Act in 1830 to uproot the Native Americans. The Indian tribes included Cherokees, Chickasaws, Choctaws, Muscogee (Creek), and Seminoles.[3] The federal government decided in 1825 to move the Indians from their land in order to make room for the gold rush and white settlement. It was President Andrew Jackson who was determined to implement the Act. "The prospect of forcing Indians to the West horrified many Americans, and petitions opposing removal poured into Congress in opposition to removal, but in the end, they could not stop the ethnic cleansing that took place."[4] This moment in history is reflective of Homi K. Bhabha's foreword to Fanon's *Wretched of Earth*, in which he highlights one of "Fanon's most quoted (and quarreled over) passages":[5]

> The singularity of the colonial context lies in the fact that economic reality, inequality, and enormous disparities in lifestyles never manage to mask the human reality. Looking at the immediacies of the colonial context, it is clear that what divides this world is first and foremost what species, what race one belongs to. In the colonies the economic infrastructure is also a superstructure.[6]

Fanon's quote represents not only one of America's ethical and historical challenges, but also the political, social constructs and hegemonic power being exercised domestically and globally today. The Trail of Tears unfolded from this type of conflict.

The Indians' native lands occupied Georgia, Tennessee, Alabama, Mississippi, North Carolina, and Florida.[7] President Andrew Jackson was excited about the Removal Act because of the wealth and population growth. As the gold rush grew so did the hostility in the state of Georgia. In 1831, the Cherokee Nation had major conflict with the State of Georgia and they took their suit to the United States Supreme Court. The question was whether "the Court had original jurisdiction to hear a case filed by a tribe against a

---

2. The exact length of time that the Trail of Tears lasted seems to vary from different authors. Many seem to reference Native Americans being removed from their tribal lands before the official removal Act of 1830.

3. Johnson, *Apartheid in Indian Country*, 21–23.

4. Perdue and Green, *North American Indians*, 55.

5. Fanon, *The Wretched*, xiii.

6. Fanon, *The Wretched*, xiii.

7. Johnson, *Apartheid in Indian Country*, 23.

state."⁸ In other words, was the Cherokee Nation a domestic dependent nation, sovereign state, or foreign nation? Hannibal Johnson outlines the legal aspect. The Court heard the cases under *Cherokee Nation v. Georgia* and *Worcester v. Georgia*. The Court ruled in favor of Georgia's state law, saying the Cherokees were not a state or foreign nation.

The case *Worcester v. Georgia* was the follow-up to *Cherokee Nation v. Georgia*. "Under an 1830 law, Georgia required all white residents in Cherokee country to secure a license from the governor and to take an oath of allegiance to the state."⁹ When two missionaries who supported the Indians refused to get those licenses, they were convicted by the state. They appealed their case to the Supreme Court. The Court reversed their decision in the *Cherokee Nation v. George* by making the following rulings: "1) Indian nations are capable of making treaties, 2) under the Constitution, treaties are the supreme law of the land, 3) the federal government had exclusive jurisdiction within the confines of the Cherokee Nation and 4) state law had no force within the Cherokee boundaries."¹⁰ After all of this controversy, Native Americans were still victims of white political hegemony.

President Jackson and the state of Georgia ignored the Court's ruling and moved forward, eventually approaching Indians with new treaties. The forced removal was painful for all the tribes and many resisted. Donna L. Akers investigated and "found [that] Choctaw religious beliefs about appropriate care for the bones of ancestors helped explain that tribe's refusal to sell tribal lands, sometimes even upon pain of death."¹¹ Unfortunately, much of the pain and human suffering from the terror is untold. "The Chickasaws acquiesced, the Seminoles fought removal for almost three decades, and a group of Cherokees, thought by some to be renegades, ultimately signed a removal treaty."¹² Only a small fraction of the Cherokees Nation, called the "Treaty Party," negotiated and signed the New Echota, which ceded Cherokee land to the government and sealed an agreement to move west. "The Treaty Party sold the eastern lands of the Cherokees for $5 million in exchange for seven million acres of land in present-day Oklahoma."¹³ In 1838, President Martin Van Buren initiated the treaty agreement movement with United States Army troops.

---

8. Johnson, *Apartheid in Indian Country*, 24.
9. Johnson, *Apartheid in Indian Country*, 24.
10. Johnson, *Apartheid in Indian Country*, 24.
11. Johnson, *Apartheid in Indian Country*, 21.
12. Johnson, *Apartheid in Indian Country*, 25.
13. Johnson, *Apartheid in Indian Country*, 25.

When the process began, Cherokees were moved from Georgia, North Carolina, Alabama, and Tennessee to fort stockades and later into internment camps. Finally, after an appeal to the president by one of the chiefs, they were allowed to direct their own removal. As Hannibal Johnson explains in *Apartheid in Indian Country?*, the Native Americans were divided or sectioned into sixteen different groups, each consisting of approximately one thousand people. Some traveled by the river on steamboat. Others traveled by land; the aged, sick, and many of the children were in wagons but the others walked. The map below exhibits that each of the Native American tribes traveled different routes into Oklahoma Territory on the Trail of Tears. According to Tolson, the removal lasted twenty-five years.[14] The Indian tribes were truly victims of manifest destiny.

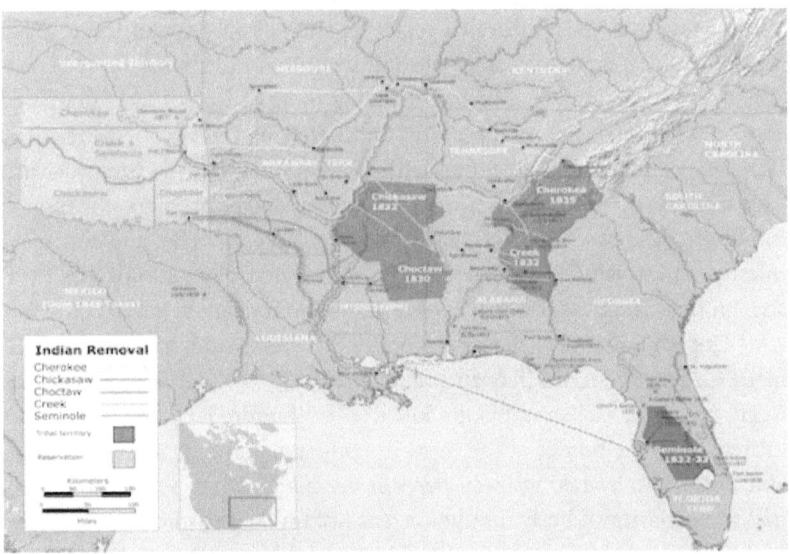

Figure 1. Trail of Tears Map. Scale not given. In: William C. Sturtevant, Wilcomb E. Washburn, eds., *Handbook of North American Indians*. Vol. 4: *History of Indian-White Relations* (Washington, DC: Smithsonian Institution Press, 1988).

Manifest destiny is best described by the terms *hegemony* and *imperialistic expansion*. It is the ability of a particular group or nation to dominate others and the power to take control. Richard Hughes explicates manifest destiny in his chapter "The Myths of a Chosen Nation," which highlights how the United States government believed they had the right to all privileges of the American land, regardless of who occupied the land or who it

---

14. Tolson, *Black Oklahomans*, 21.

belonged to.[15] Hughes and many others argue that during the formation of the American colonies in the seventeenth century, Puritans believed that their arrival on American soil was somehow connected with being a "chosen people." This ideology was embraced by the Puritans' biblical understanding and covenant with God to carry out a Christian mission living in America. By the mid-nineteenth century, the concept of manifest destiny made God a puppet in the hands of America. Puritans believed they were not only a chosen people, but rightfully a deserving people who exemplified God's will in this new nation. Manifest destiny was also derived from the myth of "Nature's Nation," which argued unalienable rights are for all men; however, that argument really meant only for certain men. Some men were more deserving of those rights than others.[16]

When we observe the Native Americans being removed from their home lands in the southeastern sector of the nation, we can understand that "manifest destiny ultimately meant the virtual extermination of Native American peoples, and no one contributed more to that process than Andrew Jackson, president of the United States from 1829 to 1837."[17] President Jackson's administration worked with people interested in profiting and gave contracts to people who provided substandard provisions for the removal of Choctaws. "Blankets were threadbare, meat rancid, and cornmeal infested with weevils. Thousands sickened and died, generating a death toll so high that Congress ordered investigation and reform."[18]

Hughes elaborates that, even before he was president, "Jackson had made a name for himself as an Indian fighter. In the 'Battle of Horseshoe Bend' in 1814, Jackson's troops killed eight hundred Creeks."[19] Jackson looked on as the bodies of the men, women, and children were massacred and mutilated, by taking body parts as tokens.[20] This type of white, animalistic behavior of body mutilation was not unlike the treatment of Black bodies during public lynchings. I will further address this in chapter 4. Historian Howard Zinn states that Jackson managed to be appointed as treaty commissioner and then constructed a treaty that took half of the Creek nations' land.[21] "Then, in 1818, Jackson's troops inflicted a devastating defeat

---

15. Hughes, *Myths America Lives By*, 109–10.
16. Hughes, *Myths America Lives By*, 109–10.
17. Hughes, *Myths America Lives By*, 114.
18. Perdue and Green, *North American Indians*, 57.
19. Hughes, *Myths America Lives By*, 114.
20. Hughes, *Myths America Lives By*, 114.
21. Zinn, *A People's History*, 127, quoted in Hughes, *Myths America Lives By*, 114.

on the Seminoles (Creek refugees), thereby preparing the way for Florida to become a territory of the United States in 1821."[22]

The Trail of Tears narrative, which has been told over the years, unfortunately is not limited to just the horrifying experiences of Native Americans. The other half of the untold story includes their relationship with African-Americans, some of whom were enslaved by the Native Americans and others who were freedmen and freedwomen. The relationship of Native Americans and African Americans has a long history of intermingling. In fact, by the end of the Civil War, many African-Americans acquired tribal citizenship rights within the Five Civilized Tribes. As the Native Americans left their lands in the eastern sector of the United States and traveled to the new Indian Territory, which would later become the State of Oklahoma, many enslaved African Americans were part of that arduous journey. Taylor writes, "Slaves who traveled along the Trail of Tears performed labor that reduced the suffering experience by slaveholding Indians during the removal. They hunted game, worked as teamsters, cooks, and nurses, tended livestock on the trail, and guarded the camps at night."[23]

Africans were a part of the Indian culture and they also knew Indian languages; they were able to move between the red and white world. Quintard Taylor explains that Black slaves in Indian Territory also had special skills as language translators. "An unnamed African-American woman in 1832 translated for Washington Irving and Charles Latrobe when they visited the home of a Cherokee farmer."[24] Another Black woman who interpreted for the Cherokees was puzzling to some onlookers as they observed her skills and recorded, "The spectacle seems strange . . . no doubt, the coal black girl speaking both English and Cherokee and keeping the old woman informed as to what was being said."[25] African-Americans made great contributions to the Indian culture and certainly on the Trail of Tears but many African-American lives were lost on the journey.

Johnson records, "Indeed some claim African-Americans made up some 15 percent of those who died on the Cherokee Trail of Tears."[26] He explains,

> We can rest assured that whenever faces gathered around the campfire, there were Africans there to serve as spiritual guides

---

22. Hughes, *Myths America Lives By*, 114.
23. Taylor, *In Search of the Racial*, 64.
24. Taylor, *In Search of the Racial*, 67.
25. Taylor, *In Search of the Racial*, 67.
26. Minges, *Beneath the Underdog*, 9–10, quoted in Johnson, *Apartheid in Indian Country*, 28.

into a different kind of wilderness. When there were dances to celebrate, deaths to mourn, or festivals to mark the passing of the seasons, there were Africans present. In addition, we must never forget that on the 'trail where we cried' there were also African tears. This we can never forget.[27]

Cherokee Indians reference their Trail of Tears with the name *Nunna daul Tsunyi*, which means "the trail where we cried."[28] This is how the first African-Americans entered into Indian Territory.

OKLAHOMA DURING THE ANTEBELLUM PERIOD

African Americans had a significant presence among the Indian Nations because "Indian Territory comprised the second largest slaveholding region in the West."[29] Taylor outlines that the Five Civilized Tribes were the only Native Americans out of 500 other tribes that held Blacks in bondage.[30] Indian Territory at this point in history was much larger than just Oklahoma; the land occupies several non-formed states in the West. Although the Seminoles fought for a while, when they were defeated by US troops in 1842, they brought the largest percentage of Black slaves to Indian Territory among the Five Nations. By 1860, there were approximately 10,000 enslaved African-Americans in Oklahoma and the treatment they received varied from kind to harsh.[31] "The Chickasaws, for example, were known as avid slavecatchers, hunting down black fugitives with special vigor. The Seminoles, by way of contrast, never practiced chattel slavery . . . Seminoles never enacted slave codes, which prevented slaves from carrying weapons or owning property."[32] Other slaveholders in the Nation feared the Seminoles' practices and better treatment of their slaves because of these looser restrictions.

Eventually some slave revolts occurred, but the Seminoles experienced less resistance because of their more humane treatment to their slaves. Several of the Indian Nations experienced revolts; the Cherokee Nation had three: 1841, 1842, and 1850. The Creek and Choctaw slaves participated in the 1842 revolt. According to *African-American Women Confront the West*,

---

27. Johnson, *Apartheid in Indian Country*, 28.

28. Mankiller and Wallis, *Mankiller*, 46, quoted in Johnson, *Apartheid in Indian Country*, 22.

29. Taylor, *In Search of the Racial*, 62.

30. Taylor, *In Search of the Racial*, 62.

31. Johnson, *Apartheid in Indian Country*, 67.

32. Johnson, *Apartheid in Indian Country*, 67.

"Approximately four thousand black women were held in bondage by Native Americans in Indian Territory in 1860."[33] The fate of African-American slaves would drastically change following the Civil War.

On the heels of the Civil War, Indian Territory was established with capitals for each tribe and forts were established to be maintained by US troops for protection, according to the Indian treaties. The conflict of slavery divided the nation; the war was fought over four million slaves from 1861 to 1865.[34] "When the Civil War began, the South wanted to secure an alliance with the Five Civilized Tribes in Indian Territory, who numbered about 62,500."[35] It appears the Five Civilized Tribes wanted to remain neutral because the majority of them were not slaveholders, only an elite group of about 1,338 owned 7,369 Black slaves.[36] The neutrality did not last long, though; the Indians were pressed from both the Confederate and the Union sides. The tribes were split with their alliances. The Choctaws had about 3,000 slaves and they allied with Confederacy to the end of the war. The Cherokees' Black slaves were down from 2,504 to about 1,500 when the war began. Creeks and Seminoles were forced to leave for Kansas seeking protection from the war.[37] The Civil War was a battle in which Native Americans, former slaves, and whites fought with, and against, one another:

> The Civil War exacted a terrible toll on the nation. Native Americans could not escape the suffering. Virtually all the tribal communities that fought in the Civil War suffered death and destruction as a direct consequence. In fact, greater losses occurred in Indian Territory than in any state. Of the 3,530 men from Indian Territory who served in the Union Army, a staggering 1,018—nearly one third—died during enlistment.[38]

The results following the Civil War changed our nation forever. The Five Civilized Tribes would sign new treaties with the United States, former enslaved Africans would receive tribal citizenship rights, and Black slaves would be emancipated.

The Emancipation Proclamation in 1863 was slightly ambiguous in the execution because it did not free all slaves simultaneously. The Thirteenth Amendment, which was later adopted in 1865, freed all remaining slaves except those in Indian Territory. Slavery continued in Indian Territory until

33. Taylor and Moore, eds., *African-American Women Confront*, 6.
34. Tolson, *Black Oklahomans*, 32.
35. Tolson, *Black Oklahomans*, 32.
36. Tolson, *Black Oklahomans*, 32.
37. Tolson, *Black Oklahomans*, 36–37.
38. Johnson, *Apartheid in Indian Country*, 37.

1866, when the Five Nations signed treaties with the US government.[39] "The Post-Civil War Treaty of 1866 guaranteed most of the 7,000 emancipated persons of African descent tribal citizenship rights within the Five Civilized Tribes."[40] All of the tribes except the Chickasaw shared tribal citizenship rights with the freedmen and freedwomen; however, initially the Choctaws refused. Each Nation provided different degrees of acceptance. Seminoles elected Blacks to their Seminole Council. Blacks built homes, churches, schools, and businesses. In other Indian Nations, they worked for land ownership. Blacks rarely left their Nation because the treatment within could not compare to what they would experience in white society.

The government signed treaties with the various Nations. The following is an example of how "Article 4" read in the Treaty of 1866 with the Cherokee Nation:

> All the Cherokees and freed persons who were formerly slaves to any Cherokee, and all free negroes not having been such slaves, who resided in the Cherokee nation prior to June first, eighteen hundred and sixty-one . . . shall have the right to settle in and occupy . . . a quantity of land equal to one hundred and sixty acres for each person who may so elect to reside in the territory above-described in this article.[41]

Under the new treaties among Creeks, Seminoles, and Cherokees, Blacks thrived in building business, homes, churches, and so forth in a way they could not have in the white community.

The Treaty of 1866 made a significant difference in the lives of newly freed African-Americans through land ownership, council opportunities, and even through the right to sue in court disputes against the Cherokee Nation. The Treaty had importance for over one hundred years, especially to freedmen and freedwoman; but as time elapsed some challenges developed around race authenticity. When Hannibal Johnson writes the chapter on "A Legacy of Mixing and Matching" among the Indian and Black race relations, he explores their interaction prior to the Civil War. Johnson found that although race mixing was taboo in early American history, for years the Native Americans and African-Americans cohabitated through marriage, tribal citizenship, and the like.

They even worshipped together: "The first Baptist Churches—Amohee Baptist Church with the Cherokee Nation, and Ebenezer Baptist Church within the Creek Nation were mixed congregations often led by Black

---

39. Johnson, *Apartheid in Indian Country*, 37–39.
40. Johnson, *Apartheid in Indian Country*, 38.
41. Johnson, *Apartheid in Indian Country*, 39.

Baptist preachers."[42] The Fountain Baptist Church (also known as Ebenezer Baptist Church) was the first church established in Oklahoma.[43] The church was built in 1832 by people of African descent living in community with Muscogee (Creek). The location later became one of the all-Black towns, called Marshalltown. They were still having services as of 2012.[44] Following European incursions, things began to change. "Clan and national identities, rather than race, defined individuals in early native cultures. Whites infected Native Americans with the plague of racism. Once exposed, too few Native Americans sought to check the spread of this scourge."[45] Racism definitely created a wedge between two cultures that, prior to the Civil War, lived amiably together.

THREE RACES AND OKLAHOMA STATEHOOD

White supremacists were the carriers of an infectious plague, called racism, and the plague spread everywhere. I introduce two thinkers who are helpful in offering clarity for the plague, which distorted race relations between these two cultures. First, George Kelsey, in the book *Racism and the Christian Understanding of Man*, offers a theological perspective for a sociological analysis on racism when he argues, "racism is a faith."[46] He explains racism as a form of idolatry and alienation that divides human beings by defining one as the "out race,"[47] while defining the dominant race as the acceptable race. With this perspective, white Americans influenced the Native Americans to believe the African-Americans were the out race. Kelsey continues to posit this by explaining the "faith character of racism" through H. Richard Niebuhr's definition of faith, which states "trust in that which give value to the self,' on the one hand; and on the other, 'it is loyalty to what the self values.'"[48] Finally, Kelsey posits a way to understand the "meaning of racism" as disclosed in Ruth Benedict's *Race: Science and Politics*:

> The dogma [is] that one ethnic group is condemned by Nature to hereditary inferiority and another group is destined to hereditary superiority. It is the dogma that the hope of civilization

---

42. Minges, "The Keetoowah Society," quoted in Johnson, *Apartheid in Indian Country*, 103.
43. Johnson, *Apartheid in Indian Country*, 209.
44. Johnson, *Apartheid in Indian Country*, 209.
45. Johnson, *Apartheid in Indian Country*, 209.
46. Kelsey, *Racism and the Christian*, 9.
47. Kelsey, *Racism and the Christian*, 24.
48. Kelsey, *Racism and the Christian*, 26.

depends upon eliminating some races and keeping others pure. It is the dogma that one race has carried progress throughout human history and can alone ensure future progress.[49]

Richard Hughes accentuates the same development and evolution of the racist plague when he writes on "Nature," arguing that America's "Myth of Nature's Nation" created absolutes or claims of entitlement for only the white race. Kelsey writes of the concept that "Nature has condemned inferior races and blessed the superior race."[50] This ideology of whiteness as superior is what gives value to the white self; that value is the faith.

Second is the work of Peter Berger and Thomas Luckmann, found in *The Social Construction of Reality*, that provides an analysis and framing for understanding how human activity constructs reality, which is both relational and reciprocal. They analyzed the "sociology of knowledge" as social reality, which has operated to construct a social order that is a product of repetitive human activity. The white influence of racism on the Indian Nations constructed a bias that made African-Americans the "out race." They convinced the Natives to see the Black race from a negative perspective; Natives then began odious treatment with perennial behavior over time. As a result, one can see how the repetitive praxis of alienation and exclusionary treatment toward African-Americans institutionalizes a bias, which is racism.

Europeans also had a motive when befriending the Natives; they wanted to extract from the Indian race and culture benefits that would support their greed. Europeans began to invade Native American culture by marrying Indian women and as a result they were able to gain access to their land. Once white supremacist philosophy penetrated the Nations and started to influence how they intermingled with the Black race, the Indians changed their laws by prohibiting marriage for African-Americans within the Nations. The impact of white power and hegemony becomes more visible and critical in the Dawes Act because white dominance instituted racism against the Black Indians.

The Dawes Act was the vehicle that government used to determine how the tribal lands would be divided. This is significant because the Dawes Act explains how African-Americans would later become land owners in Oklahoma.

> The federal government forced the Five Civilized Tribes to sell vast amounts of land for minimal payment. Prior to the land

---

49. Kelsey, *Racism and the Christian*, 29.
50. Kelsey, *Racism and the Christian*, 29.

sale, the government empowered the Dawes Commission to set up rolls of tribal citizens so each tribal citizen would receive a share of the tribal resources in accordance with agreements between the tribe and the government.[51]

The problem the Native Americans and Blacks experienced through the implementation of the Dawes Act was who and how people were identified on the rolls. "Traditional tribal rolls did not record the degree of Indian blood."[52] By the twentieth century, though, this changed. The Dawes application wanted the degree of blood, but many freed people just indicated they had an Indian father. Unfortunately, the agents did not list them as such; if people were freedmen and freedwomen they were put on a separate roll. Whites, on the other hand, if mixed with Indian blood, were treated better. The agents listed white people by showing the different degrees of Indian blood and then placing them on a "blood roll" list. This double standard echoed the racial politics of the day. "It fueled the myth that Indian ancestry is, in effect, 'Africanless.'"[53] Race played a significant role as relationships began to change between Native Americans and African-Americans; however, the 1866 Treaty and the Dawes Act has always been at the center of Black freedwomen and freedmen maintaining their status and benefits as part of the Nations.

Following the Emancipation Proclamation, white settlers and others pushed to occupy the Oklahoma Territory. After the 1866 Treaty was signed, for the next twenty years, Oklahoma was a potential consideration for freedmen and freedwomen of Indian Tribes. The circumstances revolved around the federal government being unsure about the tribal rights being extended to their former slaves.[54] "The United States acquired the area known as the Oklahoma District or Unassigned lands from the Creeks and Seminoles."[55] The purpose of the government was "to use the Oklahoma District as a settlement zone for Black freedmen of Five Civilized Tribes, Indian tribes from Kansas, other Western states and territories."[56] During these twenty years, settlers would debate over this land because many different people wanted access to this area, not just freedman from the Indian Tribes. Initially, the Choctaw and Chickasaw wanted to settle their former

---

51. Kelsey, *Racism and the Christian*, 106.
52. Kelsey, *Racism and the Christian*, 107.
53. Kelsey, *Racism and the Christian*, 107.
54. Tolson, *Black Oklahomans*, 41.
55. Tolson, *Black Oklahomans*, 41.
56. Tolson, *Black Oklahomans*, 41.

slaves in 1870 but there was no reply from the US Secretary of Interior and Congress.

By 1878, white political leaders were pushing to control this land. The following leaders of the Five Civilized Tribes were concerned: Choctaw P. P. Pitchlynn; Cherokees W. P. Adair and Daniel H. Ross; Muscogees (Creeks) John R. Moore, P. Porter, D. M. Hodge, and Yarteke Harjo; Seminoles John F. Brown and Thomas Cloud; and Governor of Chickasaws B. F. Overton.[57] These Indian leaders asked Congress to reject the outlined measures to, "1) open the land to white settlement; 2) extend United States legal jurisdiction to matters between and among Indians; 3) abolish tribal relations and grant United States citizenship to Indians, and 4) move Indians from a communal property system to a private property system."[58] Congress was unresponsive to the plea from the Indian Tribe leaders.

In 1879, white political leaders were pushing the Oklahoma District to open for white homesteaders; however, Black separatists also wanted the land as a resettlement for Blacks from the South even though they were not directly associated with freedman from the Five Tribes.[59] In 1881, a spokesman by the name of Hannibal Carter organized the Freedmen's Oklahoma Immigration Association in Chicago; he said he would bring thousands to Oklahoma. Another Black colonization leader said he would bring thousands from Missouri and the Freedmen's Oklahoma Immigration Association advertisement stated that those Blacks who were willing to go would receive 160 acres of land free.[60]

The Secretary of the Interior had Curtis Holcomb investigate the treaties to see what rights Black freedmen actually had. Holcomb's research "maintained in 1881 that colored persons who were never held as slaves in the Indian country, but who may have been slaves elsewhere, are like other citizens of the United States and have no more rights in the Indian country than other citizens of the United States."[61] In other words, the land was only for persons freed from Native American bondage.

African-Americans resisted this exclusion for land opportunities. Tolson outlines the details: the Negroes held a convention in Parson, Kansas in April 27, 1882, with forty-five delegates led by three ministers, claiming to represent 60,000 Blacks. The purpose of the convention was to ask Congress if every third section of land could be occupied by Black emigrants from

---

57. Johnson, *Apartheid in Indian Country*, 59.
58. Johnson, *Apartheid in Indian Country*, 59.
59. Tolson, *Black Oklahomans*, 41.
60. Tolson, *Black Oklahomans*, 42.
61. Tolson, *Black Oklahomans*, 43.

the South.[62] Other states sent petitions to the government with the same request. In 1882, Senator Henry W. Blair introduced a bill and wrote a letter to the Secretary of Interior requesting this permission.[63]

Hiram Price, the Commissioner of Indian Affairs, communicated to Hannibal Carter that the Indian Councils of 1866 clearly stated only Indian freed people would have access. As time continued, the land in the western portion of Indian Territory was leased to ranchmen in the 1870s and 1880s. White settlers and the Boomers[64] pushed to occupy the land; they were continuously removed. Letters continued to flood Congress over the years. Between 1885 and 1888, bills were introduced to open the land for settlement. In 1889, the government renegotiated with the Creek and Seminole Nations and paid for the District. A rider was attached to the Indian appropriations bill and passed in both houses. The land was opened in 1889.[65]

OKLAHOMA'S LAND RUNS

The Oklahoma Territory was the second migration area for disenfranchised Blacks after Kansas. People continued to come from the South, as well as many moving from Kansas; and a whole movement came from Tennessee in protest connected with Ida B. Wells-Barnett's anti-lynching campaign. Edwin P. McCabe was another separatist leader in the movement responsible for the migration to Oklahoma, along with William Eagleson, and both men had been living in Kansas. Edwin P. McCabe was one of several African-Americans attracted to the Nicodemus settlement in Kansas. McCabe was born in New York, had worked on Wall Street, and, prior to the Kansas location, lived in Chicago. He also desired to hold political positions and would later push to be governor in Oklahoma. While McCabe was in Kansas, he held positions as county clerk and state auditor, which also made him the highest elected Black official. When he was not elected for a third term in Kansas, McCabe turned his attention to Oklahoma.

Langston's land run opened on September 21, 1892 with thousands of African-Americans armed and assembled to claim their land. Some white settlers did drive away some Black settlers that day; even Edwin McCabe was caught in the crossfire and had to be rescued. The Cheyenne strip opened the following year in 1893. Just prior to this opening, the *Langston*

---

62. Tolson, *Black Oklahomans*, 43.

63. Tolson, *Black Oklahomans*, 43.

64. Boomers where those settlers who tried to occupy the unassigned Oklahoma land before the official opening.

65. Tolson, *Black Oklahomans*, 45.

City Herald advertised "Everyone that can should go to the strip and get a hundred and sixty [acres], all you need is a Winchester, a frying pan and the $15.00 to file."[66] Several other areas opened in Oklahoma between 1889 and 1906, with Negro and white populations; however, the number of Negro settlers were much smaller than anticipated. Arthur Tolson created a chart which highlights the mixed populations from the land runs. I will outline just a few of the land runs that occurred over the years.

Table 1. Land Runs

Openings	Census Year	Negro	White
Oklahoma District, 1889 Sac, Fox and Iowa, and Shawnee	1889	1,800	48,200
Pottawatomie, 1891	1900	2,973	20,000
Cheyenne-Arapaho, 1892	1900	1,379	25,000
Cherokee Outlet, 1893	1900	1,553	100,000

Source: Data from Arthur Tolson, *Black Oklahomans, A History: 1541–1972* (New Orleans: Edwards Printing, 1966), 89.

Taylor describes the process toward the end of the land runs in this way:[67]

> Black settlement in rural Oklahoma was much more extensive than in Kansas. By 1900 African-American farmers in the territory owned 1.5 million acres valued at eleven million dollars. Many of these landowners were freed people or "state negroes" married to former slaves who acquired allotments in Indian Territory after the Dawes Act terminated communal landholding among the Five Nations. But an equal number of blacks gained homesteads in various runs in Oklahoma between 1889 and 1895.[68]

In fact, McCabe desired to be the governor and believed by positioning Blacks they would have greater power to exercise political rights. McCabe's hope was to develop an all-Black state of Oklahoma,[69] at the very least developing several Black towns that would give Blacks the opportunity to be full American citizens. "Evidently the white society's rejection of Blacks led as a consequence to the growth and development of Black nationalism

---

66. Taylor, *In Search of the Racial*, 147.
67. Tolson, *Black Oklahomans*, 89.
68. Taylor, *In Search of the Racial*, 147.
69. Tolson, *Black Oklahomans*, 73.

among them."⁷⁰ Although McCabe could not make Oklahoma a Black state, he spent nineteen years creating many Black towns.

The other booster, Eagleson, "was the editor of *Topeka American Citizen*... In 1889 Eagleson founded the Oklahoma Immigration Association, headquartered in Topeka."⁷¹ He dispersed agents throughout the South to advertise the prosperous land and economic opportunities in Oklahoma. Eagleson promised a new type of freedom, "Oklahoma is now open... the soil is rich, the climate favorable, water abundant and there is plenty of timber. Make a new start. Give yourself and children new chances in a new land, where you will not be molested and where you will be able to think and vote as you please."⁷² Eagleson did have some good results; one of his representatives "reported in April 1890 that seventeen hundred African-American settlers had already left Atlanta for Oklahoma."⁷³ Several hundred more came from Mississippi and Little Rock, Arkansas. Eagleson and McCabe really became the leaders of the migration, but it was McCabe who became the icon of the Oklahoma movement.

When Indian Territory finally opened on April 22, 1889, known as the Oklahoma land run, about 50,000 people gathered on the borders.⁷⁴ The majority were white and some were Black. Until then, McCabe had spent most of the 1880s in Kansas; with his political interest, he relocated with his wife to Oklahoma in 1890. McCabe wanted to establish an all-Black state and he partnered with "Charles Robbins, a white land speculator, and Eagleson in founding Langston City, an all-black community."⁷⁵ McCabe began to advertise land in the *Langston City Herald*, which encompassed readers in Kansas, Arkansas, Texas, Louisiana, Missouri, and Tennessee.

McCabe's newspaper ad reads as follows: "Langston City is a Negro City and we are proud of that fact... her city officers are all colored. Her teachers are colored. Her public school furnish thorough educational advantages to nearly two-hundred colored children."⁷⁶ The advertisements also boasted that the land was excellent for growing crops such as wheat, cotton, and tobacco. "By 1891 Langston City had two hundred people."⁷⁷ Langston City was named after John Mercer Langston, a Black Congressman from Virginia.

70. Tolson, *Black Oklahomans*, 93.
71. Taylor, *In Search of the Racial*, 144.
72. Taylor, *In Search of the Racial*, 144.
73. Taylor, *In Search of the Racial*, 144.
74. Tolson, *Black Oklahomans*, 50.
75. Tolson, *Black Oklahomans*, 145.
76. Taylor, *In Search of the Racial*, 146.
77. Taylor, *In Search of the Racial*, 146.

He believed in the immigration to Oklahoma and pledged the support to have a Black college in Langston. They also advertised for prosperous Blacks to come to Langston, stating in the *Herald*, "Come prepared or Not at All," warning that if Black freed people did not have enough money saved to help them through their first crop, the transition would be difficult to survive.

CONCLUSION

This chapter explored the terrorism of manifest density, a function of white supremacy, and the greed for Native American land, exhibited through the implementation of the Indian Removal Act. I further explored the tragedy of the Trail of Tears and the amalgamation of two cultures, Native Americans and African Americans, for survival during this time and following the Civil War. The impact of the 1866 Indian Treaty for African Americans brought release from enslavement, future possibilities of tribal citizenship, and land ownership opportunities; however, the repercussions of the plague of racism eventually and negatively influenced the unity of these two cultures. I outlined the early formation of Oklahoma's land runs that opened for settlement and ultimately Statehood in 1907.

CHAPTER 2

Agents of Resistance
The Black Migration Continues—Protest, Black Towns, and Race Theories

> Wells sounded an alarm regarding the tendency to classify a group of people based on unsubstantiated claims. For her, silence was not an option. Rather, she asks that we question the relationship between identity and justice in a society when extreme forms of torture become moments for public celebration.
> —ANGELA D. SIMS
> *Womanist Theological Ethics: A Reader*

IDA B. WELLS-BARNETT'S MEMPHIS PROTEST

DURING THESE SAME YEARS of Oklahoma's early formation, there was another Black migration blooming in the east horizon from Tennessee. Racial violence and tension had escalated to a level such that Blacks felt they could no longer remain in Memphis. The Colored Press Association had encouraged Blacks to leave Memphis since the 1886 Carrollton Massacre in Mississippi.[1] This Carroll County Massacre occurred in the courtroom during a trial for attempted murder. Two brothers of mixed African-American and Native American blood, Ed and Charley Brown, took a white man to

---

1. Giddings, *IDA*, 190.

court for shooting them. The situation occurred when two brothers were transporting molasses to saloons and they accidently spilled some molasses on a white man. The man thought the mistake was intentional, an argument erupted on the street, and the bystanders stopped the dispute. Later, the white man's attorney returned to resolve the situation by shooting the brothers.

During the trial, fifty to one hundred white men rode into town on horseback, walked into the courtroom (which was filled with mostly Blacks, some whites), and shot approximately twenty-three Black people, including the two Brown brothers. Ten Blacks died immediately and thirteen more died later from their wounds. No white people were injured. Many whites had been warned not to attend the trial. There was only one way into the courtroom and one way out; even the Blacks who tried to escape through the windows were killed.[2] The white race mob left as fast as it came.

The critical observations in this situation have three components. First, there is no respect for Black ontology and as a result the complete disregard for the value of Black life makes it disposable. Second, the law did not protect African-Americans. Third, the historical precedent set from discriminatory colonial laws dating back to 1680, and the "social order" of construction, perpetuates the way terrorism operates within systemic structures. The Brown brothers were shot and terrorized in the process of trying to legally protect themselves through the court system but the hegemony of the ruling class that historically defined Black identity and the treatment thereof still holds the discriminatory practices in place, which tortured these men and their Black community.

Unfortunately, the murders of African-Americans have occurred over and over in our history, usually forgotten as each generation dies out, and the historical narrative is never told for the future generations. The Carrollton County Massacre was never recorded in the Mississippi history books and soon forgotten. Six years later, in 1892 in Memphis, Ida B. Wells-Barnett's best friend Thomas Moss and two other men, Calvin McDowell and Henry Stewart, were lynched.

According to Paula Giddings's *IDA: A Sword Among Lions*, the lynching of Moss, McDowell, and Stewart were the results of racial violence and white men exercising the law through their own hands. On March 2, 1892, two boys, one Black and the other white, were playing marbles and ended in a disagreement; the conflict was followed by a fight. As the fight continued, the white boy's father jumped in and began to beat the Black boy. Will Stewart and Calvin McDowell came out of the People's grocery store (which

---

2. Ward, "The Carroll County Courthouse," lines 1–25.

was owned by Thomas Moss and other stockholders) to rescue him. As the situation escalated, Black and white men engaged in the fight, taking their respective racial sides, which resulted in a charged mob.[3]

The next day William Barrett, a store proprietor and one of Moss' competitors in this neighborhood called "Curve," returned with the police to Moss' grocery store. They came to arrest Will Stewart, who they claimed was responsible for clubbing Barrett. They encountered McDowell, a young, two-hundred pound, twenty-two-year-old in the militia group, the same group Moss belonged to. After learning Stewart was not in the store, Barrett had words with McDowell and then hit him with his revolver, knocking him to the ground. Over the next several days, incidents of shootings occurred; the Black men prepared to protect themselves. After reporting the incidents, they were told the law would not protect them since the "Curve" neighborhood was outside the city limits. Later, hundreds of white men were deputized; according to the *Nashville Daily American*, "Every white man in town is a walking arsenal."[4] They came for Moss, claiming he was the ringleader. Eventually, Stewart, McDowell, and Moss were all arrested and put in jail.

On March 7, Thomas Moss' wife, Betty, came to visit with food. She was five months pregnant, but the judge would not allow her visitation and instructed her to return in three days.[5] On March 8, confusion still gathered around the jailhouse lawn. The lawyers for the men were trying to file writs of habeas corpus, but the judge would not allow it. When the word spread that the white deputies would not die from their injuries in the earlier shooting, the news coverage quieted down around the jail and the Black militiamen decided that to cover or guard the jail that night would not be required.

On March 9, 1892, seventy-five men with black masks surrounded the jail at 2:30 AM. Nine men entered the jail and took Moss, Stewart, and McDowell. The men were put on a rail track that ran a mile out of city limits, into the railroad yard; they were shot there and then hung. The men were tortured with multiple gun shots through the face and neck. The *Appeal-Avalanche* and the *Memphis Commercial* newspapers explained the details with such intensity it was assumed they were invited to witness the murders. It was written that McDonnell had the strength of ten men, he struggled and reached for someone's gun and as a result the white men shot his fingers, one by one. It was also reported that Moss pleaded for his life because of his pregnant wife and daughter. Few comments were made about Stewart.

3. Giddings, *IDA*, 177–178.
4. Giddings, *IDA*, 180.
5. Giddings, *IDA*, 181.

Ida B. Wells-Barnett was extremely distraught over the lynching incident, particularly considering her friend Moss, and she could not deny her consciousness to respond. Paula Giddings provides a window into Well's "Anti-Lynching Protest" and departure out of Memphis in her chapter "Exodus." Giddings's work offers a clear view through the window directly into the Black community's values and cultural experiences in Memphis. As Katie Cannon explains, "Black women writers function as continuing symbolic conveyors and transformers of the values acknowledged by the female members of the Black community."[6] After the lynching of Moss and the others, Wells-Barnett was paralyzed with disbelief but she pressed through because of her commitment as a journalist. Acknowledging within herself that she had a responsibility to the public, she wrote:

> The City of Memphis has demonstrated that neither character nor standing avails the Negro if he dares to protect himself against the white man or become his rival. There is nothing we can do about the lynching now, as we are outnumbered and without arms. The white mob could help itself to ammunition without pay, but the order was rigidly enforced against the selling of guns to Negroes. There is therefore only one thing left that we can do; save our money and leave a town which will neither protect our lives and property, nor give us a fair trial in the courts, but takes us out and murders us in cold blood when accused by white persons.[7]

Once this editorial was released, thousands of Black Memphians began to prepare for the newly opened Oklahoma Territory. In the process, a note written by Moss found saying, "go West—there is no protection or opportunity for you here in Memphis." The people in Memphis had received lots of information about Langston City and the other Black towns in Oklahoma.

The reports conveyed that Blacks had been moving into Oklahoma since 1891, and one year later were still arriving almost daily.[8] People had heard about the new Strip of Cheyenne and Arapaho land openings. According to Wells-Barnett Memphians had worked in the city through some difficult times and been good colored citizens; they wanted the city to take responsibility for the murders and they asked for justice. Wells-Barnett wrote again, "We ask this in the name of God and in the name of the law

---

6. Cannon, *Katie's Canon*, 60.
7. Wells, "Crusade for Justice," 52, quoted in Giddings, *IDA*, 189.
8. Giddings, *IDA*, 190.

we have always obeyed and upheld and intend to uphold and obey in the future,"[9] but they did not believe justice would be served.

In the meantime, the *Langston City Herald* advertised these words: "Why invest any money in a city where their lives were constantly in danger? It asked. Why not come to Oklahoma, 'where you can develop whenever manhood or womanhood you possess. Here you can be all that God intended you to be.'"[10] According to the *Nashville Daily American* on March 27, 1892, thousands gathered to send 649 men, women, and children off to Oklahoma.[11] Funds were raised from several different sources for those who wanted to leave from Memphis. "The black businessman Robert Church gave $10,000 to the *Central Oklahoma Emigration Society*, which claimed to have four thousand Memphis blacks organized to go West."[12] Wells-Barnett's partner, J. L. Fleming of the *Free Speech* paper, was responsible for holding the funds raised by Black churches for people who wanted to leave.[13]

Wells-Barnett thought it was important that people make good decisions regarding the move. She also felt an obligation to give accurate information in her paper, so she visited Oklahoma for herself. She stayed for three weeks, visiting several places including Langston, Guthrie, Oklahoma City, and Kingfisher. Wells-Barnett's report reflected numerous thoughts: the conditions in Oklahoma were good; however, they were best for those who had skills, otherwise there would be a tough struggle. In addition to Oklahoma's option, Wells-Barnett leaned slightly toward a new Black Nationalist vision, that Bishop Henry McNeal Turner in the *AME Church Review* was suggesting, for people moving to Liberia. Finally, the last possibility was to consider other places such as New Mexico, Colorado, Oregon, Washington, and Wyoming.[14] All of these ideas were to help people think carefully about the migration. In the April 19 land opening in Oklahoma, "thousands of homesteaders were poised to make claims along the five-hundred-mile boundary of the Cheyenne and Arapaho lands, among them black Memphians hoping to take advantage of the 'last chance for a free home' as booster put it."[15]

9. Giddings, *IDA*, 191.
10. Giddings, *IDA*, 192.
11. Giddings, *IDA*, 192.
12. Giddings, *IDA*, 193.
13. Giddings, *IDA*, 192.
14. Giddings, *IDA*, 198, 199.
15. Giddings, *IDA*, 200.

Three church congregations in Memphis wanted to make the move to Oklahoma. The first was Union Avenue Baptist Church, with Pastor William F. Morgan. The *Langston City Herald* reported:

> They arrived in Guthrie on a Friday, purchased land on Saturday, and by the following Sunday had erected a church "all finished and paid for" where services were held for three hundred people. . . . Morgan planned to return to Memphis to arrange the removal of his congregation who "are to come as a colony."[16]

The Living Way Church evidently became impatient and moved to Wichita, Kansas. Pastor Brinkley of Washington Street Baptist Church sold his church to a Jewish community. Prior to departing, Pastor Brinkley said these words regarding Memphis, "he was leaving in order to help 'depopulate this hell created for colored.'"[17] Wells-Barnett estimated about 6,000 of the African-American citizens participated in the exodus.

Establishing All-Black Towns in Oklahoma

Figure 2. Source: The Oklahoma City Historical Society Museum. Black Towns in Twin Territory and Black Nationalism.

---

16. Giddings, *IDA*, 200.
17. Giddings, *IDA*, 201.

The drive to create all-Black towns in Indian Territory and Oklahoma territory was an excellent representation of Black Nationalism in early Black history. The ratification of the Emancipation Proclamation in 1865 and the treaty signing of the Five Nations in 1866 freed Negroes who had longed for the opportunity to escape oppressive conditions and racial hatred. Although Negroes were free, they had been terrorized across the country and particularly in the South; the migration to Oklahoma provided them an opportunity to separate from the abusive treatment of white supremacy and racism. "Many of the Black towns were not constituted as racial ghettoes. Blacks of this era felt that this kind of isolation from the whites formed the only positive and workable solution to their difficulties."[18]

McCabe had desired an all-Black state but, realizing he would not achieve that goal, he continued to work for the next nineteen years to establish Black towns. Black Nationalism was the response to white supremacy and structural oppression that freed Negroes were experiencing. Black nationalism was the counter-resistance to lynching, Jim and Jane Crow, and economic instability. Black nationalism also represents the counter-narrative to systemic racism. According to James Cone, nationalists were different from integrationista in how they defined freedom and strategies, and yet neither group was 100 percent pure to their classifications. "For nationalists, freedom was not black people pleading for integration into white society; rather it was separation from white people so that blacks could govern themselves."[19]

James Cone posits many years later in *Malcolm & Martin in America* a broader understanding for integrationist and Black nationalism. Cone explains that the spirit of Black nationalism is found in the early history of slavery with people such as Gabriel Prosser, Denmark Vesey, and Nat Turner during the slave revolts, because they knew they had not been created for servitude.[20] I would include with this same spirit of Black nationalism Black women such as Harriet Tubman, Sojourner Truth, Anna Julia Cooper, and Ida B. Wells-Barnett. Black nationalism was clearly exhibited during the years of Reconstruction and, in Oklahoma, the development of Black towns and Black Wall Street.

In 1870, a few years just prior to the migration west, Sojourner Truth had worked toward the same efforts of "isolation to the west" for the purpose of economic opportunity for African-American people. Later, in the

---

18. Bittle and Geis, "Racial Self-fulfillment," 248, quoted in Tolson, *Black Oklahomans*, 92.

19. Cone, *Martin & Malcolm & America*, 10.

20. Cone, *Martin & Malcolm & America*, 9.

midst of the migration from Memphis, Ida B. Wells-Barnett represented and exhibited the same rebellious resistance as she encouraged the Memphians to protest and leave. Whether leaving Memphis meant the Negro race would go west or follow Bishop Henry McNeil Turner's offer of Blacks returning to Liberia, the purpose of establishing these all-Black towns was to create self-sustaining towns apart from a racist, white America and live in peace.

Oklahoma State Map

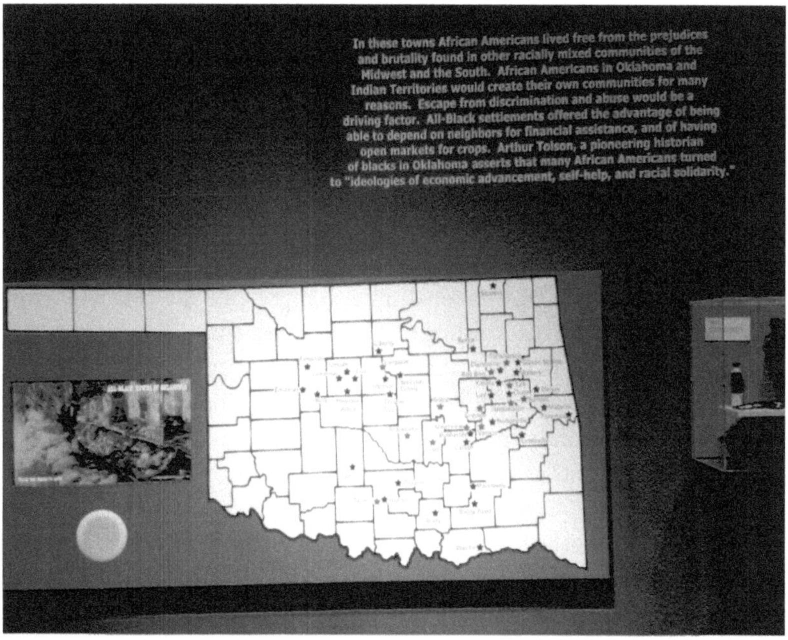

Figure 3. Source: The Oklahoma City Historical Society Museum. Map of all Black Towns in Oklahoma.

The All-Black towns established in Oklahoma occupied both the Indian Territory and Oklahoma Territory. In 1907, these two territories became the State of Oklahoma.

All-Black Towns in Twin Territories

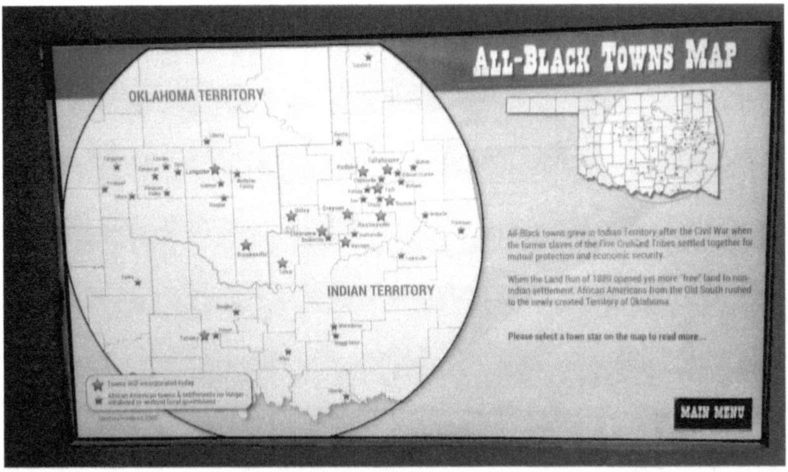

Figure 4. Source: The Oklahoma City Historical Society Museum. Map of Oklahoma Twin Territories.

The number of all-Black towns grew to at least fifty towns over the years. According to Tolson,

> The following Black towns and colony were founded in Oklahoma Territory: Lincoln City, Langston City, Liberty, Ferguson and Wellston Colony. Those established in Indian Territory were: two unnamed Seminole Nation Black towns, Tullahassee, North Fork Colored, Arkansas Colored, Canadian Colored, Gibson Station, Wybark, Marshalltown, Overton, Lincoln, later renamed Clearview, Rentiesville, Red Bird, Boley Taft, Bailey, Tatums, Wild Cat or Grayson Forman, Chase, Summit, Lewisville, Vernon Bookertee, and Lima.[21]

Despite the years of terror, Black towns in Oklahoma became places of peace and communal presence for the newly freed Negro race.

Langston City was founded in 1890 by McCabe and located near Guthrie.[22] McCabe advertised Langston in his newspaper, the *Herald,* as "the Negro's refuge from lynching, burning at the stake and other lawlessness and [it] turns the Negro's sorrow into happiness."[23] Langston University was founded in 1897 under the name Colored Agricultural and Normal University. It is the only historical Black school in the state.

21. Tolson, *Black Oklahomans,* 94.
22. Tolson, *Black Oklahomans,* 94.
23. Tolson, *Black Oklahomans,* 94.

Langston City and Langston University

Figure 5. Source: Greenwood Cultural Center in Tulsa, Oklahoma. Langston University History.

The state of Oklahoma was supposedly responsible for offering a promised land to some, or at least a new start for many. Native Americans had been forced to Oklahoma through the Indian Removal Act. Whites had come seeking new opportunities; a large percentage had come from difficult economic conditions in the East. African-Americans had come, either as slaves of the Natives, freedmen and freedwomen, or later, from the South in order to escape violence and terrorism. David Chang described pre-statehood Oklahoma this way:

> Oklahoma means "red man" in the Choctaw language, is run through by a "Black Belt," and has been claimed by some as "white man's country." It has been termed an Indian homeland, a black promised land, and a white heartland. All these competing racial claims to one place . . . reveal much about how the struggle over land has given shape to the way Americans indigenous, black and white—created and gave meaning to races and nations.[24]

---

24. Chang, *The Color of Land*, 1, quoted in Johnson, *Apartheid in Indian Country*, 60.

Whites soon dominated Oklahoma in the social, economic, and political realms.[25] They also quickly segregated Oklahoma. Whites often married Native Americans to have access to their land and worked to assimilate Indians into their way of being. "At the time of Oklahoma statehood, whites conferred upon Native Americans honorary whiteness. They regarded Native Americans as 'white' for purposes of Oklahoma's black/white segregation laws."[26] The cost of this concession was less self-governance; they also lost "Sequoyah," the Indian state within Oklahoma they lobbied for.[27] Whites ostracized Blacks and classified them with pejorative characterizations. Both Native Americans and whites feared Black migration from the South. By the time of statehood in 1907, African-Americans had long been marginalized. For the new state celebration, the planners created a mock wedding, representing the "Oklahoma Territory" with a white man and representing the "Indian Territory" with a Native American woman.

A mock wedding happened in Guthrie, the capital of Oklahoma at the time. "The new Governor, a lawyer named Charles Nathaniel Haskell, regaled the inaugural crowd with a vision of Oklahoma as a land of collaboration between red and white citizens."[28] African-Americans were completely excluded as if they did not even exist; this would be their fate going forward in the new state, separated and unable to participate.[29] The ostracism and exclusionary intent represented in the mock wedding demonstrates the power of white privilege but also the desire for permanent marginalization of African-Americans' participation in Oklahoma.

During the time that Oklahoma was opened in 1889, the ethos and social landscape was changing for African-Americans around the country. For African-Americans, the "Great Migration" represented a diverse range of challenges and opportunities related to social issues occurring in American society. The Great Migration is described through multiple lenses, usually highlighting several distinct time frames that characterize the movement. There were several segments of the Great Migration movement that spanned the late nineteenth century and the early twentieth century. The movement was precipitated by changing laws, new Black freedom, economic challenges, racial violence, lynching, religious belief, and church praxis in social activism. Benjamin Mays discusses the sociological perspectives of the movement, emphasizing the rural transition into the cities, relocations from

25. Johnson, *Apartheid in Indian Country*, 60.
26. Johnson, *Apartheid in Indian Country*, 62.
27. Johnson, *Apartheid in Indian Country*, 60
28. Johnson, *Apartheid in Indian Country*, 67.
29. Johnson, *Apartheid in Indian Country*, 60–62.

the South to the North, and church growth. Mays uses T. J. Woofter, Jr.'s work on the Negro economic status, saying the Negro city-ward movement was slow from 1900 to 1910, but explains:

> From 1910 to 1920, the Negro city population increased sharply and from 1920 to 1930, more than a million Negroes migrated from the Southern rural district—650,000 to Southern cities and 450,000 to Northern cities.[30]

Mays also posits that the changing landscape in the Negro population drastically changed the urban churches and increased the northern churches.

> According to the Federal census of Religious Bodies, there were in 1916 a total of 127 Negro Baptist churches in Chicago, Detroit, Cincinnati, Philadelphia, and Baltimore. In 1926 the Federal census Religious Bodies reported 319 Negro Baptist churches in these five cities and [an] increase of 151 per cent.[31]

Eddie Glaude describes the "Great Migration" movement in his chapter "African-American Christianity: The modern phase (1863–1935)" this way:

> [With] violence in the South, the reality that Jim Crow was fast becoming the law of the land, and catastrophic economic events in the region contributed to the massive departure of more than 2.5 million African-Americans from the South between 1890 and 1930. The movement greatly transformed cities throughout the country. Chicago saw its black population increased by 114% more than 65,000 black migrants moved to the city. Detroit experienced a 611% increase, Cleveland, 308%.[32]

The massive number of people who migrated from the South to northern cities shifted the landscape for Negroes in America.

The intentional migration would create a new horizon for the growth and expansion of Black churches, the arts, and the founding of Black political organizations such as "the short lived Afro-American League (1890); the National Council of Negro Women (1896); the American Negro Academy (1897); the National Association for the Advancement of Colored People (1910) and the National Urban League (1911)."[33] Many of the Black educational institutions were formed earlier in the nineteenth century. For example, "Shaw University in Raleigh, North Carolina was founded in 1865;

---

30. Mays, *The Negro's God*, 5.
31. Mays, *The Negro's God*, 5.
32. Glaude, *African American Religion*, 58.
33. Glaude, *African American Religion*, 54.

Morehouse College in Atlanta, Georgia, in 1867; Fisk University in Nashville, Tennessee, in 1866 and Hampton Institute in Hampton, Virginia in 1868."[34] Acknowledgement of the impact from the Great Migration is important; however, I want to focus specifically on the migration west, which began approximately a decade before the Great Migration.

When the first Black migration west began (1879–1880), from the South to Kansas, it was known as the "Great Negro Exodus to Kansas." American society at this time was characterized by less than two decades of freedom for Black people. Black Reconstruction was underway, and white America was trying to answer what they defined as the "Negro Problem." In other words, what could America do with the thousands of freed slaves? These were freed slaves who, by then, should have had access to participate in an American system consisting of economic opportunities, land ownership, and educational access but, unfortunately, continued to be excluded.

W. E. B. Du Bois wrote, in *Souls of Black Folk,* in the chapter "Of the Dawn of Freedom," that America was struggling with the question, "what shall be done with the Negroes?"[35] The Freedmen's Bureau was conflicted in representing these newly freed Negroes with inadequate plans and money in a nation that saw the Negro as less than human and still desired them as slaves. Few Blacks, particularly those in the South, owned their land. Many were indebted to a system of "land slavery," better known as "debt slavery," although they were free. A large percentage of the Negro population lived as sharecroppers, farming someone else's property. After the harvest was completed and the expenses were paid on the advancement of seed and supplies, Negroes owed all of their profits back to the actual land owners. Each season this process continued to leave the Black sharecroppers and their families in financial hardship. This system of "debt slavery" demonstrates one of the early economic structural oppressions that functioned as terrorism within the African-American family.

The Civil Rights Act of 1875, also called the Enforcement Act, was established to provide equal treatment for Negroes in public accommodations and public transportation. "By 1880 blacks were separated on trains, in depots, and on wharves. After the Supreme Court declared the Civil Rights Act of 1875 unconstitutional in 1883, blacks were banned from public and private establishments, including hotels, restaurants, theaters, parks and libraries."[36] As a result, racial violence and terrorism escalated across the country, particularly in the South. The unconstitutional ruling against the

---

34. Glaude, *African American Religion,* 49.
35. Du Bois, *The Souls,* 14.
36. White, *Too Heavy a Load,* 26.

Civil Rights Act turned this country around and upside down, intensifying white supremacy and opening the doors to Jim and Jane Crow laws. The court case *Plessy v. Ferguson* would uphold the "separate but equal" law, which remained in place for the next fifty-eight years (1896–1954). During this era, lynching African-Americans would become a frenzy around the country.

USING RACE THEORIES TO UNDERSTAND ANTEBELLUM AND POST-BELLUM OKLAHOMA

Intentional racial construction of social inequality is explicit in the Tulsa tragedy—a massacre against innocent and helpless African-American people causes one to question the very humanity and morality of white Tulsans who performed the violent acts of terrorism in this two-day event. Exploring the racial bias and social constructs inherent within our American society and systems is both alarming and challenging because they were theologically conceived in the early formation of American colonies and instituted by laws.

White America has always treated Black people immorally and white Tulsans were no different. The deep proclamations of white superiority entrenched within our social constructs have always been further perpetuated by approved government and reinforced by legal power. This gives value to whiteness and authority to the practice of immoral behavior against Blacks, which has functioned since slavery. Reflecting on the early years of laws, race theories, science, and philosophers brings clarity to the institution of practiced discrimination.

The "typifications" that define Black ontology are the codification of prejudice, which identified and labeled Black bodies during the Colonial period through the rules of laws and legislative process. Even though this is historical information, it is significant for understanding how the legal perception of Black ontology was viewed and shaped in America. For example, A. Leon Higginbotham posits, *In The Matter of Color,* that the first major slave codes created, over the years, a number of legislative acts passed to dehumanize and oppress African-Americans in Virginia prior to the 1680 codes; however, the "1680 Act" actually combined the previous twenty years of legislation and added new ones. "The 1680 statute would become the model of repression throughout the South for the next 180 years . . . [T]he provisions in the statute attempted to make sure that blacks would be recognized as legally inferior."[37]

---

37. Higginbotham, *In the Matter*, 39.

The summation of this statute establishes, "If blacks could not leave the owner's plantation without a certificate, their mobility was destroyed; if blacks could not carry arms, the potential to resist was reduced. And if Blacks could be whipped for lifting up a hand against any Christian regardless of the provocation then the dehumanization process was complete..."[38] Many of these statutes also pertained to Mulattoes and Indians.

Christianity was also at the center of Black's rights; those Blacks who were considered Christian and had been baptized were categorized according to the earlier 1667 statute, which stated slave status would not be altered by baptism.[39] Higginbotham continues to explicate the historical laws:

> With each succeeding decade, the Virginia legislators, expressing mixture of fear, greed, and prejudice, simply reduced the privileges and rights of blacks. They rationalized their actions on the ground of security, without religious or moral qualm whatsoever. They no doubt convinced themselves that blacks were so inferior that their subhuman status deserved no recognition of human rights.[40]

These laws demonstrate how Black Americans were labeled and positioned solely by race—this is the early construct of American formation.

Around the same time in the colony of Massachusetts, changing legal concepts stated, "With each passing decade, black, Indian and mulatto slaves were more and more closely identified as chattel, not people in the colony's tax assessment statutes."[41] Once this legal "identity of inferiority" for Blacks was established, the social construct was deeply embedded into American culture and the praxis was perpetuated for years; as a result, we have a nation shaped by pejorative identities of Blackness.

Berger and Luckman theorize that there is a dialectical relationship between human action and societal construction. The precedence for establishing a racial construction of social inequality is discussed in their analysis on the "social construction of reality," which explicates how society functions from a humanly produced construction of repetitious behavior. According to their theory society is a human product—"Social order exists only as a product of human activity."[42] The identifying components of their method includes consciousness, social interaction, and language, which symbolizes our human experiences.

38. Higginbotham, *In the Matter*, 39.
39. Higginbotham, *In the Matter*, 37.
40. Higginbotham, *In the Matter*, 38–39.
41. Higginbotham, *In the Matter*, 78.
42. Berger and Luckmann, *Social Construction*, 52.

The "typifications" create a pattern in the face-to-face situation. These "typifications" are the perennial patterns of how we, as a society, categorize people or how we as humans identify with others. As a result, "social structure is the sum total of these 'typifications' and of the recurrent patterns of interaction established by means of them."[43] The human action from whites during the formation of America and the years that followed implemented biased perspectives against Blacks, Indians, and Mulattos, and then instituted laws to reinforce racial hierarchy.

The other human activity that must be included in this discussion is exercising power and economic hegemony. The evidence of social order, which is produced by human action and social construction, can be found in the enslavement of Africans through the laws that confined them. Moreover, we have a nation that successfully constructed social, economic, political, and legal systems, which operate as forms of terrorism by continuous discrimination against African-Americans and treatment that is substandard to the privilege of whiteness. Unfortunately, this ideology has been perpetuated through American history.

As time progressed over the centuries, the science of "white beauty," interrogated in Nell Painters's *The History of White People*, demonstrates how white beauty was further apotheosized, giving social value and superiority to whiteness and dehumanizing Blackness. The white ruling powers, defined as the empire, have constructed a social order that excludes African-Americans. White American society has not only constructed but taught a nation how to treat Black people in America, while exhibiting that African-Americans in society, particularly in Tulsa during the massacre, were a disposable people and could be terrorized with impunity.

Even this question of the American Dream that Lee Butler raises, regarding "who can have access?" is clarified in the Tulsa tragedy. Butler posits, "The Dream remains very much alive as a guiding image and ethos of the American way of life."[44] Butler, however, explains—"The 'American Dream' has meant terror and despair for many who have experienced its influence."[45] African-Americans were certainly victims of this terror as they sought to find a "land of opportunity," while trying to escape violence in the South by moving west and north. The Negro race in Tulsa was not a race with permissible access to the American dream; this is why their possessions were taken by the white looters and their homes destroyed. According

---

43. Berger and Luckmann, *Social Construction*, 31.
44. Butler, *Liberating Our Dignity*, 24.
45. Butler, *Liberating Our Dignity*, 24.

to white Tulsans, they did not deserve those homes, ownership privileges, or luxuries.

The sociological landscape of Tulsa is quite impressive for the early twentieth century. Tulsa became a boom city because of the oil rush; in fact, it became one of the largest oil producing cities in the world. The largest population growth occurred between 1890 and 1920. Prior to the oil boom in the early 1900s, Tulsa was a sleepy town with fewer than 2,000 people. "By 1910, the Census Bureau listed Tulsa's population at 18,182, in 1920 at 72,075."[46] Tulsa was ranked in a later census with other cities such as San Diego, Wichita, Wilkes-Barre, Pennsylvania and Troy, New York as the ninety-seventh largest city in United States, all because of rapid oil growth.[47]

Oil in Oklahoma was discovered in 1897 near a town called Bartlesville, located in Indian Territory, about fifty miles north of Tulsa. The discovery that made Tulsa explode happened in 1905 when Ida Glenn No. 1 gushed in Glenn Pool, an area approximately fourteen miles from Tulsa. This area became known as "the richest small oil field in the world."[48] Over the next two years, derricks were constructed all over the area "and from some of Glenn Pool's five hundred producing wells flowed more than two thousand barrels of oil per day."[49] In 1907, Oklahoma became a state. Much to my surprise, Oklahoma was also then the leading oil producer in the nation. "Six years later, Oklahoma was producing one quarter of all the oil produced in the nation, and by 1915, the young state was producing up to 300,000 barrels of oil per day."[50]

Following the Glenn Pool discovery, Tulsa began to change, people flocked to the area, and hotels were built to accommodate the many men that worked in the oil fields. The men who worked in the oil field were so numerous that a special train called "Coal Oil Johnny" picked up the workers and dropped them off at the different oil fields and then returned at the close of the work day to take them back to Tulsa. According to the telephone directory, at least 126 oil companies were in Tulsa by 1909.[51] "'Tulsey Town' had grown into one of the Southwest's largest cities in practically no time at all. Local boosters called it the 'Magic City'"[52]

46. Ellsworth, *Death in a Promised*, 9.
47. Ellsworth, *Death in a Promised*, 9.
48. Ellsworth, *Death in a Promised*, 9.
49. Ellsworth, *Death in a Promised*, 9.
50. Ellsworth, *Death in a Promised*, 10.
51. Ellsworth, *Death in a Promised*, 11.
52. Boosters were the men who promoted Tulsa as an exciting place for relocation. McCabe was an African American booster who advertised all over the South to African Americans that moving to Oklahoma would offer a fresh start with land and

Dorothy DeWitty outlines significant details of Oklahoma's early history beyond the massive oil explosion in *Tulsa: Tale of Two Cities,* which includes some of the expansive building projects white Tulsans engaged in over the next several years. They are as follows:

> Wagon Bridge at 11th Street over the Arkansas (1904) to access Redfork Oil; Trinity Episcopal Church, 1906; Exchange National Bank, 1910; the Mayo Building, 1910–1917; the Hotel Tulsa, 1912; eighty blocks of pavement, 1910; the Kennedy Building, 1915; the Cosden Building (Mid-Continent), 1913; Central High School, 1916; the Holy Family Cathedral (the first permanent church building), 1914; Lyon's Indian Store, 1916; the Sinclair Building, 1919; the municipal building, 1919, the first modern hospital (Oklahoma Osteopathic), 1915; the first recreational park (Swan Lake, Orcutts), 1908; and the Reunion Center, 1919.[53]

The challenges with all of this new development and the massive oil expansion in Tulsa were the biased praxis of the social, political, and economic climate, integrated with the laws that established exclusion and structural oppression, which operated discriminatorily against the Negro race. "The new Oklahoma legislature confirmed segregation in 1907, when the first bill presented to the Oklahoma senate provided for segregated public transportation and a penalty for disobedience."[54] Additional Jim Crow laws implemented through legislation confirmed no mixed marriages or land ownership, separate schools and public facilities. Black protest organizations fought against the state. Representatives even traveled to Washington, DC; however, Black citizens could not prevent the state from restricting their rights.

George Kelsey postulates that racism is an idolatrous faith that positions whiteness as god. He further explicates his argument in *Racism and the Christian Understanding of Man*:

> It [racism] is a form of idolatry. It is an abortive search for meaning. In its early modern beginnings, racism was a justificatory device. It did not emerge as faith. It arose as an ideological justification for the constellations of political and economic power which were expressed in colonialism and slavery. But gradually the idea of the superior race was heightened and deepened in meaning and value so that it pointed beyond the historical opportunity.

---

53. DeWitty, *Tulsa*, 32.
54. DeWitty, *Tulsa*, 32.

structures of relation, in which it merged to human existence itself. The alleged superior race became and now persists as a center of value and an object of devotion. Multitudes of men gain their sense of the "power of being" from their membership in the superior race. Accordingly, the most deprived white man, culturally and economically, is able to think of himself as "better'n any nigger."[55]

Kelsey contends that "racist faith" manifests in identifying the alienation of others and engaging in negative judgment of God's creation. I agree that the African race has certainly been alienated from the moment of their involuntary docking upon American shores. By white culture, they were regarded as inferior and treated with contempt through terror and torture. Kelsey also critiques that the concept of the "out race," in this case the Negro, seems to imply there was some creative error in God's creation. I argue God made no errors in the creation of Blackness or Black bodies, but the evil of white supremacy has always been able to challenge the goodness and purity of Blackness through the hegemony of social, political, and economic power and privilege.

What is critical to remember in this racist ideology is the "value" that was given to whiteness. The American culture valued whiteness so highly that it became their god. This further implemented apotheosis and justified worship of themselves. Unfortunately, in the nineteenth and early twentieth centuries other incoming European immigrants wanted to be included in this American ethos of white power, privilege, and unity of inclusivity.

Emilie Townes defines the "produced misery and suffering" as structural evil that African-Americans experience. She argues,

> This is the proper realm of womanist discourse based on an inter-structured analysis that includes class, gender and race within the framework of social ethics. It provides a helpful framework to do the necessary critical and analytical work that can expose the ways in which a society can produce misery and suffering in relentlessly systematic and sublimely structural ways. This is what I call the cultural production of evil.[56]

Analyzing the interior worlds of Blacks who lived in Tulsa, and the systemic structures that terrorize African-Americans nationally is critical for understanding what necessitated the creation of the Greenwood District and Black Wall Street.

---

55. Kelsey, *Racism and the Christian*, 9.
56. Townes, *Womanist Ethics and the Cultural*, 12.

The following are a few examples that dig deeper into the interior worlds of the Negro race in Tulsa and the systemic structures. These examples display how the social codification of prejudice was embedded into Tulsa's structures. They illuminate not only white America's social ethic regarding racism, economic opportunity, but also the demoralization of Black ontology. In 1907, an article describing race in Tulsa was written in a national scholarly magazine—*The Independent*:

> The negro of Indian Territory is also a land-owner. The exslave of the Five Tribes are protected in their holds as are the Indians... So in both divisions of the State there are probably a larger percentage of negroes who own their own homes and are in comfortable circumstances than elsewhere in the United States. So it will be seen that Oklahoma's negro population is hardly to be termed improvident.
>
> An Oklahoman will give you reason for disliking the negro. [The negro] is immoral, improvident, lazy, and with all at times inclined to be impudent. After talking with many men, college graduates, professors and Northern men of education and station, I have yet to find the Oklahoman who does not admit a strong personal antipathy toward the blacks. That is, they much prefer not to come in personal contact with negroes and regard the so-called "white towns" of the Territories as progressive, for the single reason that negroes are not allowed to reside there.[57]

In 1912, the local newspaper the *Tulsa Democrat*, today known as the *Tulsa Tribune*, wrote this: "Tulsa appears now to be in danger of losing its prestige as the whitest town in Oklahoma."[58] Hannibal Johnson writes, "With like venom, the paper declared: 'Does Tulsa wish a double invasion of criminal Negro preachers, Negro shysters, crap shooters, gamblers, bootleglegs[sic], prostitutes and smart elecs [sic] in general?'"[59] These quotes provide great insight for the social ethic of white Tulsans, but they also demonstrate the extreme hatred and racism exhibited toward the Negro race.

Racism positioned the lives of Negroes as acceptable only for white servitude. As long as Negroes were working as servants for white people, they were permitted into the white areas of Tulsa. Obtaining access to economic opportunities also positioned the interior lives for many Black people who were not business owners into the submissive roles that marginalized

---

57. Johnson, *Black Wall Street*, 7.
58. Larsen, "Tulsa Burning," 48, quoted in Johnson, *Black Wall Street*, 8.
59. Johnson, *Black Wall Street*, 7.

their existence. Black women often experienced an even greater loss because the domestic service positions in white homes required more time away from their own children and families in order to perform the jobs and earn adequate income. This statement describing economic challenges mirrors the extreme sacrifice Black women had to make during slavocracy:

> African-Americans were welcome as servants in any part of Tulsa. Indeed, it was common for African-American maids to live in so-called "maid's quarters"—garage apartments adjacent to the homes of their white employers. But the welcome mat so graciously extended to them in their subservient roles disappeared when they attempted to navigate the waters of the white world. African-Americans could neither live among whites as equals nor patronize white businesses in Tulsa.[60]

Trying to fully comprehend and understand the magnitude of how Negroes were ostracized, perceived, or viewed by white culture, and then actually treated is horrifying. The dehumanizing behavior toward Black ontology clearly establishes the reason for the Greenwood District and Black Wall Street. One can probably imagine that Black nationalism functioned as their only form of Black resistance and their means of survival. If Negroes did not love themselves and each other, they would never have survived.

I want to analyze the ideology of freedom for African-Americans in contrast to the sociological landscape in the United States, particularly in Tulsa during the early twentieth century. Let me begin by asking, what does it mean to be free? I ask this question because I wonder if the Negro race of the early twentieth century in the United States was actually free. For that matter, when we observe the social, political, and legal challenges in our nation, are Black Americans today even free at the hands of white supremacy and white privilege, which continually guns them down at will?

I realize that the Emancipation Proclamation was signed in 1863, the Thirteenth Amendment was ratified in December of 1865, and the 1866 Indian Treaty was signed with the US government, all of which freed Negroes from being slaves according to the law. However, if a race of people is denied access to the daily required goods and services sold or provided by white business owners, or if they are prohibited from freely moving around a city, or restricted by law from accessing services such as the same education and health care as the white race, are they actually free?

I interrogate ideology because it is critical to understanding freedom in the United States and certainly in Tulsa. Ideology can be defined in multiple ways from various perspectives. Ideologies are illusionary concepts,

60. Johnson, *Black Wall Street*, 8.

defined and dominated by the ruling class in society. Mike Cormack offers several definitions, including, "Ideology is how the existing ensemble of social relations represents itself to individuals, it is the image a society gives of itself in order to perpetuate itself."[61] In other words, it is how individuals, groups, or even nations construct beliefs and practices within society to make sense of their surroundings or transfer information.

For example, in the formation creed of America, the Declaration of Independence states, "we hold these truths to be self-evident, that all men are created equal, that they are endowed by their Creator to certain unalienable rights, among those are the right to life, liberty and the pursuit of happiness." The ideology and myth perpetuated by this creed conveys that America is a place of equality for all men; unfortunately, they only meant equality for white men, and the creed does not speak to women's existence at all. Cormack quotes another definition of ideology "as a term used to describe the 'social production of meanings.'"[62] This definition further reiterates that hegemony of the white ruling society; those with privilege, financial wealth, and positions of power control the production of meanings.

Another way to describe ideology is in relation to the material or the economic conditions. This definition is associated with Marxism. Karl Marx and Friedrich Engels moved the term "ideology" from its French philosophical origin into the realm of material distortion, or obscurity, and related it to the "mode of production." The details are found in Marx and Engels's early work, *The German Ideology*, first written in 1840s and then later published in 1924.[63] They believed "just as the *camera obscura* distorts its image by inversion, so ideology distorts our ideas about society by inverting (and thus concealing) the relationships of the social structure."[64] As a result, society is subjected and controlled by the power of the dominant class that shapes the beliefs and ideas that perpetuate ideologies of equality, freedom, and others for citizens in America.

Still another way of exploring ideology and the continued development from Marx and Engels is with Louis Althusser, who analyzes ideology in structures. Althusser departs from ideology as the traditional concepts of ideas and beliefs and is concerned with how ideology functions in the structures and institutions of society. He makes two thesis claims. First, ideology is a representation of the imaginary relationship of individuals to their real conditions of existence. Second, ideology has a material existence. When

---

61. Nichols, *Ideology and the Image*, 1, quoted in Cormack, *Ideology*, 9.
62. Cormack, *Ideology*, 9.
63. Cormack, *Ideology*, 9.
64. Cormack, *Ideology*, 10.

the illusions created from ideologies are blended with the limitations and constraints of freedom, and when ideologies are operative within structures of society or institutions, the interior lives of Black people not only reveal but magnify the oppressive conditions that terrorize and the existential realities of Black life fighting structural evil in order to defy fact over truth.

Examining the freedom for educational opportunity in Oklahoma Territory (1894) is another example which allows us to explore ideology of freedom and ideology in structures against Blacks. In the early 1900s, for African-Americans in Oklahoma and throughout the United States, freedom meant Black bodies were no longer physically shackled; albeit, they were not free from the authority and control of the hegemonic power of white supremacy and racism. Given these circumstances, is one actually free? On the other hand, the ideologies of beliefs and legal documents constructed by society and the nation conveyed that African-Americans were free. However, subsequent to freedom, the early laws in Oklahoma segregated the education with the support of power brokers and the constitution.

When President Theodore Roosevelt signed to make Oklahoma a state (1907), he limited Black Oklahomans' education in the Oklahoma State constitution and claimed "separate and equal" in Article XIII. They imposed fines for commingling the races for teaching or allowing whites to attend schools with Black students. "These statutes were still in place in 1961, in spite of the 1954 separate and equal mandate of the U.S. Supreme Court."[65] The legal fight for equal and quality education persisted "from 1904 until 1965, including the landmark Ada Lois Sipuel v. Oklahoma Higher Education."[66] These are some examples that demonstrate how the ideology of freedom operates in contention with authority and control, while ideologies become deeply etched into structures of oppression.

CONCLUSION

This chapter traced Black migration from the South to Oklahoma, in connection with the American ethos of lynching and terrorism around the nation. I specifically highlighted the protest movement by Memphians to Oklahoma, which was initiated by Ida B. Wells-Barnett, in direct response

---

65. DeWitty, *Tulsa*, 33.

66. *Ada Lois Sipuel v. Oklahoma Higher Education* is a United States Supreme Court case of racial discrimination against the University of Oklahoma Law School in 1946, which was all-white at the time, for denying African Americans admissions into a state school based on race. Thurgood Marshall of New York and Amos Hall from Tulsa represented Lois.

to three lynchings in 1892. In all the migration movements, African-Americans were seeking to escape the terror and torture of white supremacy and racial hatred, particularly in the South. The all-Black towns in Oklahoma became a place of peace, representing a form of traditional communalism found in Black Nationalism. Moreover, I used critical race theory to explore the ideology of freedom, the racial construction of social inequality, and the interior world of the Black race.

CHAPTER 3

Black Wall Street and the Greenwood District

> I take Toni Morrison's probing distinction between truth and fact seriously. Rather than argue for a simplistic notion of history as fact, I am more interested in getting into the interior worlds of those who endure structural evil as well as the interior worlds of structural evil itself to discover what truths may be found there.
>
> —EMILIE M. TOWNES
> *Womanist Ethics and the Cultural Production of Evil*

> One is astonished in the study of history at the recurrence of the idea that evil must be forgotten, distorted, skimmed over. We must not remember that Daniel Webster got drunk and only remember he was a splendid constitutional lawyer. We must forget that George Washington was a slave owner, or that Thomas Jefferson had mulatto children, or that Alexander Hamilton had Negro blood, and simply remember the things we regard as creditable and inspiring. The difficulty, of course, with this philosophy is that history loses its value as an incentive and example; it paints perfect men and noble nations, but it does not tell the truth.
>
> —W. E. B. DU BOIS
> *Black Reconstruction in America 1860–1880*

HISTORY AND MEMORY

A competitiveness exists between history and memory because the narratives of history are often defined by who remembers or, more importantly, who has the power and authority to tell, write, and record the stories of history. For example, Emilie Townes references Toni Morrison's essay "Sites of Memory: Proceedings Too Terrible to Relate" in her book, *Womanist Ethics and the Cultural Productions of Evil*, as a way to penetrate beyond the surface to the hidden truths of Black peoples' lives. Morrison's essay is concerned that slave narratives do not tell or reveal the interior lives of enslaved people because they are written to accommodate the white reader. Morrison feels her job was to rip the veil off for truths.[1] Like Townes and Morrison, I am concerned with the truths regarding the lives of Black Tulsans in the Greenwood District and the development of Black Wall Street, which was later destroyed in the 1921 Tulsa Massacre and then rebuilt.

Over the last one hundred years, many have recounted different stories, shared memories, as well as told truths and untruths about the people of Greenwood and the Tulsa Race Massacre. Yet, I question if the history has adequately revealed who Black Tulsans were and the astounding Black resilience they demonstrated. Townes states that she is "more interested in getting into the interior worlds of those who endure structural evil as well as the interior worlds of structural evil itself to discover what truths may be found there."[2] Conveying truths and memories of Black Tulsans' lives are important history and creates sacred memory of Black culture. However, the history regarding the Tulsa Massacre blamed the innocent Black race for the tragedy. The truth is African Americans sought to escape the terrorism from the South and to live as full citizens in Tulsa. Instead, escaping the South and relocating only further instituted the horrific experiences of terrorism and painful abuses through the evil of white supremacy.

What is critical for me is to investigate the truth and memories related to the interior lives of Black Tulsans, which exhibit a great sense of communal unity, successful entrepreneurship, and extraordinary faith in order to endure the terrorism from white hegemony. To further pursue the relationship between history and memory, I employ several scholars from Townes's *Womanist Ethics and the Cultural Production of Evil* who provide clarity for the challenges. French historian Pierre Nora's essay "Between Memory and History: *Les Lieux de Memoire*," Maurice Halbwachs's contribution on collective memory, Werner Sollors's memory as possible counter-history, and

---

1. Townes, *Womanist Ethics and the Cultural*, 11.
2. Townes, *Womanist Ethics and the Cultural*, 12.

finally Carolyn Walker Bynum's *Fragmentation and Redemption* provide helpful insights.

All these scholars offer slightly different views on history and memory. Their different analyses on history help us to remember and understand better the history of the Tulsa Race Massacre. "Constructed history replaces true memory; history is a reconstruction of what no longer exists and calls for analysis and criticism, memory oozes out of a group; memory is unconscious reproduction whereas history is a conscious effort to reproduce."[3] Halbwachs posits that collective memory comes not only from the various groups but also the individuals. Sollors's view on memory is helpful for understanding Black Tulsans' experience because he suggests, "Memory may become a kind of counter-history that challenges the false generalizations in exclusionary, 'History.'"[4]

> Indeed, for oppressed or subjected peoples, memory may serve as a corrective to dominant sociocultural portrayals of history. However, it is when they are polarized and then drawn along the color lines of Black and White, Sollors observes, that history usually becomes the terrain of Whites. It is objective, rational, and true. [When] memory is the terrain of Blacks, it is subjective, emotional, and suspect.[5]

The dynamics of history and memory are helpful for interpreting Black Wall Street as well as the two-day event that occurred in 1921. Sites of memory, according to Nora, are "the places where memory 'crystallizes and secretes itself.' These include archives, museums . . . memorials, practices . . . mottos . . . basic texts and symbols."[6] I found myself doing research in all of these "sites of memory." What follows is a retelling of the experiences of Black Tulsans as gleaned from these "sites of memory."

The Beginnings of Greenwood

Although white Tulsa was booming from oil production, Tulsa was still separated by an extreme racial divide. On one side of town, white citizens

---

3. O'Meally and Fabre, "History and Memory," 5, quoted in Townes, *Womanist Ethics and the Cultural*, 13–14.

4. O'Meally and Fabre, "History and Memory," 15, quoted in Townes, *Womanist Ethics and the Cultural*, 13–14.

5. O'Meally and Fabre, "History and Memory," 5, quoted in Townes, *Womanist Ethics and the Cultural*, 13–14.

6. Nora, "Between Memory and History," 8, quoted in Townes, *Womanist Ethics and the Cultural*, 14.

were major oil producers, workers on oil rigs, and reaping the benefits of the growing massive wealth. On the other side of town, a new Black community was burgeoning on the streets of Greenwood, Archer, and Pine. Even though Black Tulsans could not directly participate in the oil industry, the Black community did benefit from general wages paid for domestic laborers, day laborers, shoeshiners, and the expanding Black population that could patronize only Black businesses. However, because of racism, Negroes were restricted to living in specific areas of Tulsa unless they were employees in the domestic profession and lived on the property of their white employers.

Racial segregation also prevented African-Americans from gaining access to the white economic growth exploding in the other areas of Tulsa. Despite the racist behavior and ethos of white supremacy and hatred, Greenwood would blossom into a successful "city within a city," eventually becoming known as the "Negro Wall Street,"[7] and later Black Wall Street.[8] But for those who despised the Black race and the Greenwood District the area was often referenced as "Little Africa," evidenced in newspapers articles.[9] The perspective of the newspapers and journalism is a critical factor highlighted here because journalists helped to shaped and convey specific identities of the Black community and Black culture. We will later see how the newspapers and other journalism were complicit in helping to ignite the massacre, which is equally important.

The Greenwood District began with the main street called Greenwood. Greenwood Street intersected Archer Street and Pine Street.[10] According to historian Scot Ellsworth, Black Tulsans started to live in the Greenwood District in 1905.[11] One of the early African-American pioneers in Tulsa was O. W. Gurley, a land owner and wealthy entrepreneur from Arkansas. He

---

7. "In Tulsa, this increasingly prominent African American entrepreneurial pool congregated primarily in a single business district, beginning at the intersection of Greenwood Avenue and Archer Street. Greenwood Avenue, likely named after Greenwood, Mississippi, became known as The Negro Wall Street. Legend has it that famed African American educator and author Booker T. Washington bestowed this moniker on Tulsa's vibrant black business district." Johnson, *Black Wall Street*, 9.

8. "'The Negro Wall Street' (later referred to as the 'Black Wall Street of America,' reflecting the African American community's changing sociopolitical identification) was well on its way to reclaiming its national reputation as an African American business center par excellence." Johnson, *Black Wall Street*, 98.

9. "This section of Tulsa was a city within a city, and some malicious newspapers take pride in referring to it is [as] Little Africa." Jones Parrish, *Events of the Tulsa*, 7.

10. Greenwood, Archer, and Pine represent the acronym GAP. The popular singing group, GAP Band, of the 1970s, derived its name from the intersection of these three street names in Tulsa.

11. Ellsworth, *Death in a Promised*, 14.

was born in Huntsville, Alabama in 1868. After graduation from Branch Normal School in Jefferson County, Arkansas in 1884, he began teaching. He taught in Jefferson County for eight years and later he married Emma Wells, from Holly Springs, Mississippi. Gurley had a presidential appointment with President Grover Cleveland. No details indicate the type of position or his length of service; however, he resigned from the appointment and moved to Oklahoma during the 1889 land run, eventually settling in Perry, Oklahoma and holding the position of principal for the city's school.[12]

Gurley later moved to Tulsa in 1906 and is considered the founder of Black Wall Street. Gurley was a wealthy man by his inheritance of 320 acres in Arkansas from his father, worth $35,000; the equivalent today would be approximately ten times this amount.[13] Gurley made significant contributions to Greenwood with both his acquisition of land and his business developments. When he moved to Tulsa, he purchased forty acres of land, which were reserved "to be sold to Coloreds only."[14] During this epoch in history, many African-Americans would have been restricted from purchasing land from white owners.

Gurley owned the first business on Greenwood; this rooming house was owned and operated with his wife Emma. Retired Senator Don Ross displays this picture in the "Greenwood exhibit" found in the Greenwood Cultural Center. Dorothy DeWitty reports in her *Tulsa: Tale of Two Cities* that Gurley's first business in Tulsa was a grocery store. Either way, Gurley is given the credit as the pioneer of entrepreneurship in Tulsa. Gurley and Emma owned other residential properties, and they built three two-story buildings. Other commercial businesses were housed in the Gurley Hotel: Brunswick Billiard Parlor and Dock Eastmand & Hughes Café. Located in one of their other two-story buildings was Carter's Barbershop, Hardy Rooms, a pool hall,[15] and cigar store.

The historic Vernon African Methodist Episcopal Church (AME) in Tulsa held their beginning years of worship in the Gurley building and Gurley was one of the founding members.[16] This is an example of how the busi-

---

12. Ross, *A Century of African-American*, 5. The Black Wall Street exhibit of history and the massacre is housed in the Greenwood Cultural Center, Tulsa. The story is largely based on *Pride and Infamy—The Black Wall Street of America*, an unpublished manuscript written by former State Representative Don Ross.

13. No information exists on how his parents became wealthy or purchased the 320 acres that he inherited.

14. Ross, *A Century of African-American*, 5.

15. The pool hall was located in another building and was in addition to the Billiard Room. Ross, *A Century of African-American*, 5.

16. Ross, *A Century of African-American*, 5.

ness owners on Black Wall Street were deeply invested in and committed to their churches and faith praxis. Vernon AME Church is the only original building that existed on Greenwood before the 1921 Massacre that remains there today. A few other historic churches from the time of the massacre still exist in the Greenwood District; however, only one other church in addition to Vernon is actually located on Greenwood.

Mt. Zion Baptist is another historic church just one street over from Greenwood; this church probably has the most significant memory related to the 1921 Massacre because the photographers captured the church on fire that night. First Baptist is another historic Black church, which is currently located on Greenwood; however, during the time of the massacre it was positioned at another intersection. I will discuss all these churches later in this chapter. According to the court records, by the time of the massacre, Gurley's properties were valued at approximately $200,000. Gurley lost everything in the massacre.[17]

Education was one of many areas divided by prejudice. In Tulsa, formal education began in 1905. "Jake Dillard, a constable and businessman, built Tulsa's first African-American school, housed in a small church at Archer and Kenosha streets, that year."[18] Additional Black schools were established. In 1908, Dunbar School was built for grades one through eight. This was a two-story, eight-room brick building. By 1912, Dunbar School also housed the high school grades. Although it was not located on Greenwood, Booker T. Washington High School opened in 1913 as a four-room structure. By 1919, Washington High School had expanded to a two-story, sixteen-room brick building.[19] Today, Booker T. Washington is no longer an all-Black school; it is an extremely diverse magnet school, with extremely competitive admission requirements.

Mary Jones Parrish,[20] who wrote the only eye-witness account of the massacre, posits that the separate school system for African-Americans in Tulsa is a reliable indicator of the progress for Black citizens. She further states, "In spite of the fact that commercial Tulsa has grown in leaps and bounds almost 'overnight,' our separate school system has been able to keep

---

17. Ross, *A Century of African-American*, 5.
18. Johnson, *Black Wall Street*, 11.
19. Johnson, *Black Wall Street*, 11.
20. Mary E. Jones Parrish wrote the only eye-witness account regarding the Tulsa Massacre in *Events of the Tulsa Disaster*. Included in this book are the events from the night of the massacre, the circumstances regarding the aftermath, and many personal testimonies from others who experienced the massacre. Parrish further outlines and records many of the losses incurred from commercial and residential property.

pace with this rapid stride."[21] I will use the literary work of Jones Parrish in much greater depth in chapters 4 and 6, drawing on her eye-witness account of the massacre.

At the same time the schools were growing so were businesses and other services for African-Americans. "In 1907, the same year Oklahoma became the forty-sixth state of the Union, two black physicians, a newspaper (the *Tulsa Weekly Planet*), three grocers and several other business and professional establishments called Tulsa's African-American community home."[22] According to Scott Ellsworth,[23] the Black population represented 10 percent of Tulsa in 1910. African-Americans even had a trade union called Hod Carriers Local 199, which was a union that represented those working in the professions as bricklayer, plasterer, and masonry.[24]

THE PROFESSIONALS OF BLACK WALL STREET

The developing expansion for Black Wall Street was most likely perceived as a threat to the "white social constructs" in Tulsa. Black businesses were growing in number and Black people's money turned over many times within their Greenwood community. African-American professionals began to build beautiful homes and have the finer things in life, which fostered resentment from everyday working whites. As the Negro race was progressing, white supremacy and the Jim and Jane Crow laws forced them to a place of "double consciousness"—ostracized and limited to their own community except for employment purposes. Many Negroes had come to Tulsa for a fresh start and with dreams they could accomplish. African-Americans built their own lives daily and excelled in professional services, supported by communal living. Many Blacks in Tulsa prospered.

The white hegemonic powers were unyielding though threatened by the Negro race as they watched the Greenwood District expand. They also envied the progress of the Negro race as multiple Black entrepreneurs acquired property and the area began to evolve into what eventually became Black Wall Street. Demonstrably, the prominent racial divide presented itself as a powder keg capable of eruption at any moment, driven by the fuel of resentment. Nonetheless, most of the literature is quick to acknowledge that, despite the growing success of the Greenwood District, many areas in

---

21. Jones Parrish, *Events of the Tulsa*, 68.
22. Jones Parrish, *Events of the Tulsa*, 14.
23. Scott Ellsworth is the author of *Death in a Promised Land*. Ellsworth wrote his dissertation on the 1921 Tulsa Race Riot; he also served on the Race Riot Commission.
24. Ellsworth, *Death in a Promised*, 14.

the District people also lived in poverty. "On some of the side streets adjacent to the famed avenue was the world of poverty that some black Tulsans shared with their racial brethren throughout America."[25] Until this point in history, white America and the white social constructs had prevented African Americans from fully utilizing their freedom or achieving success and Tulsa would prove to be no exception.

Historically, the interlocking oppressive social structures, along with social exclusions based on race and supported by unjust laws, had already set a precedent for how the Black race would be treated not just in Tulsa, but around the country. The codification of prejudice, or the "typifications of blackness," and the reinforced perennial behavior by whiteness towards the Black race established the ethos and treatment practiced long before this Negro race arrived in Tulsa. The historical existentialism regarding the privilege of white supremacy created such a moral evil and hatred against the Negro race that Blacks were prevented from the ability to live freely, or even as human beings in the eyes of white hegemony. This meant Black people were only of value when providing services for white people and beyond this servitude perspective, Blacks were not seen as valued humanity or perceived as full and equal citizens.

In the early formation of Greenwood, Tulsa had two Black physicians. Johnson posits that Dr. R. T. Bridgewater was the first doctor in Tulsa. The second, Dr. Andrew C. Jackson, was a physician and surgeon, most often remembered and highlighted in the different sources. Dr. Jackson was described as "the best Negro surgeon in America,"[26] according to the Mayo brothers. Dr. Jackson's practice provided care for Blacks and some white Tulsans. The first dentist in Tulsa was Dr. J. Littlejohn. By the time of the massacre, the directory lists fifteen physicians and two dentists. Unfortunately, Dr. Jackson was shot and killed during the massacre as he tried to surrender. "A teenage white boy murdered Dr. Jackson in cold blood as he rushed unarmed from the flaming inferno he once called home, hands held high in the air during the peak of the riot."[27] Another version of the incident states the rioters said they would protect Dr. Jackson if he surrendered from defending his home. Once he surrendered and came out with his arms lifted, they shot him twice. Jackson was later "dumped on the steps of Convention Hall and left to bleed to death."[28] He received no medical attention.

25. Ellsworth, *Death in a Promised*, 16.
26. Ross, *A Century of African-American*, 5.
27. Johnson, *Black Wall Street*, 10.
28. Ross, *A Century of African-American*, 10; Black Wall Street exhibit housed in the Greenwood Cultural Center, Tulsa.

As the Greenwood community continued to grow, Black media helped to create new forms of resistance against the social and political hegemony. A. J. Smitherman was another major figure and voice in Tulsa, most notably remembered as editor and publisher of his weekly newspaper the *Tulsa Star*. Smitherman was from Childersburg, Alabama, born in 1883. He originally moved to Muskogee, Oklahoma in 1908 and began his newspaper there, later moving to Tulsa in 1913. Don Ross writes that Smitherman was the "consciousness" of Tulsa as much as he was a leader. Mary Jones Parrish explains that Smitherman hated Jim Crowism and advocated successfully against many of the racial challenges in the state arena. Smitherman's newspaper and work ethic were similar to Ida B. Wells-Barnett's. They both used their gifts as writers to publish the vicious acts and terrorism hurled against Black people. This determination helped them spread an undeniable voice protesting racial injustice and white hegemony.

One of Smitherman's early activist movements addressed the election board. "It was necessary to redistrict the city, but this was done, and Tulsa had the distinction of being the first and only city in the country having an election board composed exclusively of colored men."[29] Smitherman was uncompromising and persistent with his tongue and pen as he fought on behalf of his people.[30] The white terrorism against the Negro race in Tulsa was extreme and even supported by Christian churches. Jones Parrish explains one aspect of terror against Blacks from a Christian leader in this way: a local pastor from one of Tulsa's leading white churches in 1914, viciously attacked the Black community with verbal assaults from his pulpit and comments that were later published in the *Tulsa World*.[31] Although Jones Parrish does not provide us with the pastor's name or the details of the slander, it was enough to elicit a response.

Smitherman defended the Black community by responding with an article, also published in the *Tulsa World*.[32] Smitherman's answers to the outrageous accusations were so well received by even some white men and women that he was commended and invited to speak at some white churches following the article.[33] Jones Parrish writes that the pastor that made these public attacks tried to form a mob that laid in wait for Smitherman. However, they were not successful. Another example of the vicious racist

---

29. Jones Parrish, *Events of the Tulsa*, 77. Jones Parrish does not provide dates, but I estimate some time between 1913 and 1918; this is the time frame in which Jones Parrish is writing about Smitherman's activism.

30. Jones Parrish, *Events of the Tulsa*, 77.

31. Jones Parrish, *Events of the Tulsa*, 77.

32. Jones Parrish, *Events of the Tulsa*, 77–78.

33. Jones Parrish, *Events of the Tulsa*, 78–79.

remarks from Christian leaders against the Black community will be made by a Methodist Bishop, printed in the newspaper immediately following the massacre. (This is highlighted in chapter 6.)

The terrorist acts of mobs, burnings, and lynchings were unrelenting. In 1917, a mob in Dewey, Oklahoma burned the homes of twenty Black families. Smitherman personally traveled to the town to investigate the incident. He later reported the findings to Governor R. L. Williams, and thirty-six men were arrested for the crime, including the mayor of the town.[34] Smitherman's activism for justice continued in 1918 when another mob, this time in Bristow, Oklahoma, attempted the lynching of a young Black man. Smitherman was serving as the justice of the peace in Tulsa County. Jones Parrish elaborates on the details:

> [Smitherman] took three willing colored men and hastened to the scene, after sending urgent telegrams to the Governor asking for state aid. The young man was saved but Smitherman was betrayed to the mob by a colored man who still lives in Bristow. After more than an hour in the hands of the mob he escaped and fearlessly published the facts in his paper.[35]

Smitherman and his *Tulsa Star* newspaper were recognized as a forceful voice to contend with, using print media for political leverage and power, all of which made outstanding contributions to Tulsa and the state of Oklahoma. His newspaper plant was valued at $40,000 or possibly more; he employed both Black and white employees.[36] Following the massacre, Smitherman was accused of influencing the "uprising of the Negro men against whites" to contest the mob that desired to lynch Dick Rowland.[37] In the end, Smitherman lost everything. According to State Representative Don Ross, Smitherman was forced into exile with his wife and five children because of the charges related to the massacre. According to history, they fled with nothing, first to Boston and later to New York, where he eventually established another newspaper.

John D. and Loula Williams owned several businesses that provided services to Black Tulsans. The Williams's reason or purpose in moving to Indian Territory was given in John's response to his young son's curious question, "why Oklahoma, Dad?": "I came out to the promised land."[38] This phrase "promised land" is an example of how African-Americans have

34. Jones Parrish, *Events of the Tulsa*, 77–78.
35. Jones Parrish, *Events of the Tulsa*, 78.
36. Ross, *A Century of African-American*, 7.
37. Jones Parrish, *Events of the Tulsa*, 79.
38. Ellsworth, *Death in a Promised*, 1.

intricately woven and framed their hopes in religious promise.[39] Loula had their son William in 1905. Black doctors were not plentiful for Black women giving birth during this time; as a result, Loula traveled to Hot Springs, Arkansas for the services of a Black physician. This probably represents their social status as well as the medical challenges Black women experienced regarding care for their bodies. John was from Mississippi and Loula from Tennessee; indeed, they had come for a new start and were quite successful.

Professionally, the Williams prospered in their business pursuits. John came to Tulsa with experience as a steam engine mechanic from working on the railroad in his hometown and these skills allowed him to find a job at Thompson Ice Cream Company, working on their engines. It was not long before John turned his talent into his own business, an automobile repair shop. In 1911, they purchased a Norwalk automobile; they were the first Blacks in Tulsa to own a car. As Tulsa exploded and others bought cars, John's side repair business became his full-time business.[40]

Loula was also gifted and had the entrepreneurial spirit. "About 1912 they built a three-story brick building at the northwest corner of Greenwood and Archer avenues."[41] Loula managed and operated a confectionary on the first floor of this building, which yielded large profits for their family. According to Ellsworth, this was Tulsa's first refreshment gathering place beyond the bootleg whiskey joints. Loula had a twelve-foot fountain and seating accommodations for almost fifty; she sold ice cream, candy, and sodas. The Williams lived on the second floor of this building and leased the third floor out to dentists, doctors, and lawyers as office space.[42]

By 1914, the Williams built another building farther up on Greenwood—two-stories, with twenty-one rooms of boarding quarters on the second floor. John had hoped to expand his garage for his auto service on the first floor in this space but was informed the city ordinance would not allow rooming houses to be located above garages. The limitations of these plans turned out to be the best business opportunity for the Williams, because instead they opened the Dreamland Theatre, which was also managed

---

39. Both Oklahoma as a whole and Tulsa in particular were often referenced and considered to be the "promised land." Important to note is that this phrase "promised land" is also associated with the biblical text referencing the Exodus story that so many African Americans adopted as their own story—of Moses leading the Hebrews out of slavery and into the promised land. Spirituals have also represented a form of oral text and sacred texts, which have further demonstrated how Black people frame their religious experience and hopes for a better tomorrow. Rev. Dr. Martin Luther King, Jr. even used this phrase in his "I've Been to the Mountain Top" speech in 1968.

40. Ross, *A Century of African-American*, 9; Ellsworth, *Death in a Promised*, 1.

41. Ellsworth, *Death in a Promised*, 2.

42. Ellsworth, *Death in a Promised*, 2.

by Loula. Many places provided the city with entertainment; however, the Dreamland Theatre was a landmark in Tulsa.

This was the first Black theatre in Tulsa, according to Don Ross—it was the first Black entertainment center in the state.[43] They purchased equipment from a theatre that went bankrupt in Oklahoma City. They showed silent movies and had live entertainment. Ross comments, "In addition to silent movies and music concerts the theater would host speakers such as NAACP firebrand W. E. B. DuBois who had urged self-defense against the tirade of lynching."[44]

The Williams Dreamland Theatre

Figure 6. The Williams on Greenwood and Dreamland Theatre. Source: University of Tulsa, McFarlin Library, Special Collection.

On the evening of the massacre, the Williams's young son Bill was decorating with classmates for the Booker T. Washington's prom in a hall on Archer Street, but there was no prom celebration on the night of May 31, 1921. The early warning of a possible lynching was first announced that

43. Ross, *A Century of African-American*, 9; Ellsworth, *Death in a Promised*, 2–3.
44. Ross, *A Century of African-American*, 9; Ellsworth, *Death in a Promised*, 9.

evening at the Dreamland Theatre; little did people realize as they rushed into the streets that it would result in the massacre. Young Bill had run into the theatre to warn his mother at work. "Inside the theater, a man got up on stage and told the audience, 'We're not going to let this happen. We're going to go downtown and stop this lynching. Close this place down.'"[45] The Williams lost everything in the massacre. "John and Loula would file more than $200,000 in court claims without success."[46]

The contributions this couple made to Black Wall Street represents significant history in Tulsa; albeit, their services exhibit how critical it was for the African-American community to be their own sustainers of all services and economic advancement. The Williams utilized entrepreneurial ability to develop economic stability in order to provide some necessities for their own Greenwood community, but white supremacy, hatred, and jealousy would terrorize the Black city to the point of destruction.

Unfortunately, when race and economics intersected and became conveniently agitated and ignited by the greed for land and jealously, the result in Tulsa was complete terrorism. The loss of property that the Williams experienced of $200,000 from their businesses in the massacre, and the loss that all the other Black Wall Street businesses owners experienced, was explicit evidence of the terror found in the conflictual intersectionality of race, economics, law, and white power. The innocent Black owners were vulnerable to the white political powers in Tulsa and the law that supported racism. Innocent Black people, both business owners and local residents, experienced terror when they lost their livelihoods and their homes while the law blamed them for the massacre. They were terrorized again economically when the insurance companies denied all their claims because the massacre was categorized as a race riot, which insurance companies do not cover.

The white powers in Tulsa were not only jealous of Black success but they wanted the land that African-Americans owned. Innocent Black Tulsans experienced terrorism when no legal resources or laws could overcome the hatred they faced or would advocate for them. African-Americans in Tulsa were building wealth and power through economic development from a Black Nationalist perspective, beyond the walls of the white social constructs that rejected and sought to oppress them. The laws, however, did not protect them. The Black nationalist perspective was represented as Negroes initially desired to build an all-Black state but continued as they built

---

45. Ellsworth, *Death in a Promised*, 3.
46. Ross, *A Century of African-American*, 9.

the Greenwood District and lived in traditional communalism and in full support of one another.

Transportation was another important component in the early twentieth century for Black Wall Street and all the hustle and bustle on Greenwood. During the early days of the Greenwood District, the streets were unpaved and public transportation was another service that African-Americans desperately needed; however, the taxi services were only for whites.

Simon Berry was yet another entrepreneur and major contributor to Black Wall Street. Berry had a business mind that made him a wealthy man and he cared for his community. He started a "jitney service" that provided transportation for Blacks. He used his topless Model-T Ford and the cost to ride was a nickel. He later developed another line, which ran up and down Lansing Street. This meant people could travel all the way to downtown and back on just one nickel. Eventually, he brought in bus services that were operated by his mechanics. It was recorded that Berry made as much as $500 per day.[47]

Berry was also an aviator and owned his own airplane. He and his partner James Lee Northington had a successful airline charter service as well. Wealthy white businessmen utilized their service in the mid-1920s. In addition to the bus system service, Berry owned the Royal Hotel in the Greenwood District. According to Johnson, the bus service lasted for about twenty-five years. The City of Tulsa eventually purchased Berry's transportation service; however, he sold his business under the restrictions "that African-Americans be allowed to ride and that African-American drivers be allowed to operate the routes running the Greenwood District."[48] Berry was known as an entrepreneur and for giving back to his Black community. After the massacre "in 1926 he acquired land and established a park on thirteen acres located on Madison Street between Virgin and Young streets, complete with a swimming pool, a dance hall, and picnic grounds."[49] Simon Berry made multiple contributions to his Black community in the Greenwood District.

Beyond the extreme racial segregation of Tulsa, both Black and white Tulsans were economically dependent on one another. The numerous Black businesses were quite successful in providing services for the Greenwood District; however, each business could only employ a limited number of African-Americans in Tulsa. The masses of the Black population were actually employed by white people. Many of the Negroes worked in some form

---

47. Johnson, *Black Wall Street*, 16–17.
48. Johnson, *Black Wall Street*, 17.
49. Johnson, *Black Wall Street*, 17.

of the service industry for whites. Fortunately, Greenwood had special days to the community. "The district would especially come alive on Thursday nights and Sunday afternoons and evenings—the traditional 'day off' for black domestic workers living in white neighborhoods."[50] Since Black people were restricted to only working in these white neighborhoods or live-ins as domestics, when the time came for purchasing goods and services and having freedom as well as fun, Black Wall Street was the place. Thursdays was the day Black women strolled up and down Greenwood shopping, going to the beauty shop, and wearing fancy clothing. Chapter 5 explores the contribution Mabel B. Little made for Black women on these special days. Black Wall Street thrived from the thousands of working-class Tulsa citizens who used and needed its services.

By 1921, the Black population in Tulsa was at almost 11,000 people.[51] According to multiple data resources, the Black businesses during this time totaled 108 (see business listings in the Appendix). However, the Tulsa Race Riot Commission reports from 2001 indicated there were 190 Black businesses at the time of the massacre. Although many of the working-class citizens in the Greenwood District earned hourly wages, the businesses profited greatly from the patronage of the growing Negro population. As Tulsa prospered from the oil boom, so did the Black community. One profession in particular which typically earned lower wages was that of the shoeshine men; however, due to the oil rush and the white oil men who regularly utilized the services, their earnings skyrocketed.

The money was so good that Dick Rowland, one of the main people the massacre ignited over, quit high school to become a shoeshine professional. "Money flowed in the Greenwood District. It became fashionable for men to dangle twenty-dollar gold pieces from their watch chains. Joe Eaton, a shoeshiner at the Palace Building sported three twenty-dollar gold pieces."[52] The economic continuity and success of Tulsa's Black entrepreneurs developed because of racial hatred and the evil deeply implemented into the daily social structures that ostracized Black people from white society. The dollars in African-Americans' possession circulated within the Greenwood District twenty to thirty times before they left the Black community.

Johnson credits John Sibley Butler, a scholar on African-American entrepreneurship, with bringing to light a phenomenon he calls "economic detour," which means anything such as race, segregation, or discrimination that would impede or prevent equal access to economic markets. I certainly

50. Ellsworth, *Death in a Promised*, 16.
51. Ellsworth, *Death in a Promised*, 14.
52. Johnson, *Black Wall Street*, 14.

agree that what Butler describes as an "economic detour" could either protect Blacks from competition with whites or hinder them. The Negro community was negatively impacted when Black doctors could not use hospital facilities or modern equipment to assist with medical needs, and when Black attorneys practicing in the courtrooms encountered prejudiced judges, etc. I would not describe Tulsa as an "economic detour," though. I believe Black Tulsans initiated a full "economic pathway," expansive in nature with provisions for the Negro culture because no one, until this point, had attempted to meet the needs of the Negro race.

When we look closely at the interior lives of Black Tulsa citizens, terrorism is found in every level of the experience. First, the social structure itself terrorized Black peoples' day-to-day existence because they were restricted from freely moving beyond their own Black community unless they were working for whites. Second, the laws supported and reinforced white supremacy. If Black people were found alone or were regarded to be acting out of what white people considered "their place," they could be lynched or killed by whites with impunity. Third, when African-American homes and businesses were destroyed by the white mobs or Klan, there were no consequences or repercussions for whites, and therefore, no justice and compensation for Black citizens. Consequently, the laws supported the radical racialized behavior against innocent Blacks. Difficult to ignore is the fact that the same biased behaviors that operated almost a century ago are still functioning today. These behaviors function through the legal rulings that are justified in courts of law regarding disproportionate incarceration and on the urban streets when police gun down innocent Black lives, which continues to criminalize Blackness.

Whites, on the other hand, were dependent on Black labor in Tulsa. Whites could not run their households or operate their businesses without the support of Black employees. Albeit whites did not want African-Americans around as equal citizens; yet they depended on the services that Negroes provided. This was probably most vividly apparent following the massacre. Black citizens were taken to detention centers, as if they had committed the looting, burning, and killing, available only for release by their employers.

Finally, a critical component of the womanist tenets, "traditional communalism," is exhibited in how the Greenwood District evolved by creating the necessary services and developing the business expansions in order to meet the African-American communal needs. The racial hatred that operated in the discriminatory Jim and Jane Crow laws of segregation required African-Americans to build their own community in Tulsa. If the Negro race in Tulsa was going to survive, sustain themselves, and flourish, they would have to contend with the social, political, and economic interlocking systems that functioned cohesively to exclude them from this growing city and fast-paced oil boom. A semblance of what womanist scholars name traditional communalism became the foundation for the Greenwood community and Black Wall Street.

CONCLUSION

This chapter reviews sites of memory and how we understand who can tell history. Toni Morrison and Emilie Townes challenges us to penetrate beyond the surface for exploring the hidden truths about Black lives. The beginning of Greenwood allows us to see the social conditions of racism and a city divided by Jim and Jane Crow laws that necessitated Black entrepreneurship and services for their community. I highlighted those who were given credit for founding Black Wall Street and the business development. I introduced many of the business owners who occupied the Black business district and provided services for the benefit of the Black community. I also investigated important details regarding the interior lives of these remarkable people and shared the contributions they made during their time. Ultimately, we can see how traditional communalism unified a community to endure.

CHAPTER 4

A Living Faith
Black Religion, Praxis, and Greenwood

> In the years after slavery was abolished, the historic Black Church became the most important institution among African Americans other than the family. Not only did churches fill deep spiritual and inspirational needs, they also offered enriching music, provided charity and compassion to the needy, developed community and political leaders—and did all of this free of white supervision.
>
> —STACEY AND JUAN FLOYD-THOMAS, CAROL DUNCAN,
> STEPHEN RAY, LYNN WHITFIELD
> *Black Church Studies: An Introduction*

BLACK RELIGIOUS FORMATIONS AND PRAXIS

ONE OF THE MOST interesting components in society and the formation of a nation has been the role of religion. For white America, the early religious beliefs that they were a chosen nation and race caused Europeans to live and operate by several myths, as detailed by Richard Hughes in *Myths America Lives By*. These myths assisted in helping to develop a new nation called America. These untruths established hierarchies in the value of humanity based on skin color, instituted whiteness as superior, and transmitted lies over generations, which created the evil of structural racism and the oppressive social structures that have terrorized the lives of the African-American race for centuries.

For Black America, religion has been the inspirational hope, strength, and traditional communalism; it has provided the Black race with persistent resilience in a constant struggle against systemic racism and the ability to overcome oppression. Religion has provided solace for African Americans, and offered what I call a universal language, regardless of denominational background. Religion through many hermeneutical lenses of God and faith praxes has been African-Americans' very power and sustainer or, to use the familiar Black religious metaphor "a rock in a weary land," in order to endure the violent acts of terrorism in a city and nation that desired to eradicate them.

Today, one hundred years later, Tulsa has beautiful historical churches from the Black Wall Street era still standing and providing worship services. This exemplifies a long history of religious praxis and faith among African-Americans in Tulsa. I did not find actual documents that can outline Black faith in Tulsa; however, so much more tells the story of faith praxis and religious history. The significant artifacts that we have include the oral tradition of Black culture, Black religious traditions, pictures, denominational history, the women's club movements birthed from the churches, and the institutions that still exist. Using the above components, investigating the historical formation and praxis, and observing the environment in which Negroes lived, we can construct an understanding of what religion and faith practices meant for the Black race and the African-American community in Tulsa.

Mary Jones Parrish gives us some immediate insight into her faith and hermeneutic of God in the opening pages of her book. She prayed on the night of the massacre for courage to endure. This represented a hermeneutic of "her God" as one who cares and is willing to provide what she needs, including the ability to be sustained. On the night of the massacre when it was time for Jones Parrish and her daughter to leave their house and run to another location, she comments, "We placed our trust in God, our Heavenly Father, who seeth and knoweth all things,"[1] and then they ran into the street toward safety as the shooting was happening. Someone screamed, "get out of the street or you and your daughter will be killed!"[2]

Faith in God and religious practice were powerful resistance tools, creating foundational support for the Black residents living in Tulsa, and Blacks across the nation. African Americans built their faith through history

1. Jones Parrish, *Events of the Tulsa*, 10.
2. Jones Parrish, *Events of the Tulsa*, 10.

from their ancestors, which they derived from various sources of influence. In the decades prior to the Emancipation, whites often used Christianity to create docile slaves. But enslaved Negroes were able to distinguish between this white Christian god, cloaked under oppressive Scriptures, which caused white slave masters to proclaim, "slaves obey your master," and their own God of power, who not only sustained them but gave them hope for a better day coming. For the enslaved Africans, an early theological understanding established God as a sustainer, but also a God who empowered them with the ability to overcome their oppressive conditions. Their biblical hermeneutics of God and African praxis created freedom and hope in a new promised land.

The biblical hermeneutic and theology of an African God provides strong insight for how Black faith has been developed and transmitted across Black culture, which can ultimately be traced to better understand early twentieth-century faith in Tulsa. Black faith is certainly not monolithic; therefore, we have many variations of Black faith praxis represented throughout multiple Black denominations. However, there are some similar religious foundational components found in most of them. I will briefly present some of the Black historical religious claims or what I call religious philosophies that helped to shape Black faith and directly influence Tulsa's faith and understanding of God. More specifically, I will trace some historical beliefs and faith praxis components of the African Methodist Episcopal Church.

From a womanist perspective Dr. Emilie Townes explains Black religious synthesis this way: "Slaves interacted with and adapted to a new land and new religion. Their blending of West African cosmology and Western Christianity produced a distinct religion that met the needs of those who sought the presence of the divine in the midst of their struggle to survive."[3] I argue that this religious philosophy would also have applied to the Negroes living in the new "promised land" of Tulsa a century ago. Townes, *In A Blaze of Glory,* offers insight regarding how many Black women demonstrated lived religious praxis, which she defines as womanist spirituality. She posits that "womanist spirituality" is a social witness; this social activism flows from the roots of surviving the injustices African Americans endure in society.[4] Townes further explains that womanist spirituality, "is born out of a people's struggle and determination to continue to find ways to answer the question, do you want to be healed? With the Yes! of our lives and work

---

3. Townes, *In a Blaze,* 19.
4. Townes, *In a Blaze,* 10.

we do for justice."⁵ Womanist spirituality will also be exhibited in the Black women's club movement.

Allan Callahan's *The Talking Book* shows that enslaved Africans adopted the Exodus story as their own. "The immediacy of African-Americans' identification with the oppressed children of Israel was seemingly spontaneous and marked the vast gulf between the religion of the master and the religion of the slave."⁶ During early Black religious formation, many forerunners, both female and male, such as Harriet Tubman, Sojourner Truth, Alexander Crummell, Bishop Henry McNeil Turner, and others, helped to shape theological perspectives of God for the many who migrated west.

Womanist theologian Jacquelyn Grant articulates a Black theological hermeneutic or a biblical interpretation through this lens in *White Women's Christ and Black Women's Jesus*: "The understanding of God as creator, sustainer, comforter, and liberator took on life as they [Black women] agonized over their pain and celebrated the hope that as God delivered the Israelites, they would be delivered as well."⁷ She continues by explaining the role of Jesus in the womanist tradition. "Chief among these . . . was the belief in Jesus as the divine co-sufferer, who empowers them in situations of oppression. For Christian Black women in the past, Jesus was their central frame of reference."⁸ The significance here is Jesus identified with the suffering of Black women and the Black community.

Another essential component of religious formation and faith claims for African Americans was the music called the spirituals. Cheryl Townsend Gilkes writes, "The 'sorrow songs,' [as labeled by W. E. B. DuBois] the Negro Spirituals or the *spirituals* came to be the musical hallmark of the African presence in the United States."⁹ Townsend Gilkes elaborates, "The spirituals speak about a wide variety of human situations, shaping our attitudes toward coping with our [Black] problems."¹⁰ Spirituals were created by the enslaved and handed down through oral tradition. There is no written form of spirituals before the Civil War.¹¹ Townsend Gilkes posits this important understanding:

> The spirituals are one of the most important sacred productions in the African American experience. These 6000-plus

5. Townes, *In a Blaze*, 10.
6. Callahan, *The Talking Book*, 86.
7. Grant, *White Women's Christ*, 211.
8. Grant, *White Women's Christ*, 211.
9. Cannon, Townes, and Sims, eds., *Womanist Theological Ethics*, 217.
10. Cannon, Townes, and Sims, eds., *Womanist Theological Ethics*, 218.
11. Epstein, *Sinful Tunes and Spirituals*, 280.

religious songs, created, and hammered out by slaves in the southern United States represent a body of religious knowledge that expresses the core values and beliefs of a dynamic religious tradition that transcends denominational boundaries and that shapes the consciousness, beliefs, and practices of African American Christians.[12]

The first written form of spirituals was published in 1867 with 136 songs in a book entitled *Slave Songs of the United States,* by William Francis Allen, a white author. The Jubilee Singers, organized in 1871, transformed the spirituals into acceptable listening music for white audiences as they traveled the world and performed.[13] Music played a critical role in religious development and faith claims; in 1905 these spirituals would have been sung in Tulsa's Black Churches.

Black religious formation and praxis is clearly expressed in C. Eric Lincoln and Lawrence Mamiya's section on the "Black sacred cosmos." The Black sacred cosmos was constituted by the cultural and religious practices that gave value to what was sacred or divine to African people and how they have functioned historically to sustain African faith. African ancestors brought their faith and cultural praxis with them. These sacred praxes were handed down over time and later infused or blended with Christianity, which is defined as syncretism. These African-Americans migrating west had a strong religious foundation based on their ancestors' praxes and their own desire for freedom and justice. This becomes evident as they quickly established their churches of various denominations.

The Black sacred cosmos in Tulsa was represented in various ways through the integration of culture and religion. As Lincoln and Mamiya explain, "culture is the form of religion and religion is the heart of culture."[14] Black Tulsans' religious praxis can be understood as a foundation of their faith life that was deeply interwoven into daily living. Jones Parrish exhibits the sacred cosmos in her testimonial expressions of faith praxis and the justice required for communal needs. Following the massacre, as Jones Parrish and her daughter stood in line for clothing and sandwiches, she saw all of the race in the same position of devastation, even those who once had great wealth had lost everything. She said, "I breathed a prayer to the Heavenly Father for strength."[15] When Jones Parrish saw a truck with a red cross on

---

12. Cannon, Townes, and Sims, eds., *Womanist Theological Ethics,* 218.

13. Information for this section was collaborated with Howard Wiley, a current PhD student writing a dissertation on spirituals.

14. Lincoln and Mamiya, *The Black Church,* 7.

15. Jones Parrish, *Events of the Tulsa,* 14.

it, she said "this meant that *The Mother of the World* was close at hand and was not forgetting any of her children in distress, even tho they had black faces."[16] When she was close enough to actually read the Red Cross sign, she stated "I breathed a prayer of thanks."[17]

The freedom, justice, and ethical concerns found in the sacred cosmos were demonstrated in the larger community when Jones Parrish writes, "About this time a body of loyal race men called a meeting at the First Baptist Church and organized *The Colored Citizens' Relief Committee* and the *East End Welfare Board*."[18] Following the massacre this group organized to help the homeless rebuild and to fight the ordinances passed that tried to stop them from rebuilding their businesses. Jones Parrish further expresses her thoughts on the disaster: "the most significant lesson it has taught me is that the love of race is the deepest feeling rooted in our being and that no race can rise higher than its lowest member."[19] The Black sacred cosmos was at the core of Black Tulsans' lives.

African-Americans also believed "the experience of oppression is more likely to find immediate resonance with the incarnational view of the suffering, humiliation, death, and eventual triumph of Jesus in the resurrection than with an abstract concept of an impersonal God."[20] Lincoln and Mamiya posit, "A major aspect of black Christian belief is found in the symbolic importance given to the word 'freedom.'"[21] They explain that "freedom" through a religious understanding has offered hope in Black lives. During the time of slavery, "freedom" meant to be unshackled; now in this nineteenth-century moment, freedom meant the opportunity for Blacks to move about the country freely[22] in the pursuit of happiness—a formidable US declaration since 1776.

Black religious faith praxis and faith claims were developed through all these mechanisms, which for me represents another way of understanding traditional communalism. Whether we highlight African-Americans blending African cosmology with Western Christian faith, Black theological interpretations of Jesus and freedom, a womanist hermeneutics, spirituals, the sacred cosmos, or the Black church, they all served to create a sense of unity and Black religious faith culture. These components were the lived

16. Jones Parrish, *Events of the Tulsa*, 17.
17. Jones Parrish, *Events of the Tulsa*, 14.
18. Jones Parrish, *Events of the Tulsa*, 20.
19. Jones Parrish, *Events of the Tulsa*, 20.
20. Lincoln and Mamiya, *The Black Church*, 4.
21. Lincoln and Mamiya, *The Black Church*, 4.
22. Lincoln and Mamiya, *The Black Church*, 4.

Black experiences in church and the communities. Traditional communalism not only represented a Black journey together, fighting to thrive against structural racism and oppressive social structures, but it also symbolizes something special for Black women.

Traditional communalism represented for Black women their unification as Black women in the struggle, with a determination to dismantle the structures that sought to define and regulate them. Black women used traditional communalism as a catalyst for modeling their social witness through activism to improve their social conditions. This is clearly demonstrated in the exemplary work of Evelyn Higginbotham's *Righteous Discontent*, as she explicates the "politics of respectability" and the major women's movement from 1880–1920 in the Black Baptist Church. This same social witness was also happening in the African Methodist Episcopal Church through their Women's Missionary Society. Finally, another movement of traditional communalism is found in Black women's efforts exhibited through the Black women's club movements across the nation. This movement is represented in Tulsa and discussed in chapter 3.

TRACING THE AFRICAN METHODIST EPISCOPAL DENOMINATION

Black religion and Black faith were essential to the resilience of African-American experiences because it offered hope in the time of constant terror and sustained the people with a determination to succeed despite the hegemonic conditions. Tracing the African Methodist Episcopal (AME) denomination is another way to explore Christian believers' praxis of Black faith. I will briefly review the denomination's inception and a few bishops' theological philosophies to better understand how the larger connectional church transmitted religious praxis for the Tulsa church.[23]

The AME church was founded in 1787 under the name "Free African Society" in Philadelphia; "it was usually their objective to provide not only

---

23. A few factors distinguished the AME Church from the Baptist Church in Tulsa. First, the AME church name incorporates the word *African* in the title. Second are the locations. Vernon AME was located on Greenwood and the two Baptist churches were on other streets. Third, the AME was slightly older. Fourth, the AME Church was a connectional church, which means it was associated with a larger church body located in many other cities across the United States. Finally, the worship services were probably different from the Baptist church. The AME Church was more guided in its worship by connectional liturgy. The AME would probably have been considered more conservative in its worship style; the praise and outward expressions of praise would have been quieter than in the Baptist churches.

for religious needs, but for social service, mutual aid, and solidarity among 'people of African descent.'"[24] In 1816, AMEs held their first annual conference. Richard Allen and his wife, Sarah Allen, were the founders of the AME Church and they had been instrumental in espousing equality, full humanity, justice for the Black society, and freedom in spiritual worship. The AME Church did exceptional work in the United States, but during the next several decades their mission field would also include Haiti, Cuba, Jamaica, Antigua, the Virgin Islands, Tobago, Barbados, Trinidad, the Bahamas, and Bermuda.[25]

The AME Churches in the north had already experienced many years of freedom and the opportunity to freely worship; however, prior to the Civil War, the AME churches were limited in the South. The reflection on God, the theological claims of who God is, and how God's immanence and transcendence were illuminated in the life of Black people over time identifies a phenomenal history of faith that sustained the Negro race and propelled them forward.

Bishop Daniel Alexander Payne was the sixth elected and consecrated bishop in 1852; he served first in Charleston, then Florida and Texas. The *AME Discipline*[26] reflects only three other bishops were serving during his time. He was a strong advocate for education and helped with the founding of Wilberforce University, the oldest private historically Black university. Wilberforce was originally founded in 1856, operating until 1862 when the Civil War impacted enrollment. The university was newly incorporated in 1863. Bishop Payne served as president from 1863–1879. "The African Methodist Episcopal Church, the first to enter the South was particularly effective in organizing congregations."[27]

Following the Civil War and during Reconstruction, Bishop Payne received thousands of new members. He was a native of Charleston and returned after thirty years to organize the South Carolina Conference in 1865. Thirty years prior, Bishop Payne had a school where he taught Black children to read and write until whites claimed it was illegal and closed it.[28] "AME growth was so rapid that by 1878 it was necessary to divide South

---

24. Wilmore, *Black Religion*, 107.
25. Wilmore, *Black Religion*, 133.
26. Forty-ninth General Conference, *The Doctrine and Discipline*, 7.
27. Raboteau, *African-American Religion*, 70.
28. Raboteau, *African-American Religion*, 70.

Carolina into two conferences."[29] By 1880, the AME Church was at 400,000 members, mostly from the South.[30]

Bishop Henry McNeal Turner was another AME clergyman and the twelfth elected and consecrated bishop in 1880. He served for forty-one years; when he became bishop, seven other bishops were serving at the time.[31] Bishop McNeal Turner established over one hundred churches in the South. He was a chaplain in the Union Army and very vocal before and after the Civil War. Bishop McNeal Turner made substantial contributions in shaping theological understanding for African Americans and his construction of what I see as a form of Black liberation theology laid a strong foundation for how African Americans understood God and were developing faith in God toward the late nineteenth century.

Bishop McNeal Turner was also an extremely controversial figure because his praxes were authentic and radical. For example, he supported women in ministry and ordained the first woman, Sarah Hughes, in 1888.[32] The Church reprimanded him and told him the AME Church did not ordain women; yet he supported the women's suffrage movement. Turner believed strongly in Black Nationalism and promoted the "Back to Africa" movement. Turner proclaimed, and often preached, that God is Black long before we named a Black theology of liberation. All of these practices made him controversial.

Bishop McNeal Turner was a strong advocate for justice, and he did not believe America would treat Black people equally or with justice. He heard "an address by [Alexander] Crummell, and from that day the mission of the church in Africa and the repatriation of African-Americans became the two great passions of his life."[33] Bishop McNeal Turner believed in mixing religion and politics. Although he held many positions in government, he did not have much respect for the country regarding the treatment of Blacks. He offered hope and a faith in possibilities for churches in Africa who were fighting against colonialism and racism. Wilmore writes, "Turner's theology culminated almost a hundred years of black theological reflection on the origin, destiny, and responsibility of blacks to demand their God-given rights in the United States and, at the same time, bring freedom and the Christian faith to Africa."[34] He was determined to confront the injustice.

29. Raboteau, *African-American Religion*, 70.
30. Raboteau, *African-American Religion*, 71.
31. Forty-ninth General Conference, *The Doctrine and Discipline*, 7.
32. Dodson, *Engendering Church*, 94.
33. Wilmore, *Black Religion*, 150.
34. Wilmore, *Black Religion*, 152.

Bishop McNeal Turner proclaimed and practiced a clear theology of resistance. "By 1880 he believed that Black religion was essentially a protest movement against the disobedient white church that had reduced African-Americans to obsequious believers in their own spiritual inferiority and the right of whites to dictate the terms of religious faith."[35] The phrase "protest movement," consolidated with the blending of religion and politics, conveys that Blacks believed that God was on their side and explicit in their fight for justice. "Blackness gained wider acceptance in religious usage when in the late nineteenth century, Bishop Henry McNeal Turner of the AME Church declared that 'God is a Negro' in response to the growing conservatism of the AME Church and African-American community."[36] One of Bishop McNeal Turner's most famous and memorable quotes follows:

> We have as much right biblically and otherwise to believe that God is a Negro, as you buckra or white people have to believe that God is a fine looking, symmetrical and ornamented white man. For the bulk of you and all the fool Negroes of the country believe that God is white-skinned, blue-eyed, straight haired, projecting nose, compressed lipped and finely robed white gentleman, sitting upon a throne somewhere in heavens . . . and why should not the Negro believe that he resembles God as much so as other people?[37]

Bishop McNeal Turner was a radical believer in God's love and powerful activism through faith that African-American people could achieve justice against a white racist America. Some think Bishop Turner was truly ahead of his time; perhaps he was just right on time.

Although the bishop referred to a growing conservatism in the AME Church, the statement was more in relation to his desire to influence others by his radically constructed self-practice and the philosophy of a "Black theology of liberation at the core of his preaching and writing"[38] in the church and larger society. Fundamentalism did not have a large impact on the AME church in 1921. The teaching from leading bishops like Turner was too strong in the AME church and always propelled toward an explicit drive to challenge injustice through social and political advocacy, rather than driven by white conservative evangelicals' rhetoric. In later years, fundamentalism may have grown to have a stronger influence on AME biblical interpretation.

35. Wilmore, *Black Religion*, 150.
36. Terrell, *Power in the Blood*, 75.
37. Wilmore, *Black Religion*, 152.
38. Wilmore, *Black Religion*, 150.

This revolutionary thinking, advocating for protest leadership, focus on education, and the demand for justice all represented the social responsibilities of what the AME denomination believed, and would have be posited and practiced in Tulsa, and across the denomination. These socio-historical faith claims, united with unmovable belief in God, created a strong Black faith and liberation for the African-Americans who belonged to this denomination.

Vernon AME Church was founded in Tulsa in 1905 under the AME revolutionary proclamation. Vernon AME was one of the first churches established on Greenwood Avenue, often referred to as one of the "mother churches," and destroyed in the massacre; it was later rebuilt and still exists today. This brief reflection and tracing of the AME founding and southern AME church expansion helps to provide insight into the Black religious faith that undergirded the migration movement west.

WHAT DOES BLACK FAITH SHOW?

The Black faith practices in Tulsa during the years of Black Wall Street evolved from a long religious history, spanning from the African shores to the American shores during enslavement and ultimately to the Black church experience. Black hermeneutics of faith and worship have been transmitted down through the generations, in response to changing social conditions, and political and ethical developments over time. There are identifiable remnants from African history and theological praxis in the forms of music, song, dance, ring shouts, unity, determination and the Spirit of God, which have not only sustained the African-American culture but made it victorious during the Black Wall Street period and beyond. This deep faith praxis, although it varies between denominations, demonstrates the ability to transcend the arduous Black struggle in a nation fraught with dehumanization and reveals the sheer stamina of Black resilience against prolonged terroristic and oppressive conditions.

One may ask, where is the evidence that remnants of African history and theological praxis made the Black race victorious not only during this time but since? Albert Raboteau explores this very question in his book, *Slave Religion: The Invisible Institution*, which outlines a debate between Melville Herskovits and E. Franklin Frazier.[39] Herskovits's research advocates to debunk five myths of the Negro past and argues that some African praxis has been retained.[40] Herskovits also states African remnants are

39. Raboteau, *Slave Religion*, 48–75.

40. "The myth that Herskovits was intent on destroying was the belief that the

visible in dance, drums, ring shouts, and the power of the Holy Spirit. He further posits remnants are found even in baptism, particularly in the Baptist tradition, which is related to African water cults. Frazier, on the other hand, disagrees with Herskovits and claims he has exaggerated his points.[41]

I believe evidence is further represented in the actual survival of African-Americans' religious praxis. The specific form of worship and distinct praxis are unique to Black churches. Another form of evidence is in the lived experience that demonstrates the theological belief that God is a sustainer. Just as their African ancestors had endured the abuse through the Middle Passage and slavery, so did African-Americans in Tulsa endure white supremacy and racism. For Black Tulsans, the evidence of theological praxes of faith was in an African God that they brought with them and through faith they constructed their "never-give-up" attitude and determination to rebuild again while continuing to fight for justice.

Historian John Hope Franklin's father, who was an attorney in Tulsa, represented the Black residents in court following the massacre. Black Tulsans had to legally fight the system for the permits and the right to rebuild their properties against new city ordinances. This deeply rooted tenacity is evidence of faith in a God who promises victory and strength to overcome all circumstances. Moreover, these Black Wall Street business owners were church members, people operating on strong faith in God. While doing my research in Tulsa, I visited First Baptist Church, among others. They showed me the plaques displayed on the wall, which represented their deacons from this era. These same deacons were also the business owners of Black Wall Street listed on the Memorial Statue housed in front of the Greenwood

---

American Negro had no past except a history of primitive savagery in Africa from which he had been delivered by contact with European civilization in America. For Herskovits the destruction of this myth was not simply a matter of detached scholarship. It also had important practical ramifications in the struggle against racism. To deny that the black American had a culture and history of significance and sophistication in Africa and to suggest that African culture was not advanced enough to endure contact with superior European culture was to imply that Negroes were an inferior people. Furthermore, Herskovits thought it important to recognize the historical relevance of African retentions in order to evaluate cultural differences between white and black Americans in scientific rather than racist terms." Raboteau, *Slave Religion*, 48.

41. "Perhaps none took him to task for it more forcefully than the black sociologist E. Franklin Frazier, the foremost spokesman for a position diametrically opposed to Herskovits'. While admitting the existence of African retentions in Latin America and the Caribbean, Frazier denies that African culture was able to survive the conditions of slavery to any significant extent in the United States. He admits that a few individual slaves remembered something of their background in Africa. However, exceptions prove the rule: African traditions and practices did not take root and survive in the United States." Raboteau, *Slave Religion*, 52.

Cultural Center, another clear form of faith evidence practiced, which gave them victory.

According to the research statistics from Scott Ellsworth, by 1921 there were twenty Black churches in Greenwood District; however, not all of the churches were located on Greenwood. The founding dates of these churches range from 1895 (with Vernon African Methodist Episcopal being listed as the oldest) to 1920 (with Mission, a Nazarene church, being the newest). One correction to these statistics—the Vernon AME Church was not founded until 1905,[42] making Macedonia Baptist the oldest church, beginning in 1897[43] or 1899.[44] The number of church denominations were categorized as follows: one Seventh Day Adventist church, seven Baptist churches, one Christian, two Church of God, two Church of God in Christ, one Holiness, five Methodist churches, and one Nazarene.[45]

The three most historic or "mother" churches are Macedonia Baptist (later changing its name to First Baptist), Vernon AME, and Mt. Zion Baptist. Among the twenty churches, these three churches had the largest memberships during the time of the massacre and all three churches still exist in 2018.[46] (See Appendix for pictures.) First Baptist's membership ranged from 300 in 1914 to 800 in 1920. By 1921, their membership had declined to only 100 parishioners with no reason given for the loss. Vernon's membership went from 203 people in 1913 to 700 by 1921. Mt. Zion had the most members, with 296 people in 1914 and 950 in 1921.[47] All the other churches had significantly fewer members than these three "mother" churches.

When the massacre occurred, the other Black churches were burned to the ground. Thankfully, the Black First Baptist Church was untouched; the rioters thought it was a white church because of where it was positioned on a cross-street bordering a white residential district that was not on Greenwood.[48] First Baptist is now located on Greenwood. Mt. Zion has the most repeated story regarding the massacre history because they had just completed the building of a brand-new edifice, which cost $92,000. Today, only a limited number of pictures are available from the two-day massacre; however, one of the pictures most often circulated depicts Mt. Zion on fire.

42. Johnson, *Black Wall Street*, 89.
43. Ellsworth, *Death in a Promised*, 113.
44. Johnson, *Black Wall Street*, 91.
45. Ellsworth, *Death in a Promised*, 113. Two AME churches, two Colored Methodist, and one American Methodist church existed.
46. See Appendix for pictures of these historical churches.
47. Ellsworth, *Death in a Promised*, 113. See Appendix.
48. Johnson, *Black Wall Street*, 92.

Prior to the massacre, the Mt. Zion congregation had raised $42,000 to build their new church and they took an unsecured loan from a Jewish contractor for $50,000. On April 4, 1921, they had their first service. Just a little over one month later, on May 31, and June 1, 1921, everything lay in ruins. By 1942, the congregation had paid off the first mortgage of a nonexistent church and they built a new edifice in 1952. However, the cost to rebuild at that point was $300,000. Mt. Zion received donations from across the nation.[49] At the time of the massacre, Vernon AME Church had only just completed their fully paid-for brick basement in 1914 and this is where they worshiped. In the years that followed, they would erect the beautiful structure that still stands today.

Reflecting on the histories of these churches, I ask the question—What does faith have to do with it? I am painfully reminded of just how difficult it must have been to live when domestic terrorism and raging white violence was the regular order of the day. I am reminded of a more recent event, with this same violence and terrorism, when I reflect on the church massacre at Emanuel African Methodist Episcopal Church in Charleston, South Carolina on June 17, 2015. Nine people were killed, including the senior pastor and state senator Clementa C. Pinckney, during a Bible study, by a twenty-one-year-old white supremacist who admitted he wanted to start a race riot. In the midst of such a hostile world, and given the seemingly incurable presence of racial hatred, religion and faith in God have been constant sustainers, representing an unrelenting hope of deliverance for a better day. This was as important to the African-American community then as it is now.

Black Tulsans and Blacks around the nation lived in socio-political and socio-economic environments that were created to exclude them and functioned daily against the Black race as a whole. I believe the question of theodicy was not a concern for Black Tulsans, particularly as it related to the massacre. African-Americans knew white Americans hated them. They understood the racial climate was biased, unfair, and filled with hostility operating through the Jim and Jane Crow systems. The laws were designed to make them invisible, appear as less than human, certainly not worthy of freedom, and always guilty when accused by whiteness, in any situation.

The political positions in government were held by whites, never representing Black interests, and therefore yielded nothing to enhance the Black milieu. Even the idea of equal citizenship was unacceptable because whites did not believe Africans Americans deserved success or opportunities that advanced their economic conditions such as ownership or occupancy in positions of prominence such as doctors and lawyers. Another important

---

49. Johnson, *Black Wall Street*, 84–87.

factor is that Black people were constantly threatened or terrorized for the smallest infractions almost daily, whether at work or just moving about in day-to-day activities. Consequently, lynching was always a possibility. Rather than Black Tulsans, and other Black people across the nation, focusing on these social and political constructs of oppression, they turned to God and their faith.

This Black ethos required a religion that had a God big enough and powerful to handle all of these circumstances. Black faith required a God that was both immanent and transcendent, a God who would not leave them or allow them to be without the ability to overcome their situation, a God who was large enough to go with them to all spaces and places. I argue that this is the theological understanding that preachers lifted up on Sunday mornings to encourage the hearts of their members. The Black churches in the Greenwood District had large memberships, a clear indication of strong religious praxis, and reliance or dependence on a God who sustained them. The weekly religious praxis, which helps to developed Black faith, offered a connectivity beyond just music, worship, or praise. Black faith and worship addressed the people of Greenwood's current social conditions and the repercussions of racism.

Understanding a God who loved them as an internalized theological claim gave rise to a posture of protest, determination to fight, and pushback against the ongoing injustice. "For many African Americans, the church did much more than attend to spiritual needs. In Tulsa, in the state of Oklahoma, and in all of America, African American churches condemned white supremacy and preached social equality and social justice. Ministers and parishioners often became social activists . . ."[50] Black faith operated in the spirituality of resistance, which provided hope and sustained a people who lived through the persistent threat of white terror. Black American religious faith is predicated on this history.

WOMANIST HERMENEUTIC

A womanist hermeneutical lens provides another epistemology for how the Greenwood community understood God and faith praxis. Clarice Martin present an excellent model to know the role of Black faith as she examines the work illuminated in proto-womanist Maria Stewart's spiritual autobiography. Stewart was a teacher, journalist, public lecturer, women's rights activist, abolitionist, and great woman of faith. Many of her speeches used Bible references to convey to her audiences her radical proclamations of equality

50. Johnson, *Black Wall Street*, 82.

and opportunity for African-Americans. Stewart was concerned with the problems of suffering and evil in relation to racism, and she was committed to social activism, as so many other proto-womanist had exemplified.

If we want to investigate through historical artifacts for answers on how faith can be understood in Tulsa, we can extrapolate from Stewart's spiritual autobiography to see how she viewed faith in God. This belief in God represented an approved agency for her but also propelled her forward as a Black woman who radically fought against racism with the Word of God. We can be confident that radical faith spawned by activism has been handed down over generations, as so many other Black women in history such as Jarena Lee, Harriet Tubman, Sojourner Truth, and Anna J. Cooper exemplified, by eliciting this same confidence in action through the power of their faith in God. Stewart "affirmed and promulgated the action of a God who fights against the oppressive evils of life."[51] Stewart's theology, grounded in the theodical question, promotes activism against the evils of racial suffering.

I posit that, with all the social challenges and evils operating against the Negro race living in Tulsa during the period of the massacre, Stewart's theological philosophy as applied to the "sites of memory" of Black Tulsans demonstrates that Black Tulsa residents of Greenwood would have engaged and used the powerful "Word of God" as their tool of defense, just as she had done. Stewart "accepted readily the notion that liberation from racial suffering and evil required a human response of participation with God in securing and encoding the realities of justice within the lives of African-American peoples."[52] I believe the people of Tulsa's Greenwood community had received this type of faith knowledge from earlier generations, like Stewart's, and utilized those tools or perspectives of theological resistance in their churches. Their human response in participation with God through their faith meant "making a way for themselves in society out of what appeared to be no way" through Black Wall Street, by entrepreneurship and community self-sustainment.

The abuse from racism would have required the ministers to preach sermons and encourage the African-American people to stand strong in the face of constant opposition and thrive as a community. Martin uses Cone's argument to reiterate Stewart's bold activist theology and I use it to argue for Greenwood's boldness. "The biblical witness of a God who is involved in history, who acts within history to advance social, economic and political justice for the poor and unwanted in society has always been a fundamental

---

51. Martin, "Biblical Theodicy," 24.
52. Martin, "Biblical Theodicy," 24.

and bedrock tenet of African-American religious faith."[53] Womanist efforts regarding religion and society continue to impact the nation.

Another significant womanist model that embodied theological, epistemological, and faith praxis during the same epoch of the Black Wall Street is discussed in Evelyn Brooks Higginbotham's *Righteous Discontent*. Higginbotham's interpretation in the chapter on "Politics of Respectability" reveals insights on how Black Tulsans might have navigated the waters of indifference. The "politics of respectability" conceptually derives from a Black Baptist women's movement, which operated across the country from approximately 1900 to 1920 under the umbrella of the Women's Convention, an auxiliary of the National Baptist Convention.

This women's movement evolved during the time that Black women's voices were resonating culturally. Contributing social influences included the migration, employment opportunities, the suffrage movement and more. In Tulsa, social particularities would have included Black women owning businesses. The Black Baptist Women's Convention created a safe place for these women of faith to discuss the social issues concerning them and their Black communities. However, "Their [Black women's] religious-political message was derived from Biblical teachings, the philosophy of racial self-help, Victorian ideology, and Democratic principles of the Constitution of the US."[54]

Critical to observe is the impact this Black women's movement had on both the white and Black society because their efforts were a direct result of their belief in God. Black women utilized their religious faith to transform stereotypes of their Black ontology, which white America had created, and the Black Baptist church was their conduit. Tulsa had seven Black Baptist churches, more than any other denomination represented there, during the early twentieth century.

I believe the Black Baptist Women's Movement reached these Tulsa churches and the Black women participated in spreading the mission and influence of faith praxis to transform their community. The movement operated as a strong form of resistance for African-American women and their communities as they challenged the social structures of injustice and discrimination against Blacks in America during a time when racial prejudice was acceptable.

Black women's resistance functioned as self-determining and self-defining by dismantling the pejorative images a white racist nation had created for them and establishing new positive perceptions of who they were. Negro

53. Martin, "Biblical Theodicy," 24.
54. Higginbotham, *Righteous Discontent*, 186.

women's resistance exhibited an ethical stance as they fought for acceptance in a white society that not only oppressed them but dehumanized them. African-American women's resistance was political as they demanded changes against white superiority in discriminatory laws that devalued and prevented equal economic opportunities. The politics of respectability was strategic; the leaders and members of the Women's Convention implemented ideas, strategies, and vocalized the power of Black Baptist women's commitment. The politics of respectability was a true activist challenge to the social structures that marginalized Black women and the terrorism that functioned daily within the systems against them.

According to Higginbotham, "professionalism became synonymous with respectability"[55] and the political empowerment of Black women's agency. The Women's Convention later partnered on projects with the National Association of Colored Women (NACW), NAACP, and developed other organizations to confront the systemic racism and the oppressive systems of social structures. I will explore in a later chapter the role of the NACW in Tulsa. Religious faith for Black women continued to demonstrate a commitment to lifting up the race and transforming society through their God-approved agency and activism.

Traditional communalism was significant to the survival and resilience of the African-American culture in the Greenwood District. Without embracing one another, creating the extreme unity demonstrated in their social milieu, and establishing the vast array of business services for each other, Black Tulsans could not have survived the social evils and torture of white supremacy. Traditional communalism is exhibited in the following exchange:

> "Committed to survival and wholeness of entire people, male and female." Not a separatist, except periodically, for health. [The young girl asked,] "Mama why are we brown, pink, and yellow, and our cousins are white, beige, and black?" [The] answer: "Well you know the colored race is just like a flower garden, with every color flower represented." Traditionally capable, as in: "Mama, I'm walking to Canada and I'm taking you and a bunch of other slaves with me." Reply: "It wouldn't be the first time."[56]

Traditional communalism is embracing Black culture, which has always included multi-culturalism based on our historical Black racial exposures in this country. Moreover, traditional communalism historically

---

55. Higginbotham, *Righteous Discontent*, 216.
56. Floyd-Thomas, *Mining the Motherlode*, 5.

includes Black determination to escape torture, rise above the oppressions of racial segregation, and survive hurt, harm, and death. Love for the Black community is exhibited in the very existence of creating a Black Wall Street. The Negro community understood they lived in a hostile environment and united in order to develop their own city within a white city, and in a nation that excluded them while concomitantly supplying all of their own communal needs. This is the portrait of a truly Black Nationalist perspective, in opposition to the evils of terrorism that haunted them daily.

Womanist work, particularly in ethics, makes a contribution to Christian ethics, as espoused by Floyd-Thomas, "by encouraging us to openly examine issues such as racism, sexism and classism as social evils in need of ethical analysis and ultimately eradication."[57] The ethical injustices of white supremacy, and the hegemonic repercussions that existed in relation to Black Wall Street, highlight these social evils and the critical role they played in understanding the challenges of living in Tulsa during this era. Unfortunately, the construction of Black inferiority set the precedent that has lasted for the past 400 years. "Womanism thus provides a fertile ground for religious reflection and practical application as a thoroughgoing analysis that attends to whatever is culturally centered, critically analytical and socially empowering."[58] What's important is that "such an analysis is not only descriptive but constructive."[59]

The womanist hermeneutic and communal spirit is traditional communalism. The epistemological praxis of Black women's faith as forms of resistance on behalf of the race demonstrates the Black communal experience of unity. As a result, Black Tulsans had an internal desire to continue to "move on" and "hold on." Black Tulsans ignited a spark that turned into a blaze that could not be extinguished. Understanding the Black historical faith praxis and some of the hermeneutics of God, which been handed down through generations, allows us to see how the Blacks in Tulsa invoked this same theological faith praxis to survive until a better day came.

In the early twentieth century, preaching and biblical hermeneutics that connected faith with justice were important historically, as they are even now. Today it appears more evident that the social conditions for African-American people have not drastically changed or there would no longer be a need for this type of theological cry or hermeneutic of God. These theological concepts and faith praxis have helped the African-American culture

---

57. Floyd-Thomas, *Mining the Motherlode*, 2.
58. Floyd-Thomas, *Mining the Motherlode*, 7.
59. Floyd-Thomas, *Mining the Motherlode*, 7.

to endure the evil, violence, and terrorism, to survive and to demonstrate resilience.

When the massacre occurred in Tulsa, even the churches were burned to the ground. I argue that the terroristic presence wanted to not only eliminate their homes and businesses, but also tried to destroy the core of their Black existence and eschatological hope by burning their temples of faith to the ground and eradicating their ability to worship. But the hope and resilience were in their souls—their very ontology, not their buildings of worship.

CONCLUSION

This chapter has focused specifically on religion, one of the most important components that has shaped our nation and more specifically how religion has impacted African-Americans. I fully engage Black religious praxis and the development of faith by reflecting on a variety religious claims that influenced Black syncretism. Reflecting from the African God to the shaping of Black Christianity the African American race has utilized their most powerful tools for resistance and survival, their religious resources. I also trace the AME denomination to better understand their religious philosophies as a denomination and how they impacted Vernon AME Church in Tulsa. A deeper engagement asked the question, what does Black faith or Black religious praxis show us? Ultimately, I explored what a womanist hermeneutic reveals about Black theological understanding and Black women's social witness through activism.

CHAPTER 5

The Hidden Secrets
Black Women's Resistance and Resilience

> From the period of urbanization of World War II to the present, Black women find that their situation is still one of struggle, a struggle to survive collectively and individually against the continuing harsh historical realities and pervasive adversities in today's world... but they have not been able to offset the negative effects of inherent inequities that are inextricably tied to the history and ideological hegemony of racism, sexism and class privilege.
>
> —KATIE GENEVA CANNON
> *Katie's Canon: Womanist and the Soul of the Black Community*

BLACK WOMEN: MEMORY, TRUTH, AND POWER

AFRICAN-AMERICAN WOMEN ARE PHENOMENAL women, particularly as the memories of truths regarding their history are unveiled. When investigating, we find an extraordinary impact from Black women's presence in the early formation of American society and Black culture. Unfortunately, these amazing truths of their power and accomplishments are usually hidden or buried deeply in historical archives, beyond most memories. This chapter seeks to explore and examine the contributions that Black women made during the latter half of the nineteenth and the early twentieth centuries in and through religion and in the larger society. Using the methodologies of womanism, sociological analysis, and womanist ethics, we will see how Black women from all regions of the country worked strategically during this time span to confront the satanic terroristic forces which sought to oppress them and the Black race, with a particular focus on Black women in the Greenwood District of Tulsa during the early twentieth century.

My womanist sociological analysis will illuminate the unique roles and significant accomplishments of Black women all across the country in developing their communities, establishing churches, performing missionary work, implementing the practice of racial self-help improvements, and creating numerous women's movements that swept the nation (such as the Black women's club movement). Their accomplishments transformed both the African-American culture and American society as a whole. Yet, race, gender, and class constraints have caused Black women to be the most subjugated in our society. As a result, their work is often unknown, unrecorded, or simply forgotten.

Black women have always been challenged in their daily socio-political, economic, and religious environments; however, the tenacity expressed in their womanish characteristics and lived agency illuminates undeniable attributes of the African American women. Alice Walker, an award-winning novelist and poet laureate, coined the original four-part definition of womanism in her book *In Search of Our Mothers' Gardens*.[1]

Katie G. Cannon introduced the womanist term into academia through the Christian social ethics lexicon in 1985.[2] Womanist, as an academic orientation, was not only a movement but was also quickly embraced by Black women religious scholars, particularly ethicists.[3] Theologian JoAnne M. Terrell states, "Walker helped black female scholars of religion to name themselves in ways that celebrate their uniqueness, providing mirrors of them to see themselves as fully capable adjudicators of the demands of their

---

1. "1) From womanish. (Opp. of "girlish," i.e., frivolous, irresponsible, not serious.) . . . Usually referring to outrageous, audacious, courageous, or willful behavior. Wanting to know more and in greater depth than in considered "good" for one . . . Responsible. In charge. Serious. 2) A woman who loves other women sexually and or non-sexually. Appreciates and prefers women's culture, emotional flexibility . . . and women's strength. Sometimes loves individual men sexually and/or non-sexually. Committed to survival and wholeness of entire people, male and female . . . Traditionally universalist . . . 3) Loves music. Loves dance. Loves the moon. Loves the Spirit. Loves love and food and roundness. Loves struggle. Loves the Folk. Loves herself. Regardless. 4) Womanist is to feminist as purple is to lavender." Walker, *In Search of*, xi–xii.

2. Floyd-Thomas, *Mining the Motherlode*, 6.

3. Floyd-Thomas, *Mining the Motherlode*, 6.

lives."[4] As a result, Black women scholars have continued to use womanist work as the analytical tools to critique the unethical praxis of society, give voices of power to the multi-dimensional oppressions of Black women including their communities, and implement a new academic consciousness that acknowledges Black women's moral wisdom.

Womanist ethics challenge the very normativity of white androcentric positioning and perspective,[5] by moving Black women to the center to analyze and eradicate the interlocking systems of oppressions that challenge them as well as their Black communities. "Womanist ethics is constructive in that it seeks to determine how to eradicate oppressive social structures that limit and circumscribe the agency of African American women."[6] The efficacy of historiography and sociological analysis in this chapter demonstrates how Black women have utilized the tenets and exhibit the virtues of womanism.

Ethicist Stacey Floyd-Thomas further expanded the original womanist four-part definition into the four tenets of womanist ethics as: "radical subjectivity," "traditional communalism," "self-redemptive love," and "critical engagement." These four tenets, as described in the Introduction, help us comprehend womanist work in greater magnitude. Radical subjectivity is the intergenerational work transmitted between mother and child, or mature women to younger women.[7] It also represents the outrageous, audacious, courageous behavior of Black women and their agency. Moreover, as it is "detected and guided by mother-wit as precious yet precarious, this process entails learning the moral lessons that will allow her not only to survive but also to subvert the triple jeopardy of racism, sexism, classism,"[8] and other forms of oppression.

Traditional communalism is the understanding and recognition of Black women's agency that embraces their entire community, both female and male. The subversive action, which is derived from Black women's radical nature and doing, is for the commitment and survival of the whole Black community. Redemptive self-love means to love oneself regardless. In spite of the "death-dealing effects of such dehumanizing stereotypes"[9] that Black women have experienced, self-love is the goal, which sometimes has been challenging. Black women loving themselves first ignites the courage and

---

4. Terrell, *Power in the Blood*, 102.
5. Floyd-Thomas, *Mining the Motherlode*, 2.
6. Floyd-Thomas, *Mining the Motherlode*, 7.
7. Floyd-Thomas, *Mining the Motherlode*, 8.
8. Floyd-Thomas, *Mining the Motherlode*, 8.
9. Floyd-Thomas, *Mining the Motherlode*, 10.

will to love another woman into wholeness. Finally, critical engagement is Black women's consciousness of their social, political, religious, and economic circumstances that marginalize their freedom and justice. This is Black women's radical willingness and engagement to address the interlocking systems that function to oppress them.

The term "proto-womanist," as defined by JoAnne M. Terrell, is used herein to connect the Black women in the nineteenth and twentieth centuries to the principles of womanism, to avoid anachronism because these historical women evinced the womanist qualities for resistance and survival. Terrell indicates that although these historical women evinced these womanist qualities for resistance and survival, using the term *proto-womanist* prevents one from being anachronistic. Through the lens of these womanist tenets, this chapter will examine and celebrate the contributions Black women made beyond the limitations of social, political, economic, Eurocentric, and hetero-patriarchal normativity.

Black women enlisted fortitude through their faith and belief in themselves, with the determination to improve their lives and communities. As Black women moved west and across the nation, they engaged in the various components of society that operated to make a difference in community, including the dismantling of towering structures that sought to oppress them. Regardless of the obstacles that most Black women encountered historically, or even face today, their profound agency and outstanding contributions to society can usually be traced as a direct correlation to their faith in God.

I begin my sociological analysis with the focus on African American women's treatment and challenges, by integrating Western frontier women's impacts in society, their faith and resilience, womanist sensibilities and virtues. Reflection on these Negro[10] women who are rarely spoken of reveals the terrorism and historical conflict (resulting from race, gender, and class concerns) that these women had to endure. Yet, their spiritual and moral groundings sustained them because they were deeply rooted in a foundation not defined by others. Further reflection provides acknowledgment and memory of their forgotten contributions, while concomitantly offering true insight into the awesomeness of Black women's ontology and existentialism. Moreover, reflection on the historical Black women in religion and society illuminates their virtue.

It is simply amazing to me the outstanding ways in which African-American women have participated in society, with all of their accomplishments, when so often they are unappreciated for who they are, what they

---

10. The term *Negro* is used interchangeably with *Black* and *African American*. I do not consider this term derogatory. *Negro* is being used as a historical racial category, the same as *Black* or *African American* is used today.

have experienced, how they have suffered, and the roles that they inhabited are marginalized or viewed as being on the underside of society and unimportant. "An untold number of black women, such as Diana Fletcher of the Kiowas, joined Native Americans on the last frontier, continuing a tradition that had begun soon after 1492."[11] Another example was a "slave named 'Mary' brought by her owner from Missouri in 1846, [she] may have been the first of her race to reach California from the East. She was the first person of African descent to sue for her liberty in the West."[12] Countless other Black women have been forgotten in history.

The body politics of their existence and survival, along with the diverse range of challenges they encountered through life, demonstrates in this chapter the multiple ways Negro women have worked to counteract terrorism. Ultimately, there have never been any laws to protect African-American women, whether from rape or abuse, gender oppression, or even to defend their character; therefore, the virtue and moral wisdom of Black women have been ignored or in many situations simply denied.

Negro women of history endured many difficult circumstances and overcame obstacles we cannot begin to imagine. The four womanist characteristics are clearly exemplified in the lives' work and efforts of these Black women. Others describe African-American women in this way: "Many [Negro women] proved as tough spirited and resilient as the wilderness they came to conquer."[13] As I explore the radical ways these women functioned in American culture and society by pushing paradigms and dismantling stereotypes, one must recognize the adverse effects of race and never forget the role of gender and class.

Too often, Negro women's bodies were compromised by white men and they endured for mere survival in their social context. At other times in history, the Black woman's body was only for negotiation, profit, and reproduction. There were still other times when Black men desired to engage Black women's bodies for family support and personal satisfaction in the West. Learning to navigate the body politic associated with being a Black woman also becomes both the resistance and resilience of Black women. A prime example of this was the struggles in the West.

Black men in the West needed Black women to move west. Black communities benefited from women's hard work after slavery and societal developments, which promoted expansion of the West. "Western black women, from the Canadian to the Rio Grande border, from Kansas to California,

---

11. Katz, *The Black West*, 282.
12. Katz, *Black Women*, 20.
13. Katz, *The Black West*, 281.

ran hotels, hairdressing parlors, restaurants, and boarding houses; they built churches, orphanages, schools and literary societies."[14] However, the Black race experienced difficulties in the West in building families because Black men in the West largely outnumbered Black women. Such a large disparity existed between the genders that some Black women were enticed to the West through "mail-order bride" advertisements.

The mail-order bride process strongly exhibits the spirit of traditional communalism because "it also takes into account the various gifts, identities, and concerns of black people in general in order to use every resource available to strengthen the community as a whole."[15] Black women made huge sacrifices by going west to build family and community but encountered even greater challenges once they arrived. According to William Katz, this "mail-order bride" system was initiated by married women in the church. This occurred through the church because evidently women feared unhealthy living situations in their town when too many Black men remained single in the Arizona Mining Camps.[16] "Letters were sent back East promising suitable females a secure marriage to an upstanding worker, and a good home."[17] According to the responses, "many [Black women] ventured forth to leave poverty and oppressive conditions behind in search of love, family life and a fulfilling marriage."[18] Demonstrably, the act of voluntarily moving to the West suggests that these proto-womanists displayed the *outrageous, audacious, courageous, and willful behavior of acting grown up, responsible, and in charge* because in so doing they forfeited familial ties in order to position themselves to start families and by extension ensure community survival.

Some of the difficulties with the mail-order bride system for Black women included the fact that the older men received first choice. This made many of the men much older than the young brides coming west; in some situations, they were old enough to be their fathers or grandfathers. In many situations, the women inherited large families from the men's previous marriages. Because the unsanitary conditions of childbirth frequently caused women to suffer and die, men usually lived through several wives.[19] Marriage for these young women certainly presented challenges larger than what they could have anticipated.

14. Katz, *The Black West*, 285.
15. Floyd-Thomas, *Mining the Motherlode*, 9.
16. Katz, *Black Women*, 34.
17. Katz, *The Black West*, 289.
18. Katz, *The Black West*, 289.
19. Katz, *Black Women*, 35–37.

Furthermore, for some of these proto-womanists,[20] the womanist definition proffered by Alice Walker would have challenged the presumed heteronormativity of the pioneer experience as it would have posed further difficulty for same-gender-loving black women in the churches as well as the communities into which they were being assimilated through mail-order marriages. Alice Walker's definition of womanist is one who "loves other women, sexually and/or nonsexually" and "sometimes loves individual men, sexually, and/or nonsexually."[21]

African American women of the late nineteenth century found in the western part of the United States were usually women newly freed from slavocracy in the South and made their marks through their own radical and tenacious determination to rise above the limits white society and white supremacy had tried to shackle them with. "'The mountains were free, and we loved them,' recalled Dr. Ruth Flowers, born in 1902 in Boulder, Colorado. On the frontier, they [Black women] stood out as an elite breed itching to challenge first slavery and then the mold set by white male society."[22] In spite of the challenges, Black women exhibited heroic efforts, often using personal success in society to propel church support. Their "outrageous, audacious, courageous, or willful," "responsible," "in charge," and "serious"[23] womanish faith demonstrated a "never-give-up" attitude in seeking the best opportunities and carving out successes that seemed impossible to accomplish in their part of the world.

The radicalism of their redemptive self-love connotes the depth and breadth of their resilience as frontier women. "Black women, recalled Dr. Flowers, 'were the backbone of the church, the backbone of the family, they were the back bone of the social life, everything.'"[24] The inter-relational components of societal life, church, family, and how Black women negotiated those strategies are the critical engagements of womanism.

African-American Western women's faith and resilience lives in the radical ways of womanism, performing with the freedom to achieve what others may perceive as unattainable, truly *outrageous, audacious, courageous,* and *interested in grown-up doings. Loves the Spirit* propelled Black women to live with the spirit of determination, which pushed beyond the limits of what many said was inappropriate for them or considered beyond their reach. Others probably contradicted their desires to purchase real

---

20. For a definition of the term *proto-womanist*, see Terrell's *Power in the Blood*, 146.
21. Walker, *In Search*, iii.
22. Katz, *The Black West*, 283.
23. Walker, *In Search*, xi.
24. Katz, *The Black West*, 281.

estate or even donate money to establish churches, but these Black women were determined to accomplish the highest level of achievement that a life of faith would allow. The crucial historical deposits that these Negro women made is not represented just in how they endured terrorism found in the physical and mental abuse of slavery, or the emotional abuse of losing husbands and children when they were sold off the plantations, or even in the early days after freedom, but in their absolute determination to somehow live above the devastation and still achieve success.

The virtues of Black women are rarely spoken about. In fact, given the pejorative historical descriptive of Black women's life, they have often been poised to be considered not virtuous at all. While womanist tenets describe how African American women operate, they do not describe their moral character. While the womanist tenets represent the pillars that hold the platform, the morality is what flows from the foundation.

Katie Cannon describes womanist virtues in three ways—*invisible dignity*, *quiet grace*, and *unshouted courage*. "Invisible dignity is black women's self-celebration and self-survival in the midst of adversity."[25] Regardless of how these pioneering women were treated or the adversity encountered, they were able to survive by using their faith in God and agency of determination. These women did not allow societal limitations such as race, gender, class, sexual orientation, or even the circumstances they found themselves in to define who they were or what they could accomplish.

The second womanist virtue, quiet grace, "is the self-knowledge of black women that operates as functional prudence—the search for truth."[26] The word *quiet* speaks to the invisibility of Black women's moral character, and their lack of privilege but still unhindered by fear in response to what was before them.[27] The Black pioneer women discussed in this chapter, in all their myriad contexts, responded with functional prudence, which operates in their moral wisdom; and this is what determines Black women's ability to survive and live. "The Black woman's very life depends upon her being able to decipher the various sounds in the larger world, to hold in check the nightmare figures of terror, to fight for basic freedom against the sadistic law enforcement agencies in her community."[28] Whether an enslaved woman, newly freed, or a woman in the church and club movement, they all lived with threats because of their race, gender, class, and potentially, given the evangelical ethos of the nation, because of their sexual orientation. What

25. Floyd-Thomas, *Mining the Motherlode*, 36; Cannon, *Black Womanist Ethics*, 99.
26. Floyd-Thomas, *Mining the Motherlode*, 36.
27. Cannon, *Black Womanist Ethics*, 125.
28. Cannon, *Black Womanist Ethics*, 125.

was important in using their agency was knowing how to make the right decisions. "As divine wisdom, quiet grace invokes spiritual discernment as a means to aid black women in distinguishing satanic forces from divine will and righteousness from iniquity."[29] Quiet grace has the components of "both spiritual and social features"[30] and is linked to the third tenet of *Loves the Spirit. Loves struggle. Loves the Folk. Loves herself. Regardless.*

The third womanist virtue Cannon posits is "unshouted courage, a virtue evolving from the forced responsibility of Black women."[31] This force is not external, although the circumstances that motivate the responsibility may be derived from there, but flows from the center of who the Black woman is and how she approaches life. Floyd-Thomas characterizes unshouted courage "as a virtue that has at the center a sense of unctuousness and self-affirmation."[32] This idea of self-affirmation comports with Walker's definition of a womanist as one who "loves herself. Regardless." The women in the nineteenth and twentieth centuries radiated this kind of courage and self-love.

African American women's confidence was an outward expression of their extraordinary faith in God; they were convinced God would journey with them. Emilie Townes argues in *In A Blaze of Glory* that Black women's witness and certainty are propelled by their spirituality. Townes states, "Spirituality is a social witness. It is born out of a peoples' struggle and determination to continue to find ways to answer the question, do you want to be healed?"[33]

This absolute belief in the power of God is what allowed Biddy Mason[34] and so many other Black women to keep pressing toward the mark

29. Floyd-Thomas, *Mining the Motherlode*, 37.
30. Floyd-Thomas, *Mining the Motherlode*, 37.
31. Floyd-Thomas, *Mining the Motherlode*, 143.
32. Floyd-Thomas, *Mining the Motherlode*, 37.
33. Townes, *In A Blaze*, 10.

34. Katz, *Black Women*, 21–22. Biddy Mason was born into slavery in Hancock County, Georgia. She had three children by her slave owner. Mason's experience with her body is one of the primary examples of how Negro women's bodies were abused and violated, a true exemplification of repetitious terrorism in the systemic structure of oppression, which relegated their bodies as property while giving slave owners full impunity. When Biddy's slave owner converted to the Mormon faith, they relocated in 1851 to Nevada and then eventually to San Bernardino, California; Biddy had walked most of those 2,000 miles since Georgia. Once in California, she filed a lawsuit and challenged the slave owner to prove he owned her. She won her case. After freedom, she became a skilled nurse, bought real estate, was the first Black woman in her region to own a home, and was a known philanthropist. In 1872, she helped found First AME in Los Angeles. In 1988, Biddy was remembered and celebrated in Los Angeles by the first Black mayor, Tom Bradley, with more than 3,000 people present.

of a true high calling. Chief among their faith, resilience, and confidence, however, was their belief in Jesus as

> the divine co-sufferer, who empowers them in situations of oppression. For Christian black women in the past, Jesus was their central frame of reference. They identified with Jesus because they believed that Jesus identified with them. As Jesus was persecuted and made to suffer undeservingly so were they. His suffering culminated in the crucifixion. Their crucifixion included rape, and babies being sold. But Jesus's suffering was not the suffering of a mere human, for Jesus was understood to be God incarnate.[35]

African-American women had the ability to hold on to a faith not shaken by the tragedies or disappointments of life, but a faith that hoped all things possible—the contributions to establishing churches, building personal financial well-being for themselves, and cultivating communal success and unity. "The spirituality that issues from Black women's lives is found in the moral wisdom of African American women. This wisdom is found in autobiographies, speeches, novels, poems, sermons, testimonies, songs, and oral histories—in their lives."[36] This moral wisdom will continue to be revealed in the life and work of African American women and is seen most clearly in the lives of two women who survived the Tulsa Massacre and were an important part of the Black women's literary tradition: Mary E. Jones Parrish and Mabel Little.

WOMANIST SURVIVORS OF THE TULSA MASSACRE

Mary Elizabeth Jones Parish

Mary Elizabeth Jones Parrish was a Black woman who lived in Tulsa during the time of the massacre. As mentioned earlier, she wrote the only eyewitness account of the two-day event. Her book is titled *The Event of the Tulsa Disaster: The Race Riot of 1921*. Jones Parrish moved to Tulsa from Rochester, New York after the positive encounters she had while visiting her brother in 1918. When Jones Parrish returned home for five months, and then experienced the passing of her mother, she relocated to Tulsa. She explains in the foreword of her book,

---

35. Grant, *White Women's Christ*, 212.
36. Townes, *In a Blaze*, 11.

> I had heard of this town since girlhood and of the many opportunities here to make money. But I came not to Tulsa as many came, lured by the dream of making money and bettering myself in the financial world, but because of the wonderful co-operation I observed among our people and especially the harmony of spirit and action that existed between the businessmen and women.[37]

Jones Parrish's statement exhibits traditional communalism in the raw sense of speaking truth to power. She saw value in the unity and prosperity of Black communal experience.

As Katie Cannon explains, Black women writers "record what is valued or regarded as good in the Black community."[38] Gleaning from the above statement, we can conclude that Jones Parrish's desire was to be immersed in the Black culture and the harmonious spirit of Greenwood and Black Wall Street. Black folks in Tulsa were instituting a new thing, and she wanted to be a part of this growing community. Jones Parrish reflects on the positive values evident in the Black community in the beginning of her book. She reflects upon her arrival to Tulsa, just as she was leaving the Frisco train station:

> One could see nothing but Negro business places. Going east on Archer Street for two or more blocks there you would behold Greenwood Avenue, the Negro's Wall Street, and an eyesore to some evil-minded real estate men who saw the advantage of making this street into a commercial district. This section of Tulsa was a city within a city, and some malicious newspapers take pride in referring to it as "Little Africa."[39]

Jones Parrish writes a counter-narrative to how some tried to negatively portray Black Wall Street. At the same time, she identifies two concepts that are important considerations for why the massacre occurred. First, the real estate men wanted to own the land of this Black business district. Second, the hatred that resided in white supremacist ideology made racists comfortable calling the Greenwood District "Little Africa."

The above quote reveals another crucial fact with the comment, "This section of Tulsa was a city within a city." This confirms that a Black Nationalist perspective existed for the purposes of being self-sufficient and flourishing as a marginalized community ostracized from mainstream Tulsa's

---

37. Jones Parrish, *Events of the Tulsa*, 7.
38. Cannon, *Black Womanist Ethics*, 78.
39. Jones Parrish, *Events of the Tulsa*, 7.

services. As partners in community, Black women in Tulsa demonstrated their unique investment in Walker's second definition of a womanist as those who were "committed to the survival and wholeness of entire people, male *and* female" and in Floyd-Thomas' interpretive framing of traditional communalism.

It is important to distinguish the Black Nationalist perspective from the politics of respectability. The Black Nationalist philosophy was an intentional communalism of racial unity. For example, when the Negro race first came to Oklahoma, they attempted initially to build an all-Black state for their protection against racism, survival, growth, and sustainability. In other words, African-Americans did not need to be embraced by white Tulsans. Racism and Jim and Jane Crow laws had already separated everything such as residential locations, social practices, and access to services; the only people not segregated were those employed by whites.

The Black business owners and Black Tulsa residents had everything they needed. This unity and harmony were features that attracted Jones Parrish to live in Tulsa. The politics of respectability was a philosophy and movement by Black Baptist women as a form of resistance, by using self-determining and self-defining agency to dismantle oppressive structures of power and gain the respect of white Americans.

Jones Parrish was motivated by the philosophy of both Black Nationalism and the politics of respectability, but without consciousness. Jones Parrish used her agency to write the Tulsa story because she valued and embraced the independence that Black Wall Street and the Greenwood District represented. Jones Parrish's social activism through her authorship models what Katie Cannon's theory teaches about the literary tradition. Cannon argues that Black women authors capture the Black community within location, time, and context, whether through fiction or nonfiction.[40]

Black women's work also mirrors the community and reflects the internal value that is usually insularity. Jones Parrish used her gift of writing because she loved and appreciated the philosophy of the Black Nationalism perspective. As a result of the massacre, almost one hundred years later, Jones Parrish demonstrates her own politics of respectability philosophy by believing that the African-American life and history were valuable enough to show the whole nation the deeply imbedded racial injustice and push for the dismantling of those structures.

Jones Parrish's book has been used by many over the years for research, such as in Scott Ellsworth's *Death in The Promised Land* and Hannibal B. Johnson's *Black Wall Street: From Riot to Renaissance in Tulsa's*

---

40. Cannon, *Black Womanist Ethics*, 77.

Historic Greenwood District. Today, only a few copies of this book are available. Originally, only a few dozen copies were made.[41] I will use her text and eye-witness knowledge as we further investigate the massacre.

Mabel B. Little

Mabel B. Little came to Tulsa from Boley, Oklahoma in 1913. She was only seventeen with $1.25 to her name, but she never looked back. She describes Greenwood this way:

> Black businesses flourished. I remember Huff's Café on Cincinnati and Archer. It was a thriving meeting place in the black community. You could go there almost anytime, and just about everybody who was anybody would be there or on their way.
>
> There were also two popular barbeque spots, Tipton's and Uncle Steve's. J. D. Mann had a grocery store. His wife was a music teacher. We had two funeral parlors, owned by morticians Sam Jackson and Hardel Ragston.
>
> Down on what went by the name of "Deep Greenwood" was a clique of Eateries, a panorama of lively dance halls, barber shops and theatres glittering in the night light, and a number of medical and dental offices.[42]

In just a few years, Mabel and her husband Pressley would become a part of all this excitement. They married in 1914 and both became business owners. Mabel opened her beauty shop; people came from all around for her services because few Black hair salons were available, and by 1918 she had so many customers she hired her first operator. This was the beginning of a long, successful career for Mabel Little.

The name Mabel B. Little is most known by Tulsans in relation to the Mabel Little Heritage House. The heritage house is a local museum and tourist site that can be toured by appointment through the Greenwood Cultural Center. The Heritage House is located in the historic Greenwood District of Tulsa at 322 North Greenwood, next door to the Greenwood Cultural Center and the Black Wall Street Memorial. The house is significant because it is the only residential home built in the 1920s that still exists on Greenwood today.

The home was built for Sam and Lucy Mackey after their first home on Greenwood was destroyed during the massacre. The architect they chose to

---

41. See Appendix for author's picture.
42. Little et al., *Fire on Mount Zion*, 26–32; and Johnson, *Black Wall Street*, 16.

design the home did such an outstanding job that he won an award and a $1,000 prize for the architectural design. The Mackeys were regular hardworking people who wanted to model that people in the domestic profession could also have nice things in north Tulsa. The home was later owned by Little. As a Black woman entrepreneur in 1918, Mabel Little exemplified all the tenets of womanism. During the "Urban Renewal" demolitions of the 1970s, Mabel Little, State Representative Don Ross, J. Homer Johnson, and Thelma Whitlow fought to save the home. In 1986 after restoration, the home was renamed in honor of Mabel B. Little.[43]

I personally toured the Mabel B. Little home and it is still beautiful. The historic site is truly a home that many would desire to live in today. The fine home has extremely large square rooms, hardwood floors, and large bright windows. The living room has a fireplace and a formal dining room. Just to the right of the living room is another open sitting room with bright windows on the first floor. The home is a two-story brick and the upstairs has three bedrooms. The huge master bedroom runs from one side of the home to the other. They had all the fine furnishings, china, and so on. The home has all the original pieces such as the sofa, chairs, dining room furniture, and record player. I was impressed by the stately presence of the home, even in 2017. The level of economic achievement had to be very significant to purchase all the fine furnishings. Mabel Little's home, then and now, manifests the invisible dignity of a particular Black woman and, by extension, Black people. The home is an absolute tribute to the accomplishments of this woman and her family. If Mabel and her family's desire was to be an exemplar on Greenwood, they certainly accomplished the task.

Mabel B. Little was a legend in Tulsa.[44] As an act of radical subjectivity, Little penned her own story in the book *Fire On Mount Zion: My Life and History as a Black Woman in America*, where she chronicles her life experiences and the 1921 Tulsa Massacre. She was born Mabel Bonner in 1896 in Spring, Texas. Her family later moved to Boley, Oklahoma, where she attended school. Following high school, Bonner attended Madam C. J. Walker's Beauty College.[45] She moved from Boley to Tulsa in 1913, hoping one day to save enough money to attend Langston University. Boley was "the largest of the twenty-five all black towns that had cropped up in the late nineteenth-century movement to make Oklahoma (then Oklahoma Territory) an all-black state."[46] Within a short time Little met and married

---

43. "Greenwood Cultural Center." See Heritage House picture in Appendix.
44. Johnson, *Black Wall Street*, 121–22.
45. Johnson, *Black Wall Street*, 121–22.
46. Little et al., *Fire on Mount Zion*, 23.

her husband, Pressley; they both worked hard as entrepreneurs. In the early twentieth century, white beauticians were not accessible for Black women, so Mabel worked to provide services to Black women in Tulsa and the surrounding towns:

> In 1917, Little opened the Little Rose Salon, which was the first establishment in Tulsa that catered to African-American beauty needs. Thursday nights saw her shop filled with young women being beautified, as Thursday was the customary "Maid's Night Out," the one night each week that young African-American domestics working in white homes had off.[47]

At the time, limited beauty shop services were available for Black women. At one point, she far exceeded her dreams with more than 600 customers. In her personal life, Mabel Little was also an active member of Mt. Zion Baptist Church and worked closely with the youth. She organized the Young Matrons for the state of Oklahoma and assisted with the National Baptist Convention. She also worked with the Young People's Department on the state and national levels. "Little organized the first church 'Woman's Day' in the state of Oklahoma,"[48] a powerful contribution to Oklahoma and Black women across the state. Little's church participation touched the youth and adults but she did not stop there as she became immersed in Greenwood's culture.

If we glean from Little's spiritual, social, and professional accomplishments, we see the determination of a woman committed to extraordinary expectations and faith. Little exhibits Black women's radical tenacity of believing "all things are possible" with faithful persistence. When their first home burned down during the massacre, they stated, "we will save and build another one." Little was radical and displayed traditional communalism when she was not afraid to be a business professional and opened her beauty shop during unpopular times of racial despair. Although she certainly must have experienced some difficult times, she embraced Black women, from all the surrounding communities, and the Black culture with cosmetology services to uplift other Black women in appearance and self-esteem. As quoted above, Black women working in the domestic profession only had one day a week to beautify and provide self-care for themselves. Because of her redemptive self-love, Little must have delighted in a sense of joy and peace to know she could extend beautician services that blessed other Black women, especially when so many others looked upon Negro women with contempt.

47. *Clio*, lines 15–18.
48. Johnson, *Black Wall Street*, 122.

Little's salons were surely the buzz of the Greenwood community, as women entered with excitement and departed with confidence. I can imagine that men stood on the street as they anticipated the women who would stroll the block, especially on Thursday. Little was critically engaged in all the social components for uplifting humanity. Inside the beauty shop, all the latest and pertinent information was probably exchanged by people looking for jobs, and newcomers looking for information and the hottest gossip. People invited each other to attend worship and sold tickets for the next church or social event. The beauty shop, even as we know today, is a communication hub of the community.

Little stayed engaged and conscious when times became difficult. "During the Great Depression Little uprooted her salon and followed the aviation boom west, moving first to Wichita, Kansas and eventually to Los Angles. Eventually Little returned to Oklahoma."[49] Mabel Little, in the true spirit of proto-womanist commitment, spent many years advocating for the Greenwood community and touched countless lives over the years. She lived to be 104.

Cannon affirms the importance of the literary contributions of women like Parrish and Little when she says, "Black woman's literary tradition capsulizes the insularity of the Black community."[50] This comment demonstrates Black Tulsa was an isolated community within the city of Tulsa. Cannon further explains, "Due to systemic, institutionalized manifestations of racism in America, the Black community tends to be situated as marginated islands within the larger society."[51] Black women writers are not only able to show the hidden aspects of truth, but they also highlight the value and good; their work mirrors the reality and parallels history.

In exercising a literary voice in the face of terrorist oppression, these Black women exemplified radical subjectivity as they used their own stories to speak truth to power. It was in the same womanist spirit that many of their sisters demonstrated redemptive self-love as they organized around the motto of the Black women's club movement: "Lifting as we climb," which translated into meeting the needs of the Black community through education, racial self-help, raising Black standards against claims of immorality, protesting unjust laws, and protection from discriminating laws against themselves and their children.[52]

---

49. *Clio*, lines 19–21.
50. Cannon, *Black Womanist Ethics*, 87.
51. Cannon, *Black Womanist Ethics*, 87.
52. Riley, "Women of Great Falls," quoted in Taylor and Moore, eds., *African-American Women*, 127.

Moreover, "redemptive self-love" allowed Black women to hold their heads up in the face of despair. They moved forward in spite of the obstacles. Otherwise, without loving themselves over the years, they would have become discouraged and these Black women could not have accomplished the outstanding contributions they made. However, I want to expand the term *redemptive self-love* to encompass more than just personal "redemptive self-love." I believe the praxis of "redemptive self-love," or the efforts that erupted from Black women who lived out "redemptive self-love" or practiced loving themselves, created an explosion, a new phenomenon, which translated into a women's movement.

Black women in history were not only able to love themselves, but they also loved other women into what we might define as "wholeness," because they understood that another Black woman's struggle was similar to their own. For the Black women who were not living out or practicing this "redemptive self-love," being loved by the other women who were actively involved in the church movement meant their hearts could be encouraged and lifted also. The expanded definition, or reflected practice of the third womanist tenet, opened the door to embrace other women who were not in the movement. The Black women who were feeling satisfied, "whole," or a sense of personal value were able to encapsulate those who were suffering and move them towards a work of empowerment. The redemption benefit here is the loving concern and caring from other women; subsequently the lives of other Black women were transformed. We can more clearly observe this concept in the women's club movement as we look at the impact on society and history.

BLACK WOMEN'S CLUB MOVEMENT

The first Black women's club was the Colored Women's League, established in June of 1892 in Washington, DC, and incorporated on January 11, 1894. They stated their purpose was to "improve the conditions of colored women."[53] Black women knew they needed unity and power. What better strategy exists than to have a national connection, They sought "to collect facts concerning the moral, intellectual, and social growth of the Negro; to foster unity among them and to promote progress; to determine methods of promoting the best interests of the colored people in directions which would be suggested by the members of the organization."[54] Their goal was to become a national organization. Mary Church Terrell, one of the

53. Wesley, *History of the National Association*, 25.
54. Wesley, *History of the National Association*, 25.

incorporators, said, "a national organization of colored women could accomplish so much good in such a variety of ways that thoughtful, provident women are strenuously urging their sisters all over the country to cooperate with then in this important matter."[55] The women were determined to start a movement that would change the social landscape for Colored women and the African-American race.

The second club was the Women's New Era Club, started in Boston in 1893. The club was led by Josephine St. Pierre Ruffin, her daughter Florida P. Ridley, and Maria Baldwin. The focus here was the support of kindergarten with the Georgia Educational League. The club membership consisted of seventy-five people. The club donated $20 per month to the kindergarten. The organization's newspaper was the *Woman's Era*, published by Colored women, and Josephine St. Pierre Ruffin was the editor. Black women started many other clubs across the nation between 1890 and 1894. The Harper Woman's Club of Jefferson City, Missouri focused on sewing, temperance, and mother's work. The Loyal Union of Brooklyn and New York emphasized better schools and employment. Other clubs include the Ida B. Wells Club of Chicago, Woman's Club of Omaha, Belle Phoebe League in Pittsburgh, Phillis Wheatley Club of New Orleans, Sojourner Club of Providence in Rhode Island, and the Woman's Improvement Club of Knoxville.[56]

The Women's New Era Club had communications primarily through the *Women's Era*, led by Ruffin, which initiated the national organization of Colored women. In response to the national attacks on Colored women, including attacks on Ida B. Wells-Barnett by James W. Jacks—the president of the Missouri Press Association—Ruffin called for a convention in Boston in 1895. "This was to be the first national conference of colored women of America and was initially called the First Congress of Colored Women which assembled on July 29–31, 1895."[57] Jacks alleged "that most colored women in the United States were 'wholly devoid of morality and that they were prostitutes, thieves and liars.'"[58] This kind of vitriolic behavior and comment against Negro women in society is what functions to demoralize their character; unfortunately, this degradation of Black women has continued beyond this epoch in history.

In response to Jacks's tirade, the women exposed his comments nationally. This audacious act of critical engagement boldly confronted the negative rhetoric designed to subjugate Black women. They published

---

55. Wesley, *History of the National Association*, 26.
56. Wesley, *History of the National Association*, 26.
57. Wesley, *History of the National Association*, 26.
58. Wesley, *History of the National Association*, 26.

Jacks's comments in the *Women's Era,* along with the call for action to the first conference for Colored women and notified their clubs throughout the country. Negro women's zeal for justice and to no longer be silent made them determined to take action. "It is to break this silence, not by noisy protestations of what we are not, but by a dignified showing of what we are and hope to become that we are impelled to take this step, to make of this gathering an object lesson to the world."[59] Hallie Q. Brown, one of the early pioneer women of the club movement also embraced the call for a national conference. In her travels as an elocutionist and in meeting with the Colored Women's League of Washington, she thought Black women needed to have closer relationships.[60]

The first national conference meeting was the National Federation of Afro-American Women in Boston. The conference had delegates from ten states and twenty clubs; sixteen states were represented by other women present. Ida B. Wells-Barnett chaired the Committee on Resolution; she had been actively campaigning against lynching and the oppression of Black women. The women focused on a broad array of topics. Jacks's comments became the least of their interests during the conference. Colored women strongly critiqued their race and any shortcomings. They advocated for action in equality for black workers and the termination of discrimination against their labor, a proposed emphasis on homemaking and home purchasing, industrial schools, mother's meetings, rights of Colored citizens of federal troops, criticism of Louisiana State Legislature on separate coaches for Blacks and whites, and the termination of mob violence, lynching, and convict leasing. The women had another conference that year in Atlanta, the Atlanta Congress of Colored Women in December of 1895.[61]

The power of Negro women in the women's club movement began to grow and connect women all across the United States. Black women had become critically engaged in all the social and political components that existed to dehumanize them and oppress the race as a whole. The radical ways in which they responded and strategized started a movement illuminating Colored women's voices that could not be silenced or ignored. Negro women practiced redemptive self-love by not only loving themselves, but also nurturing a love for other Colored women to be empowered and get on board, and by joining clubs in whatever city or state they lived in. Finally, it was the faith of these club women that substantiated their movement because they believed the scales of justice, ruled by God, would generate a new

---

59. Wesley, *History of the National Association,* 31.
60. Wesley, *History of the National Association,* 26.
61. Wesley, *History of the National Association,* 32–35.

life of possibilities for the entire race. Colored women from every region in the country joined in.

Motivated by the critical engagement and redemptive self-love on the national front, the club movement in Oklahoma found its own sense of power that not only connected to the contributions Black women were making to the movement in the far West and across the nation, but demonstrated the continuation of Negro women's determination for societal and communal change. The first women's club in Oklahoma was the Excelsior Club of Guthrie.[62] According to historical facts, following the Oklahoma land run of 1889, Guthrie gained 10,000 new residents. In 1907, the city of Guthrie became Oklahoma's first state capital; however, by 1910 the state decided to move the capital to Oklahoma City.[63]

The Excelsior Club was established in 1906 by Judith C. Horton. Mrs. Horton moved to Oklahoma before statehood and was a graduate of Oberlin College. She was truly a trailblazer and making a difference during a time when Black women's rights were limited. "The Club was also responsible for promoting the cultural enrichment of the citizens of Guthrie by bringing talented and influential groups and individuals to the city, including the Fisk Jubilee Singers, Booker T. Washington and Hallie Q. Brown."[64] Horton's contributions had significant impact on the state. The Excelsior Club founded the first library in the state for Negroes.[65] Horton and other club women in Oklahoma formed the Oklahoma Federation of Colored Women in 1910.

> She led the Federation as its second president, from 1915–1919. She brought the establishment of training schools for black boys and girls to reality. Also, during her tenure she conceived the idea of an official insignia for the Oklahoma Federation which was designed by Miss Manilla Johnson. This insignia was adopted by the national organization and became the insignia for the National Association of Colored Women Clubs in 1930.[66]

Horton's autobiography is entitled *How It Happened*. She writes in the foreword these words:

---

62. Wesley, *History of the National Association*, 506–07; Uncrowned Community Builders, "Judith Horton," lines 2–4.
63. Wilson, "Guthrie," *Oklahoma Historical Society*, lines 21, 26.
64. Uncrowned Community Builders, "Judith Horton," lines 5–9.
65. Wesley, *History of the National Association*, 507.
66. Uncrowned Community Builders, "Judith Horton," lines 12–19.

With the belief and hope that the facts and experiences herein related may lend encouragement and inspiration to many others whose chances are none brighter than mine were, and furnish a few suggestions for those older ones who are grappling with great human problems, this sketch is given to them by the author.[67]

The motto of the Excelsior Club of Guthrie was "To glorify God and uplift humanity."[68] This motto conveys the very conscious spirit that operated within to understand the commitment of Black women in the club movement. Concomitantly, the motto communicates a faith foundation constructed of cement, which we have observed from all of these pioneer women in both society and church. Moreover, the motto presents an extraordinary strength that Negro women operated in to achieve their goals.

The East Side Culture Club of Oklahoma City was another club, founded in 1907 by Harriet Price Jacobson. She moved to Oklahoma after the Cherokee Strip opening in 1883. Jacobson attended school in Emporia, Kansas at Kansas State Teachers College and served in the Oklahoma City public school system for forty years as a teacher. The club contributed financially to the Fredrick Douglass Home. They worked to create a state federation.[69]

The Frances Harper No. One of Muskogee was founded by Lois Perdue. She moved to Muskogee in 1905. Perdue was from Montgomery, Alabama and graduated from Tuskegee Institute. The members desired to build a library for Negroes and with the help of two Muskogee clubs and Mary Church Terrell in 1918 they accomplished the task. They financed three thousand dollars in three months and the Phyllis Wheatley Library was founded. The library existed for twenty-five years; once Muskogee allowed African-Americans to use the city library, it was converted into a club house.[70]

The Oklahoma Federation of Colored Women's Clubs was formed on April 16, 1910. The following clubs existed prior to the federation: "Excelsior Club, (Guthrie); East Side Culture Club (Oklahoma City); Frances Harper Club (Muskogee); Domestic Science Club (Oklahoma City); Dorcas Club (Muskogee); Ideal Reading Club (El Reno); Matron's Mutual Improvement Circle (Muskogee); and Mother's Club (Hennessey)."[71]

67. Uncrowned Community Builders, "Judith Horton," lines 22–26.
68. Wesley, *History of the National Association*, 507.
69. Wesley, *History of the National Association*, 507.
70. Wesley, *History of the National Association*, 507–08.
71. Wesley, *History of the National Association*, 508.

An interesting highlight is that when the women representatives gathered to meet and construct the constitution and bylaws, they gathered at a church. In fact, it just so happened to be at Avery Chapel AME Church in Oklahoma City.[72] Today, this is still one of the largest AME Churches in Oklahoma City and one of the larger churches in the Twelfth Episcopal District. The significance of women meeting at the church is that it continues to model the faith component, which grounded the work of Negro women in the Club movement. The Charter Officers of the Oklahoma Federation of Colored Women's Clubs were:

> Mrs. H. P. Jacobson (Oklahoma City)—President; Mrs. Myrtle F. Todd (Muskogee)—First Vice President; Mrs. Ida B. Freeman (Guthrie)—Second Vice President, Mrs. E. T. Barbour (El Reno)—Recording Secretary; Mrs. A. B. Whitby (Oklahoma City)—Corresponding Secretary; Mrs. W. H. Twins (Muskogee)—Treasurer; Mrs. J. C. Horton (Guthrie)—Organizer; Mrs. F. F. Bailey (Hennessey)—Statistician; and Mrs. Wm. Harrison (Oklahoma City)—Chairman, Executive Board.[73]

According to the table showing membership results from 1910 to 1956, the clubs and club membership of the Oklahoma Federation of Colored Women's Clubs were as follows: In 1910, the number of committees reporting active clubs was five; the number of clubs was seven, and the number of club members was 111. By 1920, which was just before the massacre, the number of committees reporting active clubs was ten, the number of clubs was thirty-four, and the number of club members was 518.[74] The number of women participating in the women's clubs represented a major commitment and determination to change the circumstances facing African Americans across the nation. The Black women's clubs in Oklahoma identified with this radical unifying power of critical engagement and embraced that vision by participating in this massive movement. Since they met in Black churches to establish many of these clubs, faith in God was their foundation and their actions of spirituality demonstrated a powerful social witness.

CONCLUSION

African-American women have made significant contributions to the Black community and American culture. This chapter has reflected the

---

72. Wesley, *History of the National Association*, 508.
73. Wesley, *History of the National Association*, 508.
74. Wesley, *History of the National Association*, 509.

outrageous, audacious, and courageous behavior of Black women's contributions through their resistance and resilience in the nineteenth and twentieth centuries in the United States. The memory and insight of the Negro, or Colored women as they were referred to during the nineteenth and twentieth, is often taken for granted and rarely spoken about. Yet, it has been the discriminatory identity politics within social constructs since slavery of Black women's value, image, and virtue that has continually operated in American society, not only to deny African-American women's value and virtue but continually to reinscribe oppression and injustice. The Black women I present here have demonstrated that their radical subjectivity evolves from their spiritual foundation and faith as the catalyst for their ability to subvert the obstacles before them.

Their traditional communalism is propelled by love, strength, and determination to uplift themselves and their communities. Redemptive self-love was a vital resource from within, which ignited a Black women's movement. All of these Black women were critically engaged in the religious, social, political, and economic work during a specific epoch in history with goals to challenge injustice. They strategized as a unified body, connecting across the nation to create a powerful resistance movement in order to change the landscape for African American culture in American society.

CHAPTER 6

White Parties of Terror
Lynching Terror, Religion, and the Laws

Nashville's Episcopal Church Remembers 1892 Lynchings in City

A mob of thousands witnessed and participated in the lynching of Ephraim Grizzard on Woodland Street Bridge in the middle of the afternoon more than 125 years ago. After seizing him on April 30, 1892 from the Nashville jail—where Grizzard was being held for the alleged assault of two girls—the crowd beat him, stabbed him and hung him before shooting him more than 50 times.

—*THE TENNESSEAN*
June 7, 2017

The Afro-American is not a bestial race. If this work can contribute in any way toward proving this, and at the same time arouse the conscience of the American people to a demand for justice to every citizen, and punishment by law for the lawless, I shall feel I have done my race a service. Other considerations are of minor importance.

—IDA B. WELLS-BARNETT
Southern Horrors

Figure 7-1. From *The Crisis*, January 1935, 27.

Figure 7. Source: *A Festival of Violence: An Analysis of Southern Lynchings 1882–1930.*

WHAT IS LYNCHING?

THE HISTORY OF WHITE supremacy set a precedent for racial hierarchy in America. The way in which this country establishes and distinguishes the hierarchy of race is best exemplified in how the interlocking systems of social, political, economic, and religious components functioned in society legally by allowing thousands of Negroes to be brutally murdered for decades through lynching. Although the memory of lynching is extremely painful, for too long the tragic historical realities have been silenced. We must acknowledge that the lynching narrative is explicit regarding the extreme hatred white America had for African-Americans, which created the hierarchical separation of these two races. This chapter demonstrates exactly how the terror of lynching raged in this nation, by investigating many of the interlocking systems that operated to oppress and subjugate the Negro race.

Black women were not lynched as often as Black men; however, Orlando Patterson records one of the most heinous acts of a Black woman's lynching. Martha Turner was eight months pregnant when her husband was murdered by lynching. Following the murder, Turner threatened the killers with legal action, which resulted in her being hung by her ankles and lynched by a mob of several hundred men and women.[1] "Her dress was doused with gasoline and burned from her body and her belly ripped open with a hog knife while she was still alive. When her baby fell to the ground and uttered its first cry, its head was crushed to pulp by the stomping feet of the frenzied men and women."[2]

In Mobile, Alabama on March 20, 1981, Josephus Anderson was on trial for allegedly killing a white police officer. The first trial concluded with a deadlocked jury and the second trial ended with another jury unable to reach a verdict. Just after 10 PM that Friday night, Michael, a nineteen-year-old technical student, Beulah Mae Donald's youngest son, was walking to the store for cigarettes when "James 'Tiger' Knowles and Henry Francis Hays, members of the Klavern 900 of the United Klan of America, were cruising through Donald's mostly black neighborhood,"[3] and decided to take out their frustration regarding Anderson's trial.

They asked young Michael for directions to a local night club. When he came near the vehicle, they forced him in the truck with a gun. They took him to a deep spot in the woods near Mobile Bay, "where they placed a noose around his neck, beat him senseless and slit his throat three times."[4] They later returned to Mobile, having dumped his body into their truck bed. "Arriving back at Henry Hays's house, the two Klansmen hung Michael Donald's lifeless body from a tree nearby, where it remained until Saturday morning."[5] Two other Klansmen later celebrated the murder by burning a cross on the lawn of the Mobile County courthouse.

---

1. Patterson, *Rituals of Blood*, 180.
2. Patterson, *Rituals of Blood*, 180.
3. Tolnay and Beck, *A Festival of Violence*, 1.
4. Tolnay and Beck, *A Festival of Violence*, 1.
5. Tolnay and Beck, *A Festival of Violence*, 1.

In Jasper, Texas on "June 7, 1998 . . . James Byrd, an Afro-American part-time musician, became America's most recent lynch victim."[6] Patterson continues, "On the picturesque country road running through the forest, he was chained by his feet to the back of a pick-up truck by three Euro-American men and dragged along the road until his spray-painted head tore away from his grated, mutilated body rolling into a ditch."[7] These are examples from America's long history of lynching violence.

African-American women, men, and sometimes children were regularly lynched in America, beginning in the 1830s. Prior to the 1830s, lynching was limited to the frontier regions and targeted primarily white Americans.[8] But following the Civil War, lynching became a horrific and evil phenomenon specifically targeting the Black race, especially during Reconstruction and continuing for decades afterwards. After the Civil War, 72 percent of all lynchings were of Black people.[9] Although lynching included Black women and children, the primary target of this terrorism was African-American men. Lynching is a principal part of the racial culture of terrorism in America against African-Americans.

Lynchings were premeditated murders and horrific acts of bodily terrorism to human beings, particularly African Americans. The Black bodies were hung from trees, railroad crossings, and bridges. While people were hanging, additional acts were often performed such as burning the bodies with a fire directly underneath where they hung. Sometimes the perpetrators shot the victims with unlimited gun shots as they hung. Still other times they cut persons' flesh and genitals off, usually for souvenirs.

These inhuman acts of torture were usually performed by mobs or large groups of people in the public square for all to see. Public lynchings were advertised or promoted events of celebration and they often attracted thousands. People gathered from near and far with a frenzy to see or participate in the so-called "festivities." These were family events and celebrations that included the children. They brought their picnic baskets, took pictures, made postcards, and obtained a souvenir by partaking in the retrieval of some article of clothing or body part from the victim.

The excuses given for lynching practices were so-called "committed crimes" or acts deemed punishable by white citizens or sometimes public officials. However, all too often, no actual crimes had ever been committed. Public lynchings were often performed by white people becoming enraged

---

6. Patterson, *Rituals of Blood*, 171.
7. Patterson, *Rituals of Blood*, 171.
8. Patterson, *Rituals of Blood*, 176.
9. Patterson, *Rituals of Blood*, 176.

for small social infractions such as not speaking or a Black person not calling them Mr. or Mrs., and sometimes for looking at whites directly in the face or simply talking back. Lynching could occur for almost anything. Other small social transgressions included not moving over or stepping off the sidewalk when white people passed by, or even accidentally bumping into someone white. In most any situation, the Negro race could be subjected to mob violence:

> In 1940 Jesse Thornton was lynched in Luverne, Alabama for referring to a white police officer by his name without the title of "mister." In 1919, a white mob in Blakely, Georgia lynched Williams Little, a soldier returning from World War 1, for refusing to take off his Army uniform.[10]

History has so many circumstances of minor and ridiculous offenses that it is difficult to limit the examples. The predominant motivation for lynching was the allegations of criminal conduct. Rarely did the white mobs wait for trials to be conducted or proof for a particular crime; they simply acted with violence. "Of the hundreds of black people lynched under accusation of rape and murder, nearly everyone was brutally killed without being legally convicted of any offense."[11] In many instances, the mobs had the wrong person for the crime, yet Blacks were without any recourse to protect themselves or their families:

> When Berry Noyse was accused of killing the local sheriff in Lexington, Tennessee, in 1918, an angry mob lynched him in the courthouse square, then dragged his body through the streets of town, shot it dozens of times and burned the body in the middle of the street below hung banners that read, "This is the way we do our bit."[12]

The challenge in confronting the history of lynching, and we have only just begun to scratch the surface, is the insanity of lynch mobs. What human beings could consistently mutilate other human bodies and call themselves Christians or even human? Lynching had to include an element of excitement and entertainment. How was that humanly possible?

Statistics for lynching vary by researcher. The most noteworthy resources are the NAACP's *Thirty Years of Lynching in the United States 1889–1918*, James Cutler's *Lynch Law* covering 1889–1903,[13] and the Equal Justice

---

10. Equal Justice Initiative, *Lynching in America*, 33.
11. Equal Justice Initiative, *Lynching in America*, 33.
12. Equal Justice Initiative, *Lynching in America*, 33
13. *Lynch Law*, although long out of print and almost unobtainable, was "the first

Initiative. The following statistics provide close estimates. The overarching numbers from the NAACP state 2,522 Blacks were lynched during 1889–1919. Another report shows 3,224 Blacks lynched during 1889–1918. The Equal Justice Initiative report shows 3,959 Blacks lynched during 1877–1950. In Oklahoma specifically, Walter White's statistics[14] in *Rope and Faggot* identify "only" forty-four Negroes were lynched during 1882–1927.[15] This number is difficult to reconcile within Oklahoma given the death toll by lynching during the Red Summer of 1919. Statistics in Oklahoma identify "sixty-one recorded lynchings of black people in 1919. In 1920, sixty-one were reported, and in 1921 fifty-seven more were recorded."[16]

A table of White's statistics categorizes lynching by individual states and within specific time frames. From 1919 to 1923, a total of 272 Negroes were lynched in all the United States. Since society often reminds us that lynching initially applied to both white and Black people, it is helpful to analyze lynching through the lens of race. In the numbers below, I have highlighted the top five lynching states between this same period of 1919–1923, with the largest number of lynchings for African-Americans, and compared them with the white lynchings in that same state.

Table 2. Lynchings by Race and State

States	Blacks Lynched	Whites Lynched
Georgia	58	0
Mississippi	44	1
Texas	35	2
Florida	34	1
Arkansas	23	1
Total	**194**	**5**

Source: Data from Walter White, *Rope and Faggot: A Biography of Judge Lynch*.

---

scientific and exhaustive study of lynching, [written] by Professor James Elbert Cutler of Yale University and Wellesley College." He complied figures from the *Chicago Tribune*, then compared and corrected them against other newspapers like the *New York Times* and *New York Tribune*. His was the "most thorough examination yet made of the years 1882–1903." White, *Rope and Faggot*, 227–28.

14. Walter White was also the assistant secretary for the NAACP. White's statistics have been compiled by "combining Cutler's and NAACP figures and checking them with the World Almanac figures to ensure maximum accuracy." White, *Rope and Faggot*, 230.

15. White, *Rope and Faggot*, 252–57.

16. Gates, *Riot on Greenwood*, 23.

These statistics, which account for only five states, demonstrate the huge disparity of lynching based on race. The total number of lynchings represented from just these five states equals 194 Blacks that were killed, while the total number of whites lynched in these states is only five. The above statistics equates to only 0.025 percent; not event 1 percent of the white population was lynched compared to African-Americans.

Moreover, an important myth that must be eradicated from history is the rape statistics against Black men, which records that the highest statistics for lynching Black men were most often rape or attempted rape of white women. Walter White's investigations and statistics in *Rope and Faggot* debunk this historical entrenched rape claim. Even though laws were in place to protect white women, history states white men were obsessed with protecting white women. As a result, the number one reason given for lynching Black men was the accusation of rape, as opposed to murder or theft or some other crime. According to the statistics, murder was the primary reason for lynching Black men. When analyzing the statistics found in *Thirty Years of Lynching in the United States 1889-1918*, we see that of the 2,522 African-Americans lynched, 900 or 35.8 percent were for alleged murder, while only 477 or 19 percent were for alleged rape.[17]

In many of the claimed rape cases between white women and Black men, the sexual involvement was consensual by both parties; unfortunately people did not believe this claim, which caused many innocent Black men to die. "Nearly 25 percent of the lynchings of African-Americans in the South were based on charges of sexual assault. The mere accusation of rape, even without an identification by the alleged victim often aroused a mob and resulted in lynching."[18]

Lynching and the obsession with believing Black men wanted white women sexually was so severe that I cite two examples to demonstrate the minor infractions that could cause a death. Keith Bowen, an innocent man highlighted in the Equal Justice Initiative, entered a room where three white women were sitting. Although no allegation for wrongdoings was made, he was lynched by the entire white neighborhood. In 1904, a Black man name General Lee knocked on the door of a white woman in Reevesville, South Carolina and the white mob lynched him.[19] Therefore, this is an important discrepancy to highlight in the historical claims of Black men attacking white women. In the Tulsa Massacre, assault or a rape accusation,

---

17. White, *Rope and Faggot*, 252; NAACP, *Thirty Years of Lynching*, 36.
18. Equal Justice Initiative, *Lynching in America*, 31.
19. Equal Justice Initiative, *Lynching in America*, 31.

by a Black man against a white woman, became the main reason cited for the massacre.[20]

Historically, lynching narratives tell a story to make some believe that after slavery Negroes were the worst criminals, and therefore needed to be controlled. White Americans hated that African-Americans were no longer slaves and now free according to the law, particularly whites in the South. The laws of the land did not operate to protect the Negro race, nor did laws see them as full citizens of the United States. The laws, rather, aggrandized the white vigilante mobs that desired to murder African-Americans, and African-Americans were neither free nor safe.

Lynching was as much about wielding tools of racial and political control as it was about fear of losing white dominance and power. Reconstruction was positioned squarely at the center of newly obtained Black freedom, changing laws, an incoming progressive Republican party, African-Americans' first-time participation in politics, and a resentful white America ruled by the evil of terror.

RECONSTRUCTION AND LYNCHING

The lynching of African-Americans following the Civil War, which had the highest concentration during 1889–1939, is certainly one of the most devastating eras for Blacks in American history. These are some examples of how insignificant Black humanity was to the white mobs.

Alabama 1894

> Three Negroes, Tom Black, Johnson Williams and Tony Johnston, were lynched at Tuscumbia, Alabama. They were in the local jail, awaiting trial on the charge of having burnt a barn. A mob of two hundred masked men entered the jail, after having enticed away the jailer with a false message, took the keys from the jailer's wife and secured the three prisoners. They were carried to a near-by bridge. Here a rope was place around the neck of each victim, the other end being tied to the timbers of the bridge and they were compelled to jump. (*New York Tribune*, April 23, 1894.)[21]

---

20. Equal Justice Initiative, *Lynching in America*, 252–59.
21. Quoted in NAACP, *Thirty Years of Lynching in the United States*, 11.

Texas 1895

News has been received of the lynching of a Negro in this part of Madison County on Tuesday night. He was accused of riding his horse over a little white girl and inflicting serious injuries on her. Later developments go to show that the mob got hold of the wrong negro. The guilty one made his escape. (*Chicago Tribune*, November 22, 1895.)[22]

Florida 1901

Will Wright and Sam Williams, charged with being implicated in a murder, were lynched without trial in jail at Dade City, by a mob of thirty or more men. Sheriff Griffin refused to give up the keys and they broke down the outer door. Unable to break down the steel doors of the cells, they opened fire through the steel bars, shooting both the Negroes to death. The Coroner's jury found that they came to their death at the hands of "parties unknown." (*New York Tribune*, February 7, 1901.)[23]

Tennessee 1901

Ballie Crutchfield, a colored woman, was lynched by a mob at Rome, Tennessee, because her brother stole a purse. The mob took Crutchfield from the custody of the sheriff, and started with him for the place of execution, when he broke from them and escaped. "This," says the dispatch, "so enraged the mob, that they suspected Crutchfield's sister of being implicated in the theft and last night's work was the culmination of that suspicion." The Coroner's jury found the usual verdict that the woman came to her death at the hands of parties unknown. (*New York Tribune*, March 16, 1901.)

South Carolina 1906

For attempting to enter a house and frightening a child who was alone in it, Willie Spain, a young Negro at St. George, S.C., was taken from jail and hung to a tree. The mob then shot five

---

22. NAACP, *Thirty Years of Lynching in the United States*, 12.
23. NAACP, *Thirty Years of Lynching in the United States*, 13.

hundred bullets into his body. (*New York Tribune*, August 24, 1906.)[24]

Oklahoma 1914

Marie Scott of Wagoner County, a seventeen-year-old Negro girl, was lynched by a mob of white men because her brother killed one of two white men who assaulted her. She was alone in the house when the men entered, but her screams brought her brother to the rescue. In the fight that ensured one of the white men was killed. The next day the mob came to lynch her brother, but as he had escaped, lynched the girl instead. No one has ever been indicted for the crime. (*The Crisis*, June 1914.)[25]

Following Emancipation and the ratification of the Thirteenth Amendment, white Southerners fought back against this new Black freedom and Reconstruction. Because whites so strongly believed the African-American race was inferior, they resisted paying Black laborers. "In numerous recorded incidents, plantation owners attacked black people simply for claiming their freedom."[26] When Andrew Johnson became president after Lincoln's assassination in 1865, he rescinded orders granting Black farmers tracts of land, which prohibited their ability to build their own farms. Johnson also opened the door for the new practice called sharecropping. This took further advantage of Black farm laborers because they still had to work white peoples' land, but unfortunately, they could not earn a profit because of the credit burden to white land owners.

Johnson further opposed Blacks' right to vote, claiming they were unintelligent.[27] Tension was growing among the races and whites began to violently attack Black communities. "The Johnson administration allowed Southern whites to reestablish white supremacy and dominate black people with impunity."[28] In May of 1866 and then again in July 1866, two different Black communities were massacred by white mobs, one in Memphis and another in New Orleans.[29] However, by the 1866 mid-term elections, the

---

24. NAACP, *Thirty Years of Lynching in the United States*, 14.
25. NAACP, *Thirty Years of Lynching in the United States*, 23.
26. Equal Justice Initiative, *Lynching in America*, 8.
27. Equal Justice Initiative, *Lynching in America*, 8–10.
28. Equal Justice Initiative, *Lynching in America*, 10.
29. Equal Justice Initiative, *Lynching in America*, 10–11.

political landscape had begun to change and this significantly impacted the status for African-Americans.

When Congress passed the Civil Rights Act of 1866 declaring Black Americans full citizens, "President Johnson vetoed the bill, but Congress—for the first time in United States history—overrode the veto."[30] Following that, the progressive Republican supermajority passed the Fourteenth Amendment, intending to rule out any doubt about civil rights and citizenship. "If ratified, the amendment would supersede the United States Supreme Court's 1857 decision in *Dred Scott v. Sandford*, which held that African-Americans were not citizens and had no standing to sue in federal court."[31] It took twenty-eight of thirty-seven states to ratify the Fourteenth Amendment, but ten of the eleven former Confederate states initially rejected it.[32]

As a result of the denial by these states, Congress passed the Reconstruction Act of 1867 over Johnson's veto, "which imposed military rule on the South and required that any states seeking readmission to the Union had to first ratify the Fourteenth amendment."[33] This Act became official in July 1868. This was major progress because "the Reconstruction Act of 1867 also gave voting rights to African-American men while disenfranchising former Confederates, dramatically altering the political landscape of the South and ushering in a period of progress."[34]

The significance of these acts changed the dynamics of the country. In the next election, Black voter turnout was almost 90 percent. The election results were outstanding, creating for the first time Black participation in politics.

> More than six hundred African-Americans, most of them formerly enslaved were elected as state legislators during this period. Another eighteen African-Americans rose to serve in state executive positions. Including lieutenant governor, secretary of state, superintendent of education and treasurer. In Louisiana in 1872, P. B. S. Pinchback became the first black governor in America. The Reconstruction states sent sixteen black representatives to the United States Congress, and Mississippi voters elected the nations' first black senators: Hiram Revels and Blanche Bruce.[35]

---

30. Equal Justice Initiative, *Lynching in America*, 11.
31. Equal Justice Initiative, *Lynching in America*, 11.
32. Equal Justice Initiative, *Lynching in America*, 11.
33. Equal Justice Initiative, *Lynching in America*, 11.
34. Equal Justice Initiative, *Lynching in America*, 11.
35. Equal Justice Initiative, *Lynching in America*, 12.

This kind of success in the political arena created white retaliation from the KKK and mobs that swept the country between 1868 and 1871. Whites were determined to regain their power.

Lynching statistics are fairly limited before 1880 to 1882, but historians estimate at least 400 African-Americans were lynched between 1868 and 1871 by white mobs.[36] Lynching during Reconstruction was only the beginning; for decades to come, political debates between the North and South would rage. White mobs would attack Black voters. Changing laws would create debate over the need for state or government protection for Negroes. White hegemony was privileged and terror would allow lynching to kill thousands of African-Americans.

The lynching statistics reveal a correlation of numbers over several years, resulting in the numbers of lynched victims shown overlapping, depending upon the number of years reported.

Table 3. NAACP: Thirty Years of Lynching in the United States

Killed by Lynch Mobs	Years	Men	Women	Total Killed
Black	1889–1918	2,472	50	2,522
White	1889–1918	691	11	702
				3,224

Source: National Association for the Advancement of Colored People, *Thirty Years of Lynching in the United States 1889–1918*, 8, Appendix 1, Table 2.

Table 4. Ritual of Blood, 1882–1968

Allegedly for Homicide	Rape	Attempted Rape	Robbery and Theft	Felonious Assault	Insult to Whites	Other Causes	Total Lynched
1,937	912	288	232	205	85	1,084	4,743

Source: Daniel T. Williams, "The Lynching Records at Tuskegee Institute," in *Eight Negro Bibliographies*, compiled by Daniel T. Williams (New York: Kraus Reprint, 1970) 15, quoted in Orlando Patterson, *Rituals of Blood: Consequences of Slavery In Two American Centuries*, 175.

36. Equal Justice Initiative, *Lynching in America*, 16.

Orlando Patterson describes lynchings after the Civil War: "Of persons lynched between 1882 and 1968—72% were Afro-Americans. It was in the South that the vast majority—80% of lynchings occurred."[37] He continues, "90% of persons lynched between 1882 and 1968 in the Deep South—the states of Alabama, Georgia, Louisiana, Mississippi, and South Carolina were also Afro-Americans compared to 78% lynched in the border states of Arkansas, Florida, Kentucky, North Carolina, and Texas."[38]

Table 5. Equal Justice Initiative, 1877–1950, Lynched in the South

Blacks Lynched by State	Numbers	Blacks Lynched by State	Numbers
Alabama	326	Mississippi	576
Arkansas	503	North Carolina	102
Florida	311	South Carolina	164
Georgia	586	Tennessee	225
Kentucky	154	Texas	376
Louisiana	540	Virginia	76

Source: Equal Justice Initiative, *Lynching in America: Confronting the Legacy of Racial Terror*, 40.

LYNCH LAW

No laws existed to substantiate Black women's value, or that commanded the worthiness for them to be protected. The colonial period established this moral injustice regarding Black women's bodies, forms of treatment, and lack of virtue during slavocracy. The legal process supported white male domination by allowing Black women to be raped and abused with impunity. Explicit ways for understanding the "typifications," from Luckman and Berger's work, that codify prejudice and the perennial behavior of white human activity is further explicated in Katie Cannon's *Black Womanist Ethics*.

Cannon argues that, initiated by slavery, Black women's status was defined as property; a "brood sow" and "work-ox," forced to function for the benefit of the white master. "Under slavery the Black woman had the status of property, her master had total power over her and she and her children

---

37. Patterson, *Rituals of Blood*, 176.
38. Patterson, *Rituals of Blood*, 176.

were denied the most elementary social bonds—family and kinship."[39] The Black woman was considered less than human, which is why her body was always subjected to abuse. Because Black women's bodies were perceived to be without value, except for reproductive purposes and sexual exploitation, white supremacy created a negative ontological identity that was deeply woven into the American fabric of culture and certainly in relation to white women's bodies. This moral obscurity toward Black women and their bodies has lived existentially for centuries. This is why white women's bodies were considered valuable and could ignite lynchings, while Black women's bodies were terrorized by rape and abuse but nothing was done, and no laws were implemented to protect them.

Ida B. Wells-Barnett was a Christian woman who had a strong commitment to and persistently advocated for social change. She participated in the women's club movement and held various positions of leadership. She was supported by various women's social groups for her anti-lynching work, including the Women's Mite Missionary Society in the AME Church and by Bishop Henry McNeal Turner.[40] Although she was not AME, she was supported by the denomination and attended some annual conferences. She also worked with leaders such as Frederick Douglas and W. E. B. DuBois to help found the NAACP.[41] Wells-Barnett's faith was the driving force and strength of her commitment to social transformation and she used her exceptional gift as a journalist to speak domestically and internationally against the injustice of lynching.

Wells-Barnett began her anti-lynching campaign in 1892 when her close friend Thomas Moss was lynched along with Calvin McDowell and Henry Stewart, his business partners at People's Grocery in Memphis.[42] Lynching had dominated the south since Reconstruction, but Moss's death made it impossible for Wells-Barnett to ignore. She believed addressing social responsibility was her Christian duty and she refused to believe it was only an African-American problem.[43] "Lynching is no longer 'Our Problem,' it is the problem of the civilized world."[44] Wells-Barnett argued both white and Black Americans must fight to end this terror. In the *Daily Inter Ocean* dispatch, Wells-Barnett made these poignant statements:

---

39. Cannon, *Black Womanist Ethics*, 31.
40. Townes, *Womanist Justice, Womanist Hope*, 158–59.
41. Equal Justice Initiative, *Lynching in America*, 49.
42. Townes, *Womanist Justice, Womanist Hope*, 140.
43. Townes, *Womanist Justice, Womanist Hope*, 116.
44. Townes, *Womanist Justice, Womanist Hope*, 116.

1) That all the machinery of law and politics is in the hands of those who commit the lynching; they, therefore, have the amending of the laws in their own hands; and that it is only wealthy white men who the law fails to reach, in every case of criminal procedure the negro is punished. 2) Hundreds of negroes including women and children, are lynched for trivial offenses, on suspicion, and in many cases when known to be guiltless of any crime, and the law refuses to punish the murderers because it is not considered a crime to kill a negro. 3) Many of these cases of "assault" are simple adultery between white women and colored men.[45]

In 1893, Wells-Barnett, with the help of Frederick Douglass's letter of introduction, took her outrage, fight, and activism to England;[46] she believed the largest importer of American cotton should be aware of the southern horrors happening in the United States. Wells-Barnett's first trip was cut short, but she returned in 1894 from March through July, speaking about the injustices to African-Americans in the United States.[47]

While abroad, she had numerous confrontations with Frances Willard, the president of Women's Christian Temperance Union (WCTU) with a membership of over 200,000 in the United States. Wells-Barnett's debates with Willard were not on temperance but racial concerns; she blamed Willard for disregarding the well-being of African-Americans and never once addressing the issue of lynching. Their debates were ongoing and carried out in the public square of Britain and the US newspapers as both made several trips to Britain.[48] "Before she [Wells-Barnett] left in July, the British Anti-Lynching Committee formed with British notables among its member. Wells-Barnett now had access to white groups in the United States previously closed to her. British opinion broke the silence of many United States leaders."[49] This spawned a new consciousness in the United States. Many began to respond to Wells-Barnett in various ways. They wrote open letters inviting her to share her concerns and articles in the newspapers, but some still argued to stop lynching was an open invitation for Black men's actions of rape and lawlessness.

Wells-Barnett's trips abroad and continued public writing had made her a constant target for attacks. Her original paper *Free Speech* in Memphis

45. Townes, *Womanist Justice, Womanist Hope*, 145.
46. Townes, *Womanist Justice, Womanist Hope*, 144.
47. Townes, *Womanist Justice, Womanist Hope*, 145.
48. Townes, *Womanist Justice, Womanist Hope*, 143–48.
49. Townes, *Womanist Justice, Womanist Hope*, 150.

had been destroyed since Moss's death while she was in Philadelphia at the AME Church General Conference.[50] Following that incident, Wells-Barnett was threatened with lynching if she returned to Memphis. T. Thomas Fortune addressed her with information written in *The Daily Commercial*, "The fact that a black scoundrel is allowed to live and utter such loathsome and repulsive calumnies is a volume of evidence as to the wonderful patience of Southern whites. But we have had enough."[51] After the public conflicts with Willard in England, "The *Memphis Scimitar* recommended Wells be tied to a stake on Main Street and branded with a hot iron."[52] So Wells-Barnett lived a life of activism under threat for what she believed. However, there were those who supported her; AME women of the Women's Mite Missionary Society of the Third Episcopal District in Cleveland rallied behind her:

> Resolved. That we, the Mite Missionary convention assembled, do hereby extend our heartfelt sympathy to Miss Ida B. Wells, who is laboring in England to create a healthy sentiment in regard to the unjust treatment, the lynchings and floggings of our people in the south. Resolved. That we especially commend her for the fearless manner in which she has entered the campaign the wholesale slaughter of Negroes in the south.[53]

The AME Bishop Henry McNeal Turner also wrote to defend Wells-Barnett's character and her crusade. He reprimanded Blacks who would not defend themselves. These are a few of his words:

> I know of editors of our colored papers who are in profound sympathy with Miss Wells, but will not say a word through their papers. . . . Whenever a people are so abnormalized by their environment that they are afraid to lift up their voices in protest against their murderers and exterminators, it is time to leave or ask for enslavement.[54]

A few African-American ministers did not support Wells-Barnett; regardless, she moved on with her calling and committed work of activism through the anti-lynching campaign. Ida B. Wells-Barnett wrote *Southern Horrors: Lynching Law in All Its Phases* in 1892; *Red Record: Tabulated Statistics and Alleged Causes of Lynchings in the United States 1892, 1893,*

---

50. Townes, *Womanist Justice, Womanist Hope*, 141.
51. Townes, *Womanist Justice, Womanist Hope*, 141.
52. Townes, *Womanist Justice, Womanist Hope*, 150.
53. Townes, *Womanist Justice, Womanist Hope*, 158.
54. Townes, *Womanist Justice, Womanist Hope*, 161.

and 1894 in 1895, and *Mob Rule in New Orleans* in 1900. In the preface of *Southern Horrors*, Wells-Barnett describes her life's work:

> The Afro-American is not a bestial race. If this work can contribute in any way toward proving this, and at the same time arouse the conscience of the American people to a demand for justice to every citizen, and punishment by law for the lawless, I shall feel I have done my race a service. Other considerations are of minor importance.[55]

Wells-Barnett performed her work of anti-lynching for forty years; however, her work alone was not enough to eradicate the lynching of African-Americans in this nation.

The National Association for the Advancement of Colored People (NAACP) was officially established in 1910. Their initial engagement was "in direct response to racial attacks in Springfield, Illinois, in 1908—an outbreak of violence that shocked Northerners and demonstrated that lynching was not only a Southern phenomenon."[56] At its founding, the NAACP's president, treasurer, board chair, and secretary were all white men, but it was one of the first organizations in which Black, white, female, and male worked together.[57]

In 1912, the NAACP made lynching their main focus; as a result, the Black support and membership rose significantly and by 1919 they had 310 chapters with 91,203 members nationwide. W. E. B. Du Bois was the editor of *The Crisis*, the NAACP's news magazine. By 1919, the magazine had a circulation of 100,000, eventually making it the most influential race publication in history.[58] Red Summer also happened in 1919; "lynching became a major national issue by the 1920s."[59] The NAACP launched a campaign to pass the Dyer Anti-Lynching Bill, which they had supported from 1919. Initially, in 1918, they disagreed with some aspects of the bill.

The Dyer Bill was an anti-lynching bill introduced by Leonidas C. Dyer, a Republican Congressman from Missouri. Under the bill, lynching would have been a federal felony. Lynching would have carried a maximum of five years in prison for state or city officials who could have protected the victim, plus a $5,000 fine; a minimum of five years in prison for those who participated in lynching; and a $10,000 fine paid to the family by the county where the act occurred. The Dyer Bill was passed by the United States

---

55. Wells-Barnett, *Southern Horrors*, 51.
56. Equal Justice Initiative, *Lynching in America*, 50.
57. Equal Justice Initiative, *Lynching in America*, 50.
58. Equal Justice Initiative, *Lynching in America*, 50.
59. Equal Justice Initiative, *Lynching in America*, 51.

House of Representatives on January 26, 1922 but stopped by the Southern Democratic filibusters of the Senate.[60] Southern lawmakers opposed the bill "resurrecting familiar objections demanding 'state rights,' alleging racial favoritism, and warning of the threat of black rapists."[61] They also claimed the bill was trying to satisfy "Negro agitators" and shield rapists from justice.[62]

A Black women's organization, called the Anti-lynching Crusaders, founded in 1922 under the NAACP, also supported the Dyer Bill by advocating the crusade within the NAACP under the leadership of Mary B. Talbert.[63] Their goal was to raise money and include white women who were sympathetic to the anti-lynching. Talbert sent out 1,850 letters to white women but they were not successful in soliciting their help. The campaign slogan was "A Million Women United to Stop Lynching." The hope was to have one million women donate one dollar. Although unable to achieve the goal, they did successfully promote awareness of lynching, in the continued tradition of Wells-Barnett's work.[64]

The Dyer Bill was again blocked by Senate filibusters in 1923 and 1924; it was not reintroduced until 1930 as the Costigan-Wagner Bill. In the meantime, the NAACP continued to support anti-lynching legislation into the 1930s. Finally, "white Southerners formed the anti-lynching Committee on Interracial Cooperation in Atlanta and in 1930 launched the Association of Southern Women to Prevent Lynching (ASWPL)."[65] A 1922 advertisement produced by the NAACP identified lynching as the "Shame of America." In 2005, nearly 200 anti-lynching bills were introduced in Congress, and three passed the House but not the Senate. Between 1890 and 1952, seven United States presidents petitioned Congress to pass a federal law against lynching. In 2005, the US Senate apologized for never passing anti-lynching legislation.[66]

CONCLUSION

Lynching African-American people is just one aspect of the most atrocious history in American culture. The diabolical characteristics of white

60. Jager, "Dyer Anti-Lynching Bill (1922)," line 27.
61. Equal Justice Initiative, *Lynching in America*, 51.
62. Equal Justice Initiative, *Lynching in America*, 51.
63. Horan, "How Did Black Women," lines 1–4.
64. Horan, "How Did Black Women," lines 1–6.
65. Equal Justice Initiative, *Lynching in America*, 51.
66. Associated Press, "Senate Apologizes for Not Passing Anti-Lynching Bill."

supremacy and racism are unrelenting in the heinous acts of lynching. This chapter has investigated the terrorism of lynching experienced by thousands of Black people in America, with particular emphasis on the extreme elevations during the Reconstruction and Post-Reconstruction periods. The changing laws and Acts of 1866 and 1867 significantly impacted the escalation of lynching statistics for decades. Lynching was not only associated with white supremacists' determination to remain in power, but they used the terror from lynchings and the threat of lynching to control African-American communities across the nation.

I explored the white obsession with Blackness and Black bodies. Many Black men were lynched by the unsubstantiated white claims of protecting white women from rape. Yet history clearly exhibits that Black women were consistently raped and abused with no laws created to protect them. I have presented the extensive anti-lynching efforts over the decades from Ida B. Wells-Barnett, the NAACP, and through anti-lynching Bills to demonstrate the significant challenges associated with terrorism, establishing new laws, and complete disregard for the humanity of the African-American race.

CHAPTER 7

White Parties of Terror Continue

> It is with no pleasure I have dipped my hands in the corruption here exposed. Somebody must show that the Afro-American race is more sinned against than sinning, and it seems to have fallen upon me to do so. The awful death-roll that Judge Lynch is calling every week is appalling, not only because of the lives it takes, the rank cruelty and outrage to the victims, but because of the prejudice it fosters and the stain it places against the good name of a weak race.
>
> —IDA B. WELLS-BARNETT
> *On Lynchings*

LYNCHING AS HUMAN SACRIFICE

THE ONTOLOGY OF BLACK life and Black bodies has always represented a valuable presence to the function of American life. Unfortunately, Black bodies have always been devalued in comparison of acceptability and equality to white existence in the formation of this American nation. Although Black people built this country, historically they were perceived as disposable and not considered fully human by most. Today, limited progress has been made in regarding Black life as valuable. The immorality of America is substantiated by an ideology of white superiority and whiteness as valuable, therefore Black people have been used as human sacrifice with impunity.

Rather than white religious leaders exhibiting a positive consciousness for Black people toward social equality and advocating Black life as valuable, they contributed and participated in lynching organizations and the destruction of Black existence. Regardless of the abuse and the sacrificial offerings of Black bodies, God continues to sustain Black existence.

When I interviewed a Special Collections librarian during my research visit in Tulsa, he insisted the KKK did not exist in Tulsa in 1921. Hannibal Johnson's *Black Wall Street* and Steve Gerkin's *Hidden History of Tulsa* present a staunchly different perspective, which supports the claim of Klan participation in the Tulsa Massacre. Johnson writes:

> Klan organizers, called "Kleagles," came to a receptive Oklahoma in 1920. Some original Klansmen had lived in the state since as early 1870. George Kimbro, Jr. and George C. Mc Carron kicked off Klan activity in Oklahoma with a meeting of local fraternal orders in Oklahoma City in 1920. They brought letters of introduction from fraternal officials in Texas with them to this initial gathering. Kimbro, calling himself the Klan's "Grand Goblin," claimed to represent territory that encompassed sixteen states, including Oklahoma.[1]

Not long after, they began recruiting across the state; in just a few months the membership was over a 1,000 in Oklahoma City.[2] "By September of 1921, the Klan's Oklahoma City membership roster alone surpassed 2,500. The activities of the Klan in Oklahoma in general and in Tulsa in particular became so notorious as to pose an imminent threat to social stability."[3]

A closer look at the "Constitution and Laws of the Knights of the Ku Klux Klan" and their articles explains the Klan's reason for existence. Reviewing one of their statements presents a distinct elevation of white supremacy and Christian belief. Here is an excerpt from their Constitution:

> I believe that God created races and nations, committing to each a special destiny and service; that the United States through its White, Protestant citizens holds a Divine commission for the furtherance of free government, the maintenance of white supremacy and the protection of religious freedom; that its Constitution and Laws are expressive of this Divine purpose.[4]

---

1. Johnson, *Black Wall Street*, 21.
2. Johnson, *Black Wall Street*, 21.
3. Johnson, *Black Wall Street*, 21.
4. Johnson, *Black Wall Street*, 36. Also see the brochure on organization and paper on the KKK coin in the Appendix.

These particular phrases or words such as, "special destiny," "maintenance of white supremacy," and "expressive of Divine purpose" again highlight Hughes's "myth of a chosen people." The Klan felt they had the right to control Tulsa. Their purpose insinuates the Klan should run the government and keep US cities under control.

Steve Gerkin presents facts about the early formation of the KKK in Tulsa. He makes a connection between the KKK and the attorney who represented Dick Rowland, the Black man accused of raping a white woman. That allegation served as the lynchpin and the principle ignitor for the massacre. First, Gerkin observed that "In January 1922, the Tulsa Benevolent Association of Tulsa, Oklahoma was officially formed as a holding company for the knights of the Ku Klux Klan, Incorporated."[5] I contend based on the rapid growth occurring, just two hours away in Oklahoma City, with over 2,500 members by September of 1921, that Tulsa's membership had been growing just as rapidly. I believe the recruitment period started long before September, especially with long-time Klan members living in the state since 1870.

Second, Gerkin writes, "They provided the financing and leadership to begin building their Klan temple, or Klavern known as Beno Hall. Locals jokingly called it 'Be No Hall' as in 'Be No Nigger, Be No Jew, Be No Catholic, Be No Immigrant.'"[6] The KKK's first purchase for a meeting place was a church, called Centenary Methodist Church and located at 501 North Main Street, that was converted for Klan business but they quickly outgrew it. (A church is in Tulsa today with this same name at this location.)

Third, the next facility for the Klan was built for $200,000. Today, the estimated cost would be $1.5 million.[7] An important fact here is the entrepreneur who helped finance the KKK's building was Tate Brady. (Today, just one street over from historical Greenwood, is a new entertainment development in Tulsa called the Brady District, named after Tate Brady.) When the new building was completed, it held over three thousand people and was the largest building in the Southwest. "Its size alone provided Tulsa with a visual reminder of the Invisible Empire's power, passion and presence."[8] This history of the KKK begins to help shape the milieu that existed in Tulsa prior to the massacre and generates more certainty of their existence prior to the riot.

5. Gerkin, *Hidden History of Tulsa*, 15.
6. Gerkin, *Hidden History of Tulsa*, 15.
7. Gerkin, *Hidden History of Tulsa*, 15.
8. Gerkin, *Hidden History of Tulsa*, 15.

Gerkin expands thoughts and facts regarding the KKK presence surrounding the time of the massacre. He explains how a Klan official and minister identified the riot as a success two months later:

> Abundant evidence points the finger at the Klan for fanning the sociological tinderbox that was 1920s Tulsa. Yearning for a spark—even an invented one—a fired-up mob of whites took the bait and burned Greenwood to the ground in the Memorial Day 1921 race riot. Two months later, a national Klan official, Caleb Ridley, who was also a Baptist minister, lectured at the Tulsa Convention Hall on the principles of the Klan, calling the riot a complete success, adding that it "was the best thing to ever happen to Tulsa and that judging from the way strange Negroes were coming to Tulsa we might have to do it all over again."[9]

White Christianity played a significant role in all the terror and torture against African-Americans. Rather than preachers or ministers working to prevent, control, or eradicate lynchings, they participated in the lynching activities. Patterson notes,

> Fundamentalist preachers not only condoned the sacrifices but actively incited many of them. They were at the vanguard of such organizations as the Ku Klux Klan. Wyn C. Wade estimates that some 40,000 fundamentalist ministers joined the Klan. "Many of them became the first Exalted Cyclopes of their local communities. In Pennsylvania, Texas, North Dakota, and Colorado they became Grand Dragons of their entire states."[10]

The preachers were complicit in the Klan movement and therefore the terrorism against African-Americans. Patterson further notes that white preachers spoke at Klan rallies, lectured for Imperial Headquarters, and preached sermons that were pro-Klan. Wade concludes, "Without these ministers and fundamentalist revivals, the KKK could never have enrolled the fantastic numbers [it did] nor have gained the remarkable power it wielded between 1922 and 1925."[11] White supremacy, supported by religious reinforcement, had no ethical consciousness or regard for social, political, or economic justice for African-Americans. The immorality of the United States built a nation that never intended for African-Americans to function as equals or participate in the "American dream," as Lee Butler argues.

---

9. Gerkin, *Hidden History of Tulsa*, 16.
10. Patterson, *Rituals of Blood*, 202.
11. Patterson, *Rituals of Blood*, 202.

I turn now to the religious aspect of lynching through Orlando Patterson's research. I highlight the ritual of lynching as human sacrifice in the South, and the role of religion and Christianity. Not all the public lynchings were considered sacrificial murders but a significant number did represent this type of horror. Patterson offers three examples; the first was a man named Henry Smith, accused of killing the young daughter of a Texas policeman. This is what a witness describes of the event in Paris, Texas:

> At 12 o'clock the train was met by a surging mass of humanity 10,000 strong. The Negro was placed upon a carnival float in mockery of a king upon his throne, and followed by an immense crowd, was escorted through the city so that all might see the most inhuman monster known in history. His clothes were torn off piecemeal and scattered in the crowd, people catching the shreds and putting them away as mementos. The child's father, her brother, and two uncles then gathered about the Negro as he lay fastened to the torture platform and thrust hot irons into his quivering flesh.[12]

Another example was in Georgia with Sam Holt, who allegedly killed his employer for wages in 1899:

> In the presence of nearly 2000 people, who sent aloft yells of defiance and shouts of joy, Sam Holt was burned at the stake in a public road. Before the torch was applied to the pyre, the Negro was deprived of his ears, fingers, and other portions of his body with surprising fortitude. Before the body was cool, it was cut to pieces, the bones were crushed into small bits and even the tree upon which the wretch met his fate was torn up and disposed of as souvenirs. The Negro's heart was cut in small pieces, as was also his liver. Those unable to obtain the ghastly relics directly, paid more fortunate possessors extravagant sums for them.[13]

These are just a few examples of how Patterson describes the highly ritualistic tortures of African-American lynchings. In each situation, the victims suffered terribly.

How can we understand these human sacrifices of innocent Black bodies unto God? Patterson quotes Durkheim's work as a way of understanding how this unifies the group: "The sacrificial ritual created not only a compact between the sacrificers and their god but a compact of fellowship

---

12. Patterson, *Rituals of Blood*, 193.
13. Patterson, *Rituals of Blood*, 194–95.

among the sacrificers themselves."[14] Theologically, I believe God received these innocent Black bodies as pure and good for the sacrificial offerings that they were. Not because the sacrificers were acting in a pleasing way to God by using Black bodies as sacrifices, but because those sacrificed were innocent and valuable to the kin(g)dom of God. These Black women, men, and sometimes children over decades had no ability to defend or save themselves from the white mobs. The biblical example in Amos is explicit regarding how God felt regarding particular sacrifices. Amos 5:21–24 reads:

> I hate, I despise your religious festivals;
> your assemblies are a stench to me.
> Even though you bring me burnt offerings and grain offerings,
> I will not accept them.
> Though you bring choice fellowship offerings,
> I will have no regard for them.
> Away with the noise of your songs!
> I will not listen to the music of your harps.
> But let justice roll on like a river,
> righteousness like a never-failing stream![15]

In this Scripture, God calls for justice not sacrifice. The sacrifice of innocent African-Americans certainly did not represent justice. Even if whites claimed their actions were reflective of religious rituals, it was not pleasing to God.

Another biblical sacrificial example, and reflection regarding how human sacrifice was seen by God, is the Cain and Abel narrative. Abel's animal sacrifice was acceptable to God, but Cain's first fruits were not. The white mobs may have conceived that they were sacrificing animals; but despite their inherent ineptitude, we know they were precious Black human beings. Genesis 4:9–11 reads as follows:

> Then the Lord said to Cain, "Where is your brother Abel?"
> "I don't know," he replied. "Am I my brother's keeper?"
> The Lord said, "What have you done? Listen! Your brother's blood cries out to me from the ground. Now you are under a curse and driven from the ground, which opened its mouth to receive your brother's blood from your hand.

This Scripture reprimands Cain for the innocent blood of his brother Abel that cries out from the ground. In this example, Cain was no different than

---

14. Patterson, *Rituals of Blood*, 202.
15. New International Version.

the mob; he killed an innocent person and God was not pleased. I posit here that there was something extraordinary about these sacrificed Black bodies.

Patterson also explains that certain sites were considered as sacred places for lynching. Trees were one primary spot because of the association with the fall of Adam and the death of Jesus.[16] "Other favored sites that had universal symbolism of transition: crossroads, railroad crossings, the border between two states, and rivers and ponds."[17] Other sacred sites often chosen were bridges, "which, as all students of symbolism and mythology know, is a universal symbol of transition, of crossing from one state, period, or form to another and hence a site for the most sacred and powerful rituals."[18] Bridges also served as a warning to others of the white power of dominance and the power of lynching executions if you stepped out of your place.

One particular lynching that occurred in Oklahoma represents this type of bridge torture. In 1911, Laura and L. D. Nelson, a mother and son, were both lynched on a bridge, close to Okemah, Oklahoma, in Okfuskee County. Accused of stealing a cow, L. D. allegedly shot the sheriff who searched their farm. After they were held in jail, the white mob came for them. Laura was raped first. The lynched bodies were photographed, and postcards were made.

Laura Nelson and L. D. Nelson Lynching

Figure 8. Source: The Oklahoma City Historical Society Museum. Laura Nelson and L. D. Nelson Lynched in 1911.

---

16. Patterson, *Rituals of Blood*, 205.
17. Patterson, *Rituals of Blood*, 207.
18. Patterson, *Rituals of Blood*, 206.

A PASTORAL PSYCHOLOGY OF LYNCHING

I want to explore the psychology of lynching. Consider Lee Butler's article "Lynching: A Post Traumatic Stressor in a Protracted Traumatic World." Butler explains that lynching should never be forgotten, nor the importance of how lynching by those who proclaimed to be followers of Jesus Christ terrorized African-Americans for generations. America's historical narrative has been presented as one of a good nation and as a claim of not being a villain or a terroristic nation. This notion of a good nation can be observed especially when the events of 9/11 and the Oklahoma City bombing occurred. Then America actually saw itself as the victim; but the truth is America has a long history of its own terrorism.[19]

Butler posits, "To live with terror is to live in constant fear so intense there is no place to feel safe."[20] That describes the psychological effects of lynching. This is what African-Americans felt for decades, through many generations during the frenzy of lynching. Butler postulates, "As a psychological condition, post-traumatic stress focuses on a single event in the past that becomes the lens and filter for interpreting present and future events and situations."[21] For African-Americans, that single event was lynching. Not only is the Black race reminded of the atrocities associated with lynching, but they are haunted by other events that trigger this memory.

Butler further elaborates, "Our protracted traumatic existence means that evil and suffering continue to inform and impact our [Black] lives."[22] He theorizes that these traumatic events have impacted the entire Black culture, not just certain or specific individuals. Therefore, African-Americans are haunted, for instance, by nooses hanging on trees, as we saw in the more recent years with "Jena 6," or when college students saw a doll hang from a fraternity house.[23] All of the historical, social, and psychological consciousness must be taken into consideration, Butler notes, when doing psychotherapeutic work.

The immorality of this American nation is best exhibited in two ways. First, in the unwillingness to repent of its sins by not admitting the long history of injustices related to torturing African Americans through slavery, lynching, racism, and a claimed precedence of Black inequality. Second, based on the above atrocities, a legislative government that continues

19. Butler, "Lynching," 11.
20. Butler, "Lynching," 10.
21. Butler, "Lynching," 20.
22. Butler, "Lynching," 20–21.
23. Butler, "Lynching," 14.

opposition to changing the laws that will protect African Americans in this country. In more recent examples, when Laquan McDonald was shot sixteen times in Chicago by a white policeman, while walking away, African Americans experienced these post-traumatic stressors. When nine people were shot and killed at historic Emanuel AME Church in Charleston, South Carolina by a young white man, who they kindly invited into Bible Study, the post-traumatic stressor continued. However, this time, the trauma happened in the sacred place of solace for African Americans, the Black church; this represented an even deeper traumatic experience. Another example is when Sandra Bland was found hanging in her jail cell in Texas—most African Americans were also traumatized by this tragedy.

Finally, there are current examples of why the traumatic stressors continue because we see today that public lynchings of African American bodies are still at the core of American ethos. Public lynchings are no longer limited to only swinging Black bodies from ropes; today public lynchings demonstrate that the ropes have been traded for guns and "violence to death" in the public square and private spaces. During just the year of 2020 several public deaths have mimicked or represented the age-old torture of lynching. Ahmaud Arbery was followed while jogging by white men, who took the law into their own hands, by shooting and killing him. Breonna Taylor was shot unlimited times and killed by police who busted into her home in Louisville, Kentucky. George Floyd was killed by a police officer who kneeled on his neck with his knee for eight minutes and forty-six seconds while other officers stood by and watched.

Over the last few years there is a long list of these public lynchings. Most of these acts of violence and terrorism have been caught on tape and shown to the public. The devastation to the African American public and to the many supporters from other ethnicities is they have not been able to elicit changes in laws or galvanize the Senate to vote that Black bodies are valuable enough to save and deserve protection. Trauma and terror are deeply embedded in the structures of this nation against African Americans, and complicit in American laws which continues to lynch African American people as history magnifies the ongoing heinous crime of public lynching. The evil propelled by racism in this country must be dismantled.

Normalization of Lynching

Another psychological interpretation that I want to explore regarding the acceptability and practice in American culture is the normalization of lynching. Exploring the components that instantiate the normalization of anything involves the consideration of how the dynamic of communal activities are established particularly, in this instance, with the emphasis on lynching.[24] Multiple threads must function simultaneously to normalize something—just one or two factors would not be sufficient. I will discuss seven factors that contributed to the normalization of lynching.

1) The act of lynching occurred on a regular basis; it was not an anomaly. Lynching was known and practiced throughout the nation, especially in the South. 2) Lynching was ritualized. I am not referring here to a "spiritual ritual" aspect, although that did exist, but those perennial acts that typically customized lynching or the repetition most often associated with it. Lynching was primarily reserved for African-Americans. If the person had been arrested and jailed, the mob would regularly take the prisoner. Sometimes lynchings included burning of the body and/or shooting of the body in addition to hanging the victim. All of these components helped to ritualize the process.

3) Lynching was a communal event, in which many participated. The public lynchings were attended by thousands of white people, men, women, and children. People came from miles around. They brought picnic baskets. They made post cards of the lynchings and sold souvenirs of flesh and crushed bones from the victim's dead body. 4) These events and processes represented for communities an aspect of the American cultural socialization. Terrorizing African-Americans became known as a part of their regular activities. Everyone knew about lynching and embraced the excitement that surrounded it.

Another critical aspect was the children. 5) Children were taught from a very young age that lynching was good, acceptable, and exciting. Lynchings were events that the entire family attended or participated in. Walter White wrote about encountering three children on the road where lynchings had occurred. The children were jubilant regarding the dead Negroes. In fact, "playing 'lynching' was so popular a pastime for Southern children that the game was named 'Salisbury.'"[25] Even the historical pictures show images of children on the shoulders of their fathers for a full view when crowds gathered. Sometimes children helped to start the fires or rekindle them as the victims burned.

6) One more thread in the normalization was the span of time in which lynching continued in American culture. Recorded lynchings began around 1865 and lasted until 1950, almost a century. If we count the non-recorded

24. A conversation with ethicist Christophe Ringer on why lynching was embraced and how it could have lasted for decades caused him to respond that lynching was "normalized." This exchange caused me to explore how something becomes normalized.

25. Equal Justice Initiative, *Lynching in America*, 67.

lynchings, those documented through the oral tradition, beginning in the early nineteenth century, it would be well over one hundred years. 7) The final thread that normalized lynching was in the hegemonic power within the American social structure. This component was an absolute requirement for lynching to be normalized. White men had the social, economic, and political control to make lynching possible.

Socially, white men held the majority of positions in the government. White men were responsible for constructing the mobs and they determined when lynchings would happen. They had the power to notify and inform the communities of upcoming lynchings. Economically, white men owned the farms, controlled the work of sharecroppers, and the paid disbursements to employees. The law and lack of legal protection is where the greatest power was exhibited. As long as lynchings were legal or could be performed with impunity, Negroes remained the targets of terror.

There were several Enforcement Acts and debates regarding the Fourteenth Amendment; however, they were ineffective in protecting African-Americans individually. "In the *United States v. Cruikshank*, decided March 27, 1786, the Court held that the Fourteenth Amendment 'prohibits a State from depriving any person of life, liberty, or property, without due process of law; but this adds nothing to the rights of one citizen as against another.'"[26] This meant only protection from actions of the state but not against individual violence. As a result, "African-Americans in the South were to be left at the mercy of white terrorists, so long as the terrorists were private actors."[27] Lynching had truly become normalized in American culture.

I argue that what was experienced in lynching is not just hatred, but an evil manifested through multiple perspectives to create an American culture called white supremacy. White supremacy was constantly being reinforced by the social and structural components that were shaping America. Walter White explains that, for generations, southern whites had believed in a mental and moral superiority over Blackness and the proclivity of the Negro race for sexual crimes. He further argues, "Added to this is the belief that any white man, no matter how inept, criminal, or depraved, is infinitely superior to the 'best Negro who ever lived.'"[28] This helps one see how the lynchers perceived themselves in relation to the Negro race; yet numerous other factors contributed to their behavior.

---

26. Equal Justice Initiative, *Lynching in America*, 19.
27. Equal Justice Initiative, *Lynching in America*, 19.
28. White, *Rope and Faggot*, 6.

Another psychological factor for the lynchers was the "human love of excitement."[29] In other words, the daily routine of life could often be drab. "Lynching often takes the place of the merry-go-round, the theatre, the symphony orchestra and other diversions common to large communities."[30] This component of "excitement" is a major element in the lynching gatherings. White describes three children walking on the road where five Negroes had been burned in Florida. The ruddy-cheeked girl of nine or ten asked him enthusiastically, "Are you going to the place where the 'niggers' had been killed?"[31] White describes the three children as animated and almost as excited as they would be for Christmas or some other joyous occasion as they explained the fun of burning them.[32]

Still another psychological factor was the inability of white people to form new ideas about the Negro.[33] Rather, when they heard the word *Negro*, they wanted to classify them in three categories. "One of these is the happy-go-lucky, improvident, shiftless Negro; the second, a habitual criminal of unrestrained appetites, kept within bounds only by extreme brutality; the third is a humble, 'befo' de wah' type, who knows 'how to stay in his place.'"[34] If they did not fit into one of these, they were not classifiable and beyond what whites could comprehend.

Walter White explores the economic element as a psychological factor that motivated lynching. The Southerners feared greatly the progress the Negro race had made and would make. To see African-Americans exceed the success of any white person was more than tradition allowed them to bear. "Ku Kluxry is the Southern poor white's answer to the progress of the emerging Negro, once his equal and now threatening to become his superior."[35] When whites saw a successful Negro business person or doctor living comfortably while they personally struggled to make good wages or still had to live in shabby housing, their self-esteem was wounded.

The economic challenge represented in Negro progress following Reconstruction and the resentment of Black success is exactly what led to Tulsa's Massacre. One of the major conflicts in Tulsa by 1921 was that the Negroes had exceeded "their place" in society as defined by white people. The night of the massacre, when homes were burning, one extremely successful

29. White, *Rope and Faggot*, 9.
30. White, *Rope and Faggot*, 6.
31. White, *Rope and Faggot*, 3.
32. White, *Rope and Faggot*, 6.
33. White, *Rope and Faggot*, 10.
34. White, *Rope and Faggot*, 10.
35. White, *Rope and Faggot*, 12.

Black doctor came out of his burning home with his hands held high and surrendering; yet, they shot him dead. So, the economic progress played a significant role in white Americans' jealously and the Klan's determination to keep Negroes in their place.

I want to further pursue my investigation regarding this violent act of lynching and terrorism of evil that so many participated in. It is conceivable that a small percentage of white people, especially those in the South, could be convinced that lynching was acceptable. Even a group of people could have been encouraged to join the "so-called" excitement of killing Negroes from time to time because they despised the race so much; but to convince thousands of people to participate over decades shows this evil was deeply imbedded into the psyche of white America culture.

Another significant aspect of lynching, which should not be overlooked or taken lightly, was the "white thing for Blackness."[36] White people had an insatiable desire for Black bodies and, although the laws did not protect Black women, the laws did protect white women. White women played a major role in the act of lynching Black men. One cry from someone whom white men considered as the pure and innocent white woman, would bring the mob running. White women contributed substantially to the justifications and acceptability of lynching in American history. The perennial claims of rape gave white women extreme power and voice in the public square. This exemplifies that white women definitely perpetuated lynching for decades.

Reddick, a Black man in the "Lynching to Belong" section below, had an alibi; even though several Black women testified to his innocence, their word meant nothing in a white court of law. Ida B. Wells-Barnett's extensive work on lynching also investigates these particular accusations made by white women. She comments in *Southern Horrors* on these very challenges:

> Nobody in this section of the country believes the old threadbare lie that Negro men rape white women. If Southern white men are not careful, they will over-reach themselves and public sentiment will have a reaction; a conclusion will then be reached which will be very damaging to the moral reputation of their women.[37]

Too often, the cries of rape coming from white women were volatile, resulting from fear either when they were caught with a Black man or thought that someone had seen them with a Black man. Even Cynthia

---

36. This phrase was inspired by one of Ida Bell Wells-Barnett's chapters, entitled "The Black and White of It."

37. Wells-Barnett, *Southern Horrors*, 52.

Nevels's research,[38] conducted by a white woman, advocates white women were complicit in sustaining the lynching terror. Ida B. Wells-Barnett's research in *Southern Horrors* examines extensively in chapter 2, "The Black and White of It," the unlimited cases and excuses of white women in relationships with African-American men.

Wells-Barnett concludes that many white women simply wanted to be with Black men and their relationships were consensual. Wells-Barnett's information also reveals that one of white women's greatest fears was having an African-American child. On the other hand, white men desired Black women as well and regularly pursued those encounters. Unfortunately, when their aggressions resulted in the rape of Black women, there were no restrictions, laws to punish them, or mob repercussions for their actions.

Lynching served in multiple ways to dominate the Black race. It had clearly become the tool of racial violence, whether used to control the labor force or try to influence political elections and outcomes. Lynching was also a way that outsiders could belong to or be embraced into white culture. Cynthia Nevels explores in *Lynching to Belong* how European immigrants such as Germans, Italians, Irish, and Bohemians or Czechs participated in Texas's lynching culture. Another challenge for African-Americans were the Democrats, who wanted to control the Black Republican vote. When the Populist Party came into existence as an alternative party, they wanted to prohibit Blacks from voting. As a result, African-Americans' voting boxes were removed in 1899 so they could not vote. Often, they had to travel longer distances to vote and by 1900 city elections were difficult to participate in at all because of the massive threats of violence when Blacks tried to vote.

Tulsa highlights an interesting dichotomy, expressed through the Black/white binary and the social culture as depicted in the newspaper. Although more details regarding the Tulsa Massacre are in the next chapter, instructive to note is that immediately following the bloody massacre in Tulsa, the front page of Tulsa's newspapers ran coverage for several days presenting the same Black/white contrast and comparison. In Tulsa, it was between white women participating in a beauty contest and the devastated lynched Black Wall Street, which was in ruins.[39] This is a continuation of the ideology that presents white as good and of value, juxtaposed with African-Americans as bad and not of value. Additionally, it elevates this idea of purity of white women in contradiction to the Black race or community.

I am convinced more than ever before that Blackness is uniquely special and extraordinary. This conviction that I carry extends beyond

38. Nevels is the author of *Lynching To Belong*.
39. See the Appendix for newspaper headlines.

ontological Blackness. However, the ontology is subjugated to the existential in the experience of Blackness: the way it breathes, the way it lives, the way it moves, how it endures, and the resilience attached to it. Blackness has a sacredness about it. It is strong, tough, precious, and tender concomitantly and something about it seems to bounce back until it is no more. Yet, Blackness seems to exist in a world that always positions it in contravention of whiteness, which is often characterized in theory as good and pure. I have difficulty seeing this purity and goodness in whiteness because of so much historical terror leveled against Black people by white people.

When I reflect upon the historical experiences of Blackness in terms of race relations, I see many who are not Black in our American society have not only needed but wanted Blackness as a part of their lives. They have wanted Blacks to be their laborers, to produce their labor capital, to be their servants, to build their country, to develop their economic capital, to make them rich, to raise their children, to be their entertainment, and to fulfill their personal and psychological needs as companions and lovers. This obsession with Blackness is phenomenologically exemplified in the ritualistic sacrifices in which Black bodies were chosen to hang on trees and over bridges. And yet, Blackness still prays, still stands, still speaks, still hopes, still shines, still shouts, still laughs, still loves, and still lives! I am absolutely convinced Blackness is a sacred resilience.

THEOLOGY OF SUFFERING

My final thoughts regarding lynching cause me to contemplate one of the womanist theological arguments related to the suffering of Jesus as an identifiable connection for Blacks in America. Jacquelyn Grant opines what it means to understand Black women's suffering in relation to Christ by explaining the very suffering of Jesus and the challenges that he experienced in both life and at the cross are what solidify the connection between Jesus and African-Americans' theology. Regarding the womanist tradition she further explains, "For Christian Black women in the past, Jesus was their central frame of reference. They identified with Jesus because they believed that Jesus identified with them. As Jesus was persecuted and made to suffer undeservedly, so were they."[40]

JoAnne Terrell notes, "Yet the reality of violence in black women's lives informs their theodical attempts to ascribe meaning to their suffering and to affirm the divine assistance to gain victory over it."[41] This means there

40. Grant, *White Women's Christ*, 212.
41. Terrell, *Power in the Blood*, 125.

is hope and encouragement to overcome the situation with divine power, no matter how difficult the circumstances. The tree was one of the places identified as sacred, in relation to Jesus' death on the cross. Many of the lynchings for Black people also occurred from trees. How can one better understand the crucifixion of African-Americans through lynching in relation to Jesus' crucifixion?

I certainly believe the body and blood of Jesus, through one event, was redemption enough for the whole world, but what do we say about the innocent blood and bodies representing thousands of lynched African-Americans over decades? The innocent "splattered blood" of African-Americans has not received retribution in this world yet, and the evil will be punishable by God. My womanist sensibilities say perhaps the innocent blood that has been splattered continues to serve as a form of redemptive covering, to continue fighting against the evil the Black race encounters. The Black race has remained under constant attack and has demonstrated resilience to rise, in spite of lynching, above discrimination, beyond police gun violence, and survive even though laws still do not protect them.

Delores Williams would disagree; she argues no redemption is in the death of Jesus on the cross, but rather, redemption is in his life. She states, "the image of Jesus on the cross is the image of human sin in its most desecrated form."[42] The image of Jesus (voluntary) or any crucified or lynched person (involuntary) on the cross is a terrible sight of torture, and all of the sins associated with the acts; however, it leaves no room for hope. For Williams, this image is one of defilement.[43] She posits "there is nothing divine in the blood of the cross."[44] I disagree with Williams. I believe there is something sacred in Jesus' blood on the cross and the hope is found in Jesus' resurrection.

Williams's perspective would also convey that there is no purpose or hope in the lynched person's death either. While I understand lynched victims are not Jesus, the theology Williams espouses concludes that lynched people's blood has no value. This reflection causes me to further advocate for the value of innocent persons and their blood. At least Jesus had a choice as well as the divine power for redemption by the sacrifice; but the lynched victim never had a choice. God's power is demonstrated in the ability to overcome death.

Terrell argues in relation to Jesus' crucifixion and the empty cross, "For many Christians, while the image of a crucifix signifies awareness of a God

---

42. Williams, *Sisters in the Wilderness*, 166.
43. Williams, *Sisters in the Wilderness*, 166.
44. Williams, *Sisters in the Wilderness*, 167.

who suffers with us in our experiences of suffering, the image of an empty cross signifies faith in the possibility of our own resurrection."[45] This says to me that the empty cross encourages people of faith to believe in the hope to lift themselves. Terrell further posits, "The empty cross is a symbol of God's continuous empowerment."[46] This shows Christ's significance for us.[47]

If Jesus' blood redeems the world and empowers us, then I believe value is in the body, blood, and life of lynched African-American ancestors not because God required the sacrifice but because God accepted their lives as good. African-Americans believe value is in their ancestors and in those who suffered before them. We regularly hear the claim, especially during Black history month, that "we stand on the shoulders of those ancestors who have gone before us." So that means innocent lynched Black bodies and their shed blood have value by giving hope and providing empowerment for Black lives. Maybe an ongoing sacredness, a holiness, is in the very existence of Blackness, which was never meant to survive the evil of white supremacy; yet Blackness still lives.

In honor of James Cone, who we lost in 2018, I would like to conclude this chapter with thoughts from his book *The Cross and the Lynching Tree*. Cone explains the time of the cross and the lynching tree are separated by almost 2,000 years and "both are symbols of death, one represents a message of hope and salvation, while the other signifies the negation of that message by supremacy."[48] Cone explicates that the cross symbolizes "divine power and black life"[49] and that at the same time the symbol of the cross is the very foundation of American Christian theological refection. On the other hand, Cone further explains that the lynching tree symbolizes "white power and black death of terror,"[50] and, although the lynching tree is similar to the cross, it has no theological discourse or reflection in America.[51]

Cone constructed a sacred parallel between Jesus' death on the cross and African-Americans' deaths on the lynching tree. In fact, he could not fathom how America, particularly twentieth century theology, missed the connection. He posits, "The crucifixion of Jesus by the Romans in Jerusalem and the lynching of blacks by whites in the United States are so amazingly similar that one wonders what blocks the American Christian imagination

---

45. Terrell, *Power in the Blood*, 125.
46. Terrell, *Power in the Blood*, 125.
47. Terrell, *Power in the Blood*, 125.
48. Cone, *The Cross*, xiii.
49. Cone, *The Cross*, 18.
50. Cone, *The Cross*, 18.
51. Cone, *The Cross*, 30.

from seeing the connection."[52] Jesus' death on the cross symbolized African-Americans' religious faith, a resurrection, hope, power, and our ability to overcome and succeed. I contend that African-Americans' lives lost on the lynching tree symbolize the same hope and power.

CONCLUSION

Since a failed lynching of Dick Rowland was responsible for the Tulsa tragedy, this chapter continues to explore some other components of lynching. I reviewed some research to highlight the early development of the Ku Klux Klan expansion into Oklahoma, particularly in Tulsa, to evaluate the role of the KKK in the massacre. The KKK involvement is important for our theological understanding associated with race. Unfortunately the research reveals that large numbers of white ministers participated extensively in the Klan movement, which integrates white supremacy and religion. I briefly reflected on human sacrifice from Orlando Patterson's work and the historical places lynchings typically occurred. I explored the psychology of lynching and the deep impact it has on the psyche from both perspectives. Finally, I examined the womanist perspective on Black suffering, blood sacrifice, and sacredness.

52. Cone, *The Cross*, 31.

CHAPTER 8

A Lynched Black Wall Street
The 1921 Tulsa Massacre

To escape white violence, many of Tulsa's African-Americans had been chased from everywhere. Their bravery was an obligation of pride. In black history, Greenwood's last stand is as symbolic as the Alamo is to America history. They may have been overpowered and imprisoned in concentration camps, but they never surrendered their hearts, minds and tenacious resilience.

—THE HONORABLE DON ROSS
A Century of African-American Experience in
Greenwood: Ruins, Resilience and Renaissance

Nab Negro For Attacking Girl in Elevator
To Lynch A Negro Tonight
—*TULSA TRIBUNE* NEWSPAPER HEADLINES

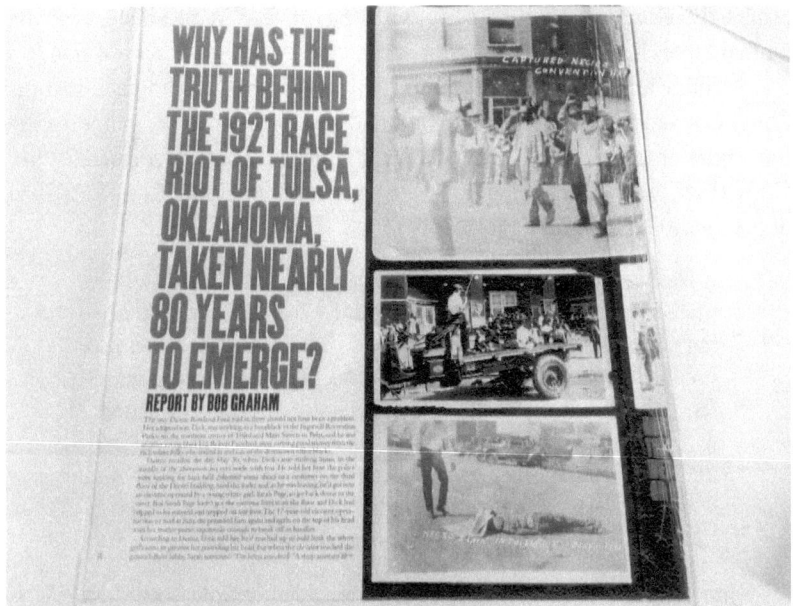

Figure 9. Source: Newspaper page in the Race Riot File—Tulsa Downtown Central Library.

BEFORE THE MASSACRE

During the summer of 1919, race riots had broken out in more than three dozen cities across the United States, including Chicago; Washington, DC; Elaine, Arkansas; and Omaha, Nebraska. The riots between May and October of 1919 were so extensive they named the period "Red Summer," but none of those riots equated in magnitude to the Tulsa Massacre.

"Roy Wilkens, former executive director of the NAACP, put the Rowland/Page incident in historical context. The Tulsa riot illustrates the classic lie of criminal assault which was used for decades to justify lynching and assaults upon Negroes in both the South and the North."[1] The culture of racial hatred against Black people was so heightened that even an innocent situation could escalate out of control. Equally significant during this epoch in American culture was the constant fear and claims by white men that Black men desired and consistently raped white women. Unfortunately, in the thousands of rape cases regarding white women, and all these claims

---

1. Johnson, *Black Wall Street*, 36.

against Black men used to justify lynching, "never in the history of the United States has a white man been executed for raping a Black woman."[2]

Alfalfa Bill Murray, president of the 1906–1907 Oklahoma Constitutional Convention, argued Blacks would always be inferior to whites. In the first Oklahoma legislative session after statehood, as some advocated for Jim Crow laws, this preview of an article was written by editor Roy E. Stafford of the *Daily Oklahoman*:

> It was never intended by the Almighty that the races should be placed upon social equality and the foolish ideas that are being placed in the black man's head to the contrary, by designing politicians, bode no good to either race. For the negro is an infant, figuratively, in intellect. His understanding of things is easily influenced. He is but so much putty in the hands of greater intelligence and he believes what he is told to believe. His mind is as much a slave to dictations of his superiors as his body was a slave to masters who owned it before the war.[3]

Jim and Jane Crow laws forbade miscegenation and separated everything: education, voting rights, public accommodations, railroad travel, and shared living spaces within the city. Actually, the Jim and Jane Crow laws operated no differently than the slave codes Higginbotham outlines in *Matter of Color*, which were used to form the early colonial laws in the United States.

In 1921 Tulsa, many young Black males worked as shoeshine boys. The jobs paid a five dollar a week wage, but the tips were "out of sight,"[4] according to Robert Fairchild, an after-school teenager who joined the shoeshine profession, or turned bootblack as they referenced it, because of the newfound wealth from rich oil men. "They didn't know what to do with their money and they'd come down there and get a shine, and they'd give you a dollar as [soon as they'd give you] fifteen cents."[5] This was the situation for Dick Rowland, also known as Diamond Dick, a nickname he was given for buying and sporting a diamond ring. The ring was a birthday gift he purchased for himself with the money made from shoeshining.

According to the *Hidden History of Tulsa*, Rowland was adopted as a child by Damie Roland Jones. She and the child lived with her parents after 1910. Dick was originally known as Jimmie Jones and, according to the 1920 census, John Roland. In high school, he reportedly changed his name to Dick and took the Roland last name out of respect for his grandparents.

2. Kovel, *White Racism*, xxxiii.
3. Stafford, "Jim Crow Laws."
4. Ellsworth, *Death in a Promised*, 45.
5. Ellsworth, *Death in a Promised*, 45.

The Booker T. High School yearbook[6] shows his name as James Jones and J. W. Jones. Following the massacre, a misspelling of his name occurred, and he became Rowland.[7]

Dick Rowland dropped out of Booker T. Washington High School to work downtown as a shoeshine boy. Due to the heavy racist environment, the owner of the shoeshine parlor had made arrangements with the Drexel building, located across the street, for the bootblacks to use the restroom facilities located on the top floor of the building.[8] On Monday, May 30, 1921, Rowland took the elevator up, as he did each day to use the facilities. A young seventeen-year-old white girl name Sarah Page was the elevator operator.

Many versions of the story exist regarding what happened in the elevator the morning of May 30, 1921. One story is the elevator shaft was not even with the floor when Rowland entered the elevator, that he stumbled into Page and she screamed. Another story is that Rowland tripped and grabbed her arm as he tried to keep from falling and Page screamed. Mary Jones Parrish writes, "A Colored boy accidentally stepped on a white elevator girl's foot. An evening paper hurled the news broadcast with the usual 'Lynching is feared if the victim is caught.' Then the flames of hatred which had been brewing for years broke loose."[9] "What actually transpired is probably forever clouded in obscurity, but many white Tulsans soon came to believe that Rowland had attacked the girl, scratched her hands and tore her clothes."[10]

Hannibal Johnson explains that Sarah Page provided her own statement regarding that morning:

> She admitted that her encounter with Dick Rowland had been inadvertent and innocent. She told officers that Rowland had come close to her on the elevator and that he had stepped on her foot. Of her own admission, she had panicked and overreacted. Page told officers that she slapped Rowland, at which time he grabbed her arm to prevent her from slapping him again. She screamed. He fled.[11]

Page's statement sounds like a possible disagreement between the two of them or an innocent accident, but certainly not like a woman who wanted to get a man arrested. The African-American community tells the story

6. Booker T. Washington High School Yearbook in 1921.
7. Gerkin, *Hidden History of Tulsa*, 43–44.
8. Ellsworth, *Death in a Promised*, 46; Johnson, *Black Wall Street*, 36.
9. Jones Parrish, *Events of the Tulsa*, 7.
10. Ellsworth, *Death in a Promised*, 46.
11. Johnson, *Black Wall Street*, 27.

that Rowland and Page knew each other. In fact, they were known to be girlfriend and boyfriend, which might be why Page made the preliminary police report but did not press charges. "Sarah Page initially accused young Rowland of assault but quickly retreated from that accusation."[12]

Ida B. Wells-Barnett suggested that many white women wanted to be with Black men. She noted that many interracial relationships were consensual, but the white communities claimed they could not believe this to be true. The possibility of Page and Rowland being in a relationship appears to be rarely considered in Tulsa's history except in the oral tradition of the Black community. This interracial taboo takes us back to the slave codes in the colonial formations that forbid Black men to be in relations with white women:

> Thus, the colonial legal system can be better evaluated by recognizing that it was a system controlled by a white male-dominated culture, a society generally antagonistic toward blacks, a society wherein white males wanted to maintain their domination over both white and black females, and finally, a society in which white males fervently desired to preclude any sexual relationships between black males and white females.[13]

The laws prohibited any contact with white women by Black men, but unfortunately no laws existed to protect the Black women from unrestrained aggressive white men. The number of rape assaults on Black women were significant for centuries. Interracial taboos certainly emphasize the atrocious lynchings that regularly occurred following Reconstruction, derived solely from the claims of Black males' desire for white women. These biased laws prohibiting mixed race interaction were deeply entrenched in American history. Even the restrictions against interracial marriage remained law in the United States until 1967.

Regardless of what happened in the elevator on the morning in question, once Page screamed, a Renberg's store clerk from next door came to her rescue. Given the racial climate in Tulsa, Rowland ran away. Of course, this made him look guilty, but Rowland knew the risk of assaulting a white woman. Critical to understand is how the words *rape* and *assault* were evaluated in society. As James S. Hirsch wrote in *Riot and Remembrance*, "'Rape' was rarely used by newspapers or in academic settings. 'Assault' was the word used, so when a white psychologist told a symposium in 1904, 'The crime of assault is the crime of the new Negro,' everyone knew what he meant."[14] Tulsa not only accused Rowland of stepping on Page's foot, they accused him of

12. Jones Parrish, *Events of the Tulsa*, 36.
13. Higginbotham, *In the Matter*, 42.
14. Hirsch, *Riot and Remembrance*, 53.

raping her. As a result, we have this comment: "Walter White [investigator for the NAACP] later wondered: why were so many people readily believing that Rowland was so ignorant as to attempt a rape in a crowded office building within earshot of many people?"[15] An innocent encounter quickly became an assault and then the larger society interpreted it as rape because everyone knew what "assault" meant. Walter White's comments represent that he knew that story was conflictual. Rowland was not arrested until the following day, but in the meantime the media made the situation explode.

The *Tulsa Tribune* ran a headline story on Tuesday, May 31, 1921 in the afternoon paper with the title "Nab Negro for Attacking Girl in Elevator." According to both Ellsworth and Johnson, the article from the above headline was written about by Loren Gill in his 1946 thesis. All of the research references this particular newspaper headline that aroused the Tulsa community. Unfortunately, the section where this article was published in the newspaper has been destroyed. Most people have concluded that someone cut the editorial from all papers before they were microfilmed. This was the article published:

> A negro delivery boy who gave his name to the public as "Diamond Dick" but who has been identified as Dick Rowland, was arrested on South Greenwood avenue this morning by Officers Carmichael and Pack, charged with attempting to Assault the 17-year-old white elevator girl in the Drexel building Early yesterday. He will be tried in municipal court this afternoon on a state charge. The girl said she noticed the negro a few minutes before the attempted assault looking up and down the hallway on the third floor of the Drexel building as if to see if there was anyone in sight but thought nothing of it at the time. A few minutes later he entered the elevator she claimed, and attacked her, scratching her hands and face and tearing her clothes. Her screams brought a clerk from Renberg's store to her assistance and the negro fled. He was captured and identified this morning both by the girl and the clerk, police say. Tenants of the Drexel building said the girl is an orphan who works as an elevator operator to pay her way through business college.[16]

In addition to this article, the *Tribune* ran the headline "To Lynch A Negro Tonight." Just like the first article, this one is missing from the newspaper archives. Soon after the papers hit the streets, about 3:15 PM, the community began to stir. Shortly after, an anonymous caller said there was

---

15. Ellsworth, *Death in a Promised*, 47.
16. Ellsworth, *Death in a Promised*, 48; Johnson, *Black Wall Street*, 38.

"lynch talk" on the street. J. M. Adkison, a fire commissioner, called Sheriff Willard McCullough to notify him. Not long after, between 6:00 and 7:00 PM, the crowd of whites began to gather at the court house where Dick Rowland was held.[17] The safety of a prisoner seemed to be of no consequence if the lynch mob wanted him.

Just nine months earlier, Roy Belton, an eighteen-year-old white boy, had been taken from the jail and hung for killing a white taxi driver named Homer Nida.[18] In another case, "just a few months before, white hoodlums took a young African-American man jailed for allegedly assaulting a white woman from his cell in Holdenville, Oklahoma, tied him to a telephone pole and summarily executed him. He was shot to death, not lynched."[19] The African-American community certainly had reason for concern as the white mob began to assemble.

THE MASSACRE

By 7:30 PM, the crowd had grown to 300 whites outside the courthouse. At 9:00 PM, the crowd had grown to 400. Sheriff McCullough told three white men who entered the court there would be no lynching and ordered them to leave. Inside, McCullough sent the elevator to the top, made it inoperable and told the guards to take precautions and barricade behind the door.[20] Johnson comments, "Sheriff McCullough took pains to protect Rowland, rendering the jail elevator inoperable, ordering his jailers to barricade themselves on the top floor where Rowland was incarcerated, and ordering the assembled whites to cease and desist. (They did not.)"[21] Just before the National Guard troops arrived at 9:15 AM the next day (June 1, 1921), "Sheriff McCullough slipped out with Rowland about eight o'clock."[22]

Shortly after 9:15 PM, a false report reached Greenwood that a white mob was storming the courthouse,[23] and the men from the Greenwood community began uniting. Later, Henry Jacobs, another man on Greenwood,

---

17. Ellsworth, *Death in a Promised*, 49.
18. Ellsworth, *Death in a Promised*, 40–43.
19. Johnson, *Black Wall Street*, 39.
20. Ellsworth, *Death in a Promised*, 61.
21. Johnson, *Black Wall Street*, 37, 38.
22. Ellsworth, *Death in a Promised*, 49. Ellsworth's chapter does not specify that the time that Dick Rowland and Sheriff McCullough left was in the morning, but since the departure is written between the paragraphs of the National Guard's arrival at 9:15 AM and martial law being declared at 11:29 AM, I am saying 8:00 AM.
23. Ellsworth, *Death in a Promised*, 50.

said he saw J. B. Stratford, an attorney and Black hotel owner, rounding up an armed group. He was heard saying to go get the Muskogee (a smaller town forty-five minutes away) crowd.[24] An unidentified man said he saw Smitherman, a Black deputy sheriff, go into the "choc" joint and gather men.[25] Barney Cleaver, one of two Black policemen, had offered his assistance to McCullough earlier but McCullough told him things were under control. Cleaver later stated that he tried to keep a group of African-American men from going to the courthouse but they only laughed and threatened him.[26] When a group of twenty-five to thirty Black World War I veterans showed up at the court house armed with rifles and shotguns, they were told Rowland was safe and were reassured the guards could handle it.[27] The police convinced the Black men to leave but the white crowd of men remained at the court house.

The white mob continued to increase and, by 10:30 PM, 1,500 to 2,000 white people were at the court house. The armed group of African-American men, this time fifty to seventy-five in number, visited the courthouse for the second time. Again, the police asked them to leave and told them everything was under control. Policeman Cleaver was among the crowd asking the Black men to leave. One Black man was disarmed by the sheriff but no one else was. Still no attempts to disperse the white mob were made.[28] According to Ellsworth and Johnson, the entire police force had not been called or summoned to the scene. By now, the Black men totaled about 200. As the Black men prepared to leave, one observer, Robert Fairchild, commented, "The white approached a tall black veteran who was carrying an Army issue 45-caliber and said, 'Nigger what are you doing with that pistol?' 'I'm going to use it if I need to,' came the reply. 'No, you give it to me.' 'Like hell I will.'"[29] The white man attempted to disarm the veteran and the gun shot exploded into the air; from that moment on, the massacre was underway.

The African-American men were clearly outnumbered and began to retreat back to the Greenwood area. "After the initial fighting had moved away from the courthouse, the Tulsa police deputized scores of whites—many of who had been part of the crowd in front of the courthouse."[30] The very men who gathered at the courthouse to strategize Dick Rowland's lynching were

24. Ellsworth, *Death in a Promised*, 50.
25. Ellsworth, *Death in a Promised*, 50.
26. Ellsworth, *Death in a Promised*, 50.
27. Ellsworth, *Death in a Promised*, 50; Johnson, *Black Wall Street*, 39.
28. Ellsworth, *Death in a Promised*, 51.
29. Ellsworth, *Death in a Promised*, 52.
30. Ellsworth, *Death in a Promised*, 54.

now the same men who became legally authorized, as deputies, to terrorize the entire Black community. The law empowered them to destroy the community. These same men broke into McGee's Hardware, stealing guns and ammunition. They also broke into fifteen other hardware stores and pawn shops, stealing guns and ammunition.[31] When Police Inspector C. W. Daley arrived about midnight, many of the men were still in front of the courthouse; their attention had moved from Rowland to the Black community.

During the first few hours of the massacre, any whites without guns were preparing by securing weapons and being armed to fight.[32] Earlier, before the fighting started, some talked about contacting the Tulsa National Guard troops but Chief Gustafson, Tulsa's police chief, said they could handle it; besides, according to Major Bell, they would need an official order. "The first fire broke out at about 1:00 AM at the intersection of Archer Street and Boston Avenue along the fringe of the Black district."[33] The white deputized mob was now beginning to move into the neighborhood of the Black community. The Frisco Railroad tracks were a dividing point for Black and white Tulsans. Much of the major fighting took place along that divide, especially as they tried to hold the whites from crossing that line. As whites tried to cross this line, they were met with great resistance from Blacks defending their property, but they persisted. During this time, the fire department arrived but the mob of more than 500 whites prevented them from doing their job; so they returned to their station.[34]

The African-American community had been warned early in the evening by the newspaper and communications circulating around town. Booker T. Washington had canceled its senior prom. Mary Parrish came home from her typewriting class about 9:00 PM and planned to finish reading a book; she explained to her daughter not to disturb her. As her little girl stared out the window, she first stated "Momma, look at the cars full of people." Parrish responded, "Baby, do not disturb me." A few minutes later her daughter said, "I see men with guns."[35] As her mother ran to look out the window, people gathered in groups talking excitedly. "Going down stairs to the street I was told of the threatened lynching and that some of our group were going to give added protection to the boy."[36] They continued to watch people move about until the late hour. Parrish could not believe

31. Ellsworth, *Death in a Promised*, 54.
32. Ellsworth, *Death in a Promised*, 54–55.
33. Ellsworth, *Death in a Promised*, 55.
34. Ellsworth, *Death in a Promised*, 55.
35. Jones Parrish, *Events of the Tulsa*, 8.
36. Jones Parrish, *Events of the Tulsa*, 8.

what was happening. She knew about the riots in Chicago and Washington, but in Tulsa, she was surprised. When Parrish realized what was actually happening, she held her daughter, read a few chapters of Psalms, and prayed God would give them courage to stand.[37] Parrish also described the Frisco tracks as the dividing line between Black and white Tulsa:

> It was here that the first battle was staged. Like mad bulls after a red flag or blood thirsty wolves after a carcass, so did these human wolves called men rave to destroy their fellow citizens. But these brave boys of ours fought gamely and held back the enemy for hours. Owing to the shortage of ammunition they were forced to retreat from Cincinnati, and immediately the advancing force began to pillage and burn that section.[38]

By 1:30 AM, the firing had quieted some and they thought perhaps it was over, when suddenly someone screamed, "Cincinnati, one of the main streets, is on fire!"[39] Parrish still had not vacated her home. At 3:00 or 4:00 AM, they could see the Midway Hotel burning. When they called the fire department, they replied that they would be right there, but of course they never came. Around 5 AM, a friend of Parrish's called the Police Department to find out when the militia would arrive in Tulsa. They replied that it would be at 7:00 AM. "Then the truth dawned upon us that our men were fighting in vain to hold their dear Greenwood."[40] People were running as the men came down the streets. Whites were looting and then burning the homes. Parrish looked out the back door and saw people fleeing and the enemy fast approaching.[41] Finally, Parrish, her daughter and a few friends ran out the south door leading to Archer:

> When Florence Mary and I ran into the street it was vacant for a block or more. Someone called to me to "get out of the street with that child or you both will be killed." I felt that it was suicide to remain in the building for it would surely be destroyed and death in the street was preferred for we expected to be shot down at any moment so we placed our trust in God, our Heavenly Father, who seeth and knoweth all things.[42]

---

37. Jones Parrish, *Events of the Tulsa*, 8.
38. Jones Parrish, *Events of the Tulsa*, 8.
39. Jones Parrish, *Events of the Tulsa*, 9.
40. Jones Parrish, *Events of the Tulsa*, 9.
41. Jones Parrish, *Events of the Tulsa*, 9.
42. Jones Parrish, *Events of the Tulsa*, 10.

As they continued what they thought was an escape, they ran right towards a machine gun positioned on the hillside. Passing others in the same frantic rush to leave town, "the question on every lip when a newcomer from town would arrive was, 'How far had they burned when you left town?'"[43] Many people were either walking or catching rides to escape the chaos that had been in effect all night and continued into the early morning hours.

The tension and conflict in Tulsa were not just about racial hatred but also the tremendous amount of envy and jealousy surrounding the success of the Negro race. Many of the white people in Tulsa despised the accomplishments African-Americans had achieved. Whether they were doctors, business owners, or just hard-working everyday people, whites believed Negroes should not have possessions better than theirs. Economic stratifications between certain African-Americans and the white population had become recognizable and both the rich and poor whites resented the success of African-Americans who had acquired wealth. During the massacre, whites desired Black people's valuables and took their property before burning their homes. Johnson highlights a Black woman who lost her home during the massacre, recalling:

> After they had the homes vacated one bunch of whites would come in and loot. Even women with shopping bags would come in, open drawers, take every kind of finery from clothing to silverware and jewelry. Men were carrying out the furniture, cursing as they did so saying "These [damn] Negroes have better things than lots of white people." . . . Some remarked that "The city ought to be sued for selling [damn] niggers property so close to the city."[44]

They took jewelry, china, furniture, and other expensive possessions; then they burned the homes. Whites often commented that Blacks had stepped out of their place or overstepped their bounds and must be put back in place.

At the Frisco Railroad station about 4:30 AM, Police Inspector Daley found the guards who were posted being overpowered by the white mob threatening to enter the Black district. Up to this point, they had invaded all the other areas of Black Tulsa; this was the last untouched space. Daley said he would shoot anyone who moved past and called for police backup, but everyone was already out. Daley and the armed Black residents held the mob for a while; however, by 6:00 AM they pressed and invaded the last untouched area of Black Tulsa.[45] The white mob burned the Greenwood

43. Jones Parrish, *Events of the Tulsa*, 11.
44. Johnson, *Black Wall Street*, 47.
45. Ellsworth, *Death in a Promised*, 55–57.

business district, homes, the schools, hotels, everything. "At the height of the Riot, carloads of marauding white Tulsans streamed into the streets, firing indiscriminately at any African-American target in sight. Women and children proved no exception."[46]

> At around 6:40 AM, fires were started in the shanties along Archer Street, and one hour later, both sides of Archer from Boston to Elgin streets were burning. "Deep Greenwood" was soon looted and put to the torch. The Mt. Zion Baptist Church, an impressive structure which had only recently been built, was burned by white Tulsans after a gun battle took place outside of it.[47]

The other Black historic church, Vernon AME, was also destroyed. Only the Black First Baptist Church, which is now located on Greenwood, was overlooked. At that time, First Baptist was positioned on a cross street. The mob thought it was a white church, so they did not burn it down. One of the most famous pictures that still circulates today is Mt. Zion on fire.

Mt. Zion Baptist Church on Fire

Figure 10. *Source*: Danney Goble, *Tulsa! Biography of the American City* (Tulsa, Oklahoma: Tulsa's Future, 1997), 125.

46. Johnson, *Black Wall Street*, 47.
47. Ellsworth, *Death in a Promised*, 57.

The debate is polemical regarding the role of airplanes during the massacre. Most of the authors write on how, or if, airplanes were used to bomb the Greenwood district. Hirsch, author of *Riot and Remembrance*, makes this statement:

> Exactly what they did has been debated ever since but numerous black witnesses have said the aircraft were used to assault Greenwood: pilots either dropped incendiary devices like "turpentine balls" and dynamite or used rifles to strafe people from the sky. If true, Tulsa was the first U.S. city to suffer an aerial assault. But police officials said the planes were used only to monitor the fires and to locate refugees. Walter White, the journalist from the NAACP, wrote: "Eight aeroplanes were employed to spy on the movements of the Negroes and according to some were used in bombing the colored section."[48]

To believe what police officials said seems contradictory, especially when the police were the ones who legally deputized members of the white mob on the courthouse grounds and then employed that mob, with full authority, to terrorize Black women, children, and men, to ultimately destroy the entire Greenwood community. Hirsch continues:

> Many black witnesses said that planes dropped explosives or "rained fire" on Greenwood. Mary E. Jones Parrish's book, J. B. Stradford's memoirs, A. J. Smitherman's poem—all provided first hand testimony of the bombing or strafing, as did black newspapers like the *Chicago Defender*. "At the signal of a whistle, more than a dozen aeroplanes went up and began to drop turpentine balls upon the negro residences, while 5,000 whites, with machine guns and other deadly weapons, began firing in all directions," a black witness told Parrish.[49]

Mary Jones Parrish, eye-witness of the massacre describes the incidents related to airplanes this way:

> After watching the men unload on First Street where we could see them from our windows, we heard such a buzzing noise that on running to the door to get a better view of what was going on, the sight our eyes beheld made our poor hearts stand still for a moment. There was a great shadow in the sky and upon a second look we discerned that this cloud was caused by fast approaching aeroplanes. It then dawned upon us that the enemy

---

48. Hirsch, *Riot and Remembrance*, 106.
49. Hirsch, *Riot and Remembrance*, 259.

had organized in the night and was invading our district the same as the Germans invaded France and Belgium. The firing of guns was renewed in quick succession. People were seen to flee from their burning homes, some with babes in their arms and leading crying and excited children by the hand; others, old and feeble, all fleeing to safety.[50]

The *Chicago Defender* reported that Tulsa's Black community was "bombed from the air by a private plane equipped with dynamite."[51] As Hirsch stated, unlike the Mt. Zion Baptist Church, no photographs or films are available to show absolute evidence. Since the Tulsa newspapers, grand juries, mayor, and even other officials said nothing, proving the bombing was difficult; however, the bombings do matter because this further demonstrates Black lives were dispensable and devalued. This debate further represents an importance in the oral traditions of the Black community, which I will discuss in more detail shortly.[52]

Regardless of the actual proof or those who chose not to believe the eye-witness accounts, personal testimonies of residents and survivors state something harmful did fall from the sky during the massacre, which further terrorized the African-Americans in Tulsa and intensified the burning destruction of the Greenwood community. Black voices appear to have been ignored and silenced regarding the massacre. However, on March 13, 1983, sixty-two years after the massacre, a newspaper article was written referencing Tulsa in the *Significa* entitled, "The First U.S. City To Be Bombed From the Air."[53]

J. B. Stradford was the first Black attorney in Tulsa. "In 1910 he built the luxurious 65-room hotel—Stradford Hotel. This lodge and other properties valued at $200,000, perhaps $2 million in today's dollars."[54] The first library in the state for Blacks was another necessary service established by Stradford's contribution. When a number of armed Black men went down to the courthouse to protect Dick Rowland, thousands of white men had already gathered. Stradford stayed behind just in case any of the black men were arrested and needed his services as a lawyer. Immediately following the massacre, the African-Americans were held in concentration camps. After the massacre, J. B. Stradford and sixty-three other Black men were

50. Jones Parrish, *Events of the Tulsa*, 10.
51. Ellsworth, *Death in a Promised*, 63.
52. Hirsch, *Riot and Remembrance*, 260.
53. See Appendix for full article.
54. Ross, *A Century of African-American*, 6. This story and pictures are exhibited in the Greenwood Cultural Center, Tulsa.

indicted on rioting charges by a grand jury.[55] Stradford, however, was able to escape from Tulsa, first to his brother's house in Independence, Kansas, and later to Chicago with his son.[56]

Stradford died a fugitive in 1935. His family tried to clear his name. "In 1995 Governor Frank Keating offered a pardon posthumously and formally apologized to the family and Tulsa's black community for the incident."[57] Stradford was publicly recognized in *People Weekly* and his name was cleared in in 1996; he made outstanding contributions to Greenwood but it took seventy-five years to clear his name.

I interviewed Lee Roy Chapman during my research in Tulsa about the massacre and the article he had written concerning the history. He was a white Tulsa resident, historian, journalist, artist, and activist. Chapman has written extensively on Tate Brady's connection with the KKK and on the Tulsa Massacre. Chapman died on October 8, 2015. He believed the conflict in the elevator was only an excuse—a smoke screen for whites to attack the Black community because whites wanted the land Blacks owned in Tulsa. The land owned by Black Wall Street and the Negro community was prime real estate in an area located right next to downtown. The African-American people that I interviewed made this same claim, that white people wanted the land and that was the real foundational source of tension.

I have concluded from the many sources that I read, that not only did whites want the land that African-Americans owned, the other point of contention existed because whites simply did not want African-Americans living in Tulsa. Eddie Faye Gates, a member of the Tulsa Riot Commission, said Blacks in Tulsa had been threatened and warned by notes on their houses to leave Tulsa.[58] Taking possession of the land is a real consideration because it addresses the motive surrounding economic gain and what the white community stood to profit if it could obtain the land once the properties were destroyed. I will further explore the land suspicion later, and the legal challenges associated with obtaining permits for rebuilding that became an obstacle for the restoration of Black Wall Street.

African-Americans concluded the massacre was intentional and strategically planned to destroy the Black community and expel Black Tulsans from the city. Many Blacks, and others like Chapman, concluded that white developers wanted the prime land the Negroes owned and the elevator incident was a smoke screen. Contemplated efforts by white Tulsans to destroy

---

55. Johnson, *Black Wall Street*, 62.
56. Ross, *A Century of African-American*, 6.
57. Ross, *A Century of African-American*, 6.
58. Gates, *Riot on Greenwood*, 32.

the Black community were not new. In fact, the *New York Times* and some Black newspapers had printed that Negroes were warned to leave Tulsa and other surrounding areas by June 1, 1921. Reportedly, these warnings had been attached to homes, threatening Blacks to leave or sell their properties. The *New York Evening World* reported the newspaper warnings ran three successive days.

A few African-Americans left Tulsa and reported the situation to the NAACP in New York.[59] Du Bois wrote in July 21 edition of *The Crisis* magazine about a small group of people that went to New York just prior to the massacre. Their names were Lizzie Johnson, Stella Harris, Josie Gatlin, and Claude Harris. These four were part of a total group of eight, arriving with basically nothing but the clothes they were wearing; all of the people were from Okmulgee, Oklahoma.[60] They proceeded to tell the terrible oppressive conditions upon Colored people and that peonage was common.[61]

Another significant action that gives credibility to the white Tulsans' desire for and threat of obtaining the land from African-Americans was revealed in the aftermath. Once the massacre was over, the City of Tulsa implemented an illegal fire ordinance, which imposed some extreme requirements in order for Blacks Tulsans to rebuild their properties. This illegal action was contested and fought in court by attorney Buck Franklin, John Hope Franklin's father, and overturned.

Further evidence of the theory that Tulsa officials planned the massacre was published by the Associated Negro Press in October 1921. The article stated, "Van B. Hurley, a former Tulsa policeman, claimed that he attended a meeting with city officials who carefully planned the attack on Greenwood by instructing local aviators to drop nitroglycerin on buildings."[62] Reportedly, Hurley signed a twenty-page affidavit for a Black attorney who represented the residents of Greenwood; however, that document could not be found.[63] Vivian Clark-Adams, another woman who served on the Tulsa Race Riot Study Commission, stated, "I know of no other riot where they had to resort to aerial assault and machine guns."[64]

The white Tulsans' story of Black Wall Street held that Blacks were out of control or living beyond their place and they wanted to teach them a lesson. Many whites who lived in the city, filled with all their privilege and

59. Hirsch, *Riot and Remembrance*, 256–59.
60. Du Bois, "The Tulsa Race Riots."
61. Du Bois, "The Tulsa Race Riots."
62. Hirsch, *Riot and Remembrance*, 260.
63. Hirsch, *Riot and Remembrance*, 260.
64. Hirsch, *Riot and Remembrance*, 260.

perceived superiority, simply thought Blacks were corrupt and disposable. An editorial on June 4, 1921 in the *Tulsa Tribune* newspaper made these comments:

> Such a district as the old "Niggertown" must never be allowed in Tulsa again. It was a cesspool of iniquity and corruption...Yet anybody could go down there and buy all the booze they wanted. Anybody could go into the most unspeakable dance halls and base joints of prostitution... In this old "Niggertown" were a lot of bad niggers and a bad nigger is about the lowest thing that walks on two feet.[65]

These types of comments provide a more comprehensive psychological understanding of how many whites had obscured views and biased feelings toward African-American people.

Another important consideration this newspaper article raises is the role that the news media and journalism played by triggering the frenzy to search for Dick Rowland after the alleged elevator encounter, with the newspaper headline "To Lynch A Negro Tonight." The massacre was propelled by media agitation and volatile race relations. In May of 2003, a lawyer named Jim Lloyd, who served on the Race Riot Commission, said he was suing the children of the late *Tulsa Tribune* editor, the heirs to its fortune:

> Lloyd argues that the newspaper incited the riot with its inflammatory front-page editorial entitled "To Lynch A Negro Tonight," of which no copy can be found. The best evidence is a hole cut out of the Tulsa public library's copy of the paper. The lawsuit also names Ku Klux Klan Grand Wizard as aiding in inciting the riot and more names are added as Lloyd continues his research. The *Tribune* stopped printing in 1992, when it was purchased by the *Tulsa World*.[66]

The ongoing investigations continue to reveal so much information regarding what happened on those two horrifying days in Tulsa. History seems to write a narrative of a Black Wall Street that was lynched. The evidence from these various perspectives indicates that all of these components contributed to the destruction of the Greenwood District.

Who was fighting is another important facet of the massacre to explore. I will begin with the philosophical and ideological debates. Given the racial and political climate in Tulsa in 1921 toward the African-American race, I believe the ideologies of freedom and supremacy were at play. Although

---

65. Gates, *Riot on Greenwood*, 34. See Appendix for full article.
66. *Archaeology*, "The Tulsa Race Riot."

the Negro race was considered free according to the law, white Americans who believed in their superiority over Black ontology still wanted to control Black existentialism. Unfortunately, most of the time whites were successful in controlling Negroes through terrorism because white hegemony monopolized the social, political, and in most situations, the economic interlocking systems that operated to dominate Black existence, primarily by unjust laws. The laws were further enforced by police, other governmental powers, and white organizations such as the KKK. Therefore, Blacks were deemed to be free; however, the unjust treatment that resulted from the Jim and Jane Crow laws, including racial bias and white superiority, constantly discriminated, oppressed, and abused the Negro race.

Perhaps another way to express who was fighting is found in the immorality of America. White power was fighting against Black equality. Whiteness had established a precedence since the early laws in America were instituted; Blacks were constitutionally considered three-fifths human and fit for slavery or servitude. Just forty years beyond Reconstruction would not change that ideology. The white power in Tulsa was imperialistic and it dominated in all the levels of government. Many of the prominent people in positions of power, such as lawyers, doctors, police, public and political figures, were members of the KKK and they did not want Black people to think they had equal rights or access what some would call the American Dream. As a result, in order to defend their white power and protect their ability to control the Black race, white mobs and the KKK were also fighting during those two days.

My final analysis on who was fighting is found in the Black woman's literary tradition through the work of Eddie Faye Gates. She served on the Oklahoma Commission to Study the Tulsa Race Riot of 1921 and was a strong advocate for reparations for Tulsa's survivors. "The Black women's literary tradition provides rich resources and a coherent commentary that brings into sharp focus the Black community's central values, which in turn frees Black folks from the often deadly grasp of parochial stereotypes."[67] Gates has written several books, particularly about the events surrounding the massacre. In *Riot on Greenwood: The Total Destruction of Black Wall Street*, she utilized the oral tradition to record the stories from hundreds of Tulsa survivors and descendants. Katie Cannon's Womanist work teaches us that the writings of Black women, both fiction and non-fiction, provide great insight; their intentionality allows one to see the Black community, understand the values within it, and how it navigates the exigencies of life.

---

67. Cannon, *Katie's Canon*, 62.

Gates has captured and preserved Tulsa's Black history with the early pioneers, based on many of the facts associated with the massacre and the testimonies from the survivors. Although she gives us great details in her book, I will summarize some of her points regarding who was fighting. She states Blacks in Tulsa and surrounding areas had been warned to leave. Gates notes that strategically "the chief of police of Tulsa, John Gustafson, deputized only whites who had gathered at the courthouse to lynch Dick Rowland."[68] The Tulsa police and government officials are culpable because they did not protect the Black citizens. They prevented many firefighters from responding to the request for help. Moreover, Gates decisively concludes that local officials and aviators flew over Tulsa dropping incendiary devices.[69]

As a Black woman who served on the Study Commission and who took the time to chronicle events in her book, Gates exemplifies why Cannon states "the Black women's literary tradition is the best available literary repository for understanding the ethical values Black women have created and cultivated in their participation in this society."[70] Gates's assessment of the massacre reiterates how the lead primary sources and drawing from the oral tradition, in which numerous factors contribute insight into who participated in the fighting, also illumine the causative elements known to Black citizens of Greenwood.

Many ask the question, who was actually defending the Greenwood District? According to Vivian Clark-Adams, another Black woman who served on the Study Commission, the Black World War I veterans were not the only ones fighting to save Greenwood. The African Blood Brotherhood (ABB) also participated in helping to defend the attack on the Greenwood District. The ABB was a Black militant group founded in 1919. The leader of the organization was Cyril Briggs; he was from the West Indies and the first Black man to join the American Communist Party. Briggs denies that the ABB "fomented" the riot, but Clark-Adams espouses the ABB did assist the Negro community in Tulsa to defend themselves. "On June 3, 1921, the *New York Times* wrote that the authorities had evidence that members of the ABB, who were 'highly aggressive in character,' were leaders of the black 'mob' at the courthouse and had 'fomented unrest among the Negroes.'"[71] According to Clark-Adams, the details of that night were published in the

---

68. Gates, *Riot on Greenwood*, 33.
69. Gates, *Riot on Greenwood*, 33.
70. Cannon, *Katie's Canon*, 61.
71. Hirsch, *Riot and Remembrance*, 161.

ABB's monthly publication called the *Crusader* in July 1921.[72] This is what the *Crusader* wrote:

> The Negro fighters early took up good positions inside and behind railroad cars, and in hastily dug trenches . . . and were under cover most of the time. The whites, on the contrary, were attacking in the open and in idiotic mass formation until the little steel bullets tripping on their errands of death by determined Negro hands [convinced] them killing Negroes wasn't such as pleasant and easy job after all . . . Especially in the attack on the Negro church held by a handful of ex-soldiers—fifty to be exact—were [whites] badly mauled and punished. Five times they came against it in mass formation, and five times they were repelled with deadly force. However, what they had not valor enough to accomplish by force, they treacherously achieved.[73]

The *Crusader*'s final comments stated, "the whites crushed Greenwood only by dropping 'incendiary bombs' from the airplanes."[74]

The narrative of who was actually fighting seems to be a little controversial. Eddie Faye Gates interviewed an elderly Black man who said "he was in Greenwood during the riot and saw ABB members prepare for the battle by unloading ammunition in Mount Zion Baptist Church."[75] However, others believed the ABB's participation was disingenuous, designed only to generate publicity for the organization. Still others believed that to remember the possibility that ABB might have been involved was important to folks' memory because it showed that they had support in fighting back against the massive attack on African Americans that night. Clark-Adams believed the accounts demonstrated Black Tulsans' bravery and sacrifice and determination not to be walked on by the white mob.[76]

On June 1, 1921, at 11:29 AM, martial law was finally declared by Governor Robertson in Tulsa. "Adjutant General Barrett and the National Guard troops from Oklahoma City arrived in Tulsa by train at about 9:15 AM."[77] At this point, Black Wall Street and the Greenwood community lay in ruins; nothing but smoke, ashes, twisted iron, and scattered bricks were left. Instead of the troops eagerly rushing to the streets to stop the chaos and

---

72. Hirsch, *Riot and Remembrance*, 261.
73. Hirsch, *Riot and Remembrance*, 261.
74. Hirsch, *Riot and Remembrance*, 261.
75. Hirsch, *Riot and Remembrance*, 261.
76. Hirsch, *Riot and Remembrance*, 261–63.
77. Johnson, *Black Wall Street*, 48.

rescue the people, they first had breakfast and Barrett set up at City Hall.[78] Once they were on the streets of Tulsa, any African-Americans found were imprisoned and taken to internment camps set up at either the fairgrounds or convention center. Over 6,000 Blacks were reported on June 1, 1921 as interned.[79] Purportedly, being interned was for the African-Americans' protection, but all were required to wear tags, which read "Police Protection." Many Negroes had left the night before during the massacre, never to return; others had escaped just outside the city limits for safety. The following morning, those outside the city limits were brought back by the Red Cross trucks to the internment camps:

> We did not enter there through our section of town, but they brought us in through the white section, all sitting flat down on the truck looking like immigrants, only that we had no bundles. Dear reader, can you imagine the humiliation of coming in like that, with many doors thrown open watching you pass, some with pity and others with a smile?[80]

The compassion for what the Negro population had suffered seemed to be rather limited.

The humiliation experienced by African-Americans the follow morning had to be horrific; not only had they lost everything but now they were being treated as the responsible parties, and under guard. Any white people found on the streets were simply disarmed by Guardsmen and sent home. The Red Cross set up to assist whites with changes of clothes and sandwiches. Parrish describes what they saw passing through town. "This is what we found to be piles of bricks, ashes, and twisted iron, representing years of toil and savings. We were horror stricken but strangely, we could not shed a tear. For blocks we bowed our heads in silent grief and tried to blot out the frightful scenes that were ahead of us."[81] The Black community had not only been devastated but terrorized by the inhuman treatment of white supremacy and hatred.

---

78. Ellsworth, *Death in a Promised*, 61.
79. Ellsworth, *Death in a Promised*, 63.
80. Jones Parrish, *Events of the Tulsa Disaster*, 13.
81. Jones Parrish, *Events of the Tulsa Disaster*, 13.

Martial Law Declared

Headquarters Oklahoma National Guard,
City Hall, Tulsa, Okla., June 1st, 1921

Following telegram from Governor J. B. A. Robertson received at these Headquarters at 11:29 a. m., places Tulsa and Tulsa County under Martial Law:

Hon. CHAS. F. BARRETT, Adjutant General,
    Care City Hall, Tulsa, Oklahoma:
    I have declared Martial Law throughout Tulsa County, and am holding you responsible for maintenance of order, safety of lives and protection of property. You will do all things necessary to attain these objects.
                    J. B. A. ROBERTSON, Governor.

THEREFORE, By authority of this order, I hereby declare the City of Tulsa and Tulsa County from and after the hour named in the telegram to be under Martial Law, which will be enforced with all the rigor necessary to accomplish the purpose of restoring peace and order within the boundaries of this City and County.

The people of Tulsa and of Tulsa County will retire immediately to their homes and remain there, so far as possible until this order is modified or revoked.

All persons, except sworn officers of the law, found upon the public streets of Tulsa or in any locality in Tulsa County, will be promptly arrested and punished as a military court may direct.

All business houses in the city will close on or before 6:00 o'clock p. m. today and will not re-open until 8: a. m. June 2nd, and will observe these hours from day to day until further orders, unless granted permission by the commanding officer of the Oklahoma National Guard.

Services of necessity, such as Grocery stores, Drug stores, Dairies, Meat Markets and other agencies that contribute to the comfort of the people will be excepted from the provision requiring permission to render such service.

It is the hope of the commanding [officer] in Tulsa or any surrounding city in Tulsa County.

Every good citizen should lend his or her best efforts to secure a prompt compliance with this order.

Automobiles, Trucks and other conveyances, except those used by Doctors, Officers of the Law, members of the Red Cross and other individuals or organizations contributing to the health and welfare of the people will not be allowed on the streets between the hours of 7:00 p. m. and 6:00 a. m.

Sufficient military forces are on hand to rigidly enforce this order, and it will be done.

Equal protection under this order is guaranteed to all persons, without regard to race or color. After the publication of this order, the man or woman, white or black, found with arms in their hands without written permission from military authority or by virtue of proper commission under the civil law, will be considered as public enemies and treated accordingly.

Figure 11. Source: Oklahoma State Library in Tulsa, Race Riot Collection.

IMMEDIATELY AFTER THE MASSACRE

The aftermath of the massacre can be described from multiple perspectives. Whether we look at pictures, the newspaper headlines, the estimated numbers of those who were killed, those injured and treated by the Red Cross, or the homes destroyed, which forced African-Americans to be homeless and live in tents during the winter of 1921, or even all of the Black businesses burned beyond repair, we see the worst massacre in American history. This pogrom was intentional toward this Black community. No riots continue over a two-day period unless the purpose is complete destruction. Whoever was responsible meant to annihilate the race, their presence in Tulsa, their possessions and livelihood.

Several Black organizations such as the NAACP, the National Association of Colored Women, and others across the country assisted with donations and sent telegrams to Tulsa and the mayor, requesting help for the Black community in Tulsa. (See Appendix for copies of telegrams.) The city blamed the African-American community for the riot and then accused W. E. B. Du Bois of being at the center of instigation. The insurance companies were also unwilling to compensate the disaster because it was classified as a riot. Most would probably have expected white churches to be sympathetic, and a few churches were as they offered assistance.

Black men were separated from the women and children and for several days many did not know the whereabouts of their loved ones. All Blacks were required to wear the tags that read "Police Protection." In order to leave the camp, each person had to be signed out by their white employer. Even African-American business owners needed someone white to vouch for them. Regardless of money or status, all Blacks were now under government authority. If any African-Americans were caught without an approved signature, they would be arrested and returned to the camp. This behavior fully exhibits and replicates the days of slavery, when no slaves were allowed to leave the plantation without a signed paper. Tulsa had become a nation-state living under the regime of white supremacy.

Aftermath of Massacre

Figure 12. Source: The Oklahoma Historical Society, Oklahoma City, Oklahoma. Pictures of the Greenwood District After the Massacre—June 1, 1921.

Newspaper Headlines

Figure 13. Source: University of Tulsa, McFarlin Library, Special Collections. Newspaper Headlines.

The statistics regarding how many people were killed and injured during the massacre have always been controversial over the years. One of the major discrepancies has been in the number of African-Americans killed. Many say they saw truckloads of bodies dumped into the Arkansas River. Others say numerous bodies were buried in unmarked graves that were never accounted for. One testimony stated the Salvation Army fed fifty-seven Negroes employed to dig graves, and they dug 120 graves, each of which had a Negro body buried in it.[82] Here are some numbers from different sources to give an approximation. When reading from most sources, the deaths for African-Americans range from thirty-six to 300. According to Ellsworth, the *Tulsa Tribune* gave two sets of numbers, reporting first that nine whites

82. Ellsworth, *Death in a Promised*, 69.

and sixty-eight blacks had died. In the same issue, they stated 175 people had been killed. The next day, the *Tribune* reported thirty-one deaths: nine whites and twenty-two Blacks.[83] Booker T. Washington School was turned into a hospital to care for many, in addition to six other private hospitals:

> Red Cross materials also revealed that 183 blacks were given surgical treatment within twenty-four hours after the riot with over 70 percent of these people being hospitalized. The organization gave first aid treatment to some 531 persons, and during the first week after the riot, about twenty doctors (eleven of whom were black) performed some 163 operations, 82 of them classified as major operations.[84]

Parrish compiled a chart of services for the Red Cross; they assisted 2,480 families from June 1 to January 1. The total number of people represented in this number is 8,624. The total number of families receiving clothing, beds, dishes, and the like was 1,941. The Red Cross closed its relief service in Tulsa on December 31, 1921.[85]

Property losses are difficult to estimate exactly. Many losses are recorded in the Tulsa Real Estate Exchange. According to Ellsworth, the losses totaled about $1.5 million, with one-third being in the business district. Personal property loss was approximately $750,000. According to the Red Cross, 1,115 residences had been destroyed during the massacre. About 314 houses were looted but not burned. Claims were also filed against the city, according to the Tulsa City Commission meeting reports from June 14, 1921 to June 6, 1922, of over $1.8 million.[86] By July 30, 1921, over 1,400 lawsuits for losses upward of $4 million had been filed. The claims ranged from $25 to more than $150,000:

> Emma Gurley, a black woman whose family owned the Gurley Hotel (the Gurley building), filed a claim for its loss in excess of $150,000. Loula T. Williams filed a claim for over $100,000 for the destruction of the Dreamland Theatre and the Williams building. R. G. Dunn and Company reportedly lost some $250,000 in goods. Other large losses included the newly constructed Mount Zion Baptist Church (reportedly built at a cost of $85,000), and the offices of both of Tulsa's Black newspapers, the *Tulsa Star* and the *Oklahoma Sun*.[87]

83. Ellsworth, *Death in a Promised*, 66.
84. Ellsworth, *Death in a Promised*, 67.
85. Jones Parrish, *Events of the Tulsa*, 76.
86. Ellsworth, *Death in a Promised*, 70.
87. Ellsworth, *Death in a Promised*, 70.

Important to remember is that these numbers are from the year 1921; one can only ponder what the estimate losses would be equivalent to today. According to the myriad of writers, 8,000 to 10,000 people were displaced after the massacre. They lived in tents for the remainder of the winter.[88]

More contemporary information, found in State Representative Don Ross's materials, lists claims filed against insurance companies at $2.7 million. The most significant reality of Black discrimination behavior and racial bias was represented in property loss and claims. The insurance companies denied all African-American claims because they were associated with a race riot. However, claims filed by white owners from the gun and ammunition businesses were paid, even though they were related to the riot. "In a verdict denying insurance claims, the Oklahoma Supreme Court acknowledged that after breaking into stores for guns and gathering at the police station, white men were sent out to different parts of the town ostensibly to guard the town."[89] This is a false statement; the white men used the guns during the massacre to participate in the burning, looting, shooting, and destruction of the Black Greenwood community.

The newspapers blamed the Negro community with ugly headlines such as "Acres of ashes lie smoldering in what but yesterday was 'Niggertown.'"[90] The Tulsa Ministerial Alliance boldly stated that African-Americans were the root cause of their own misfortune. One well-known minister publicly blamed W. E. B. Du Bois for the massacre in his sermon. Du Bois had been in Tulsa just a short time before the massacre and he stated:

> I have never seen a colored community so highly organized as that of Tulsa. There is complete separation of the races, so that a colored town is within the white town. I noticed a block of stores built by white men for negro business. They had long been empty, boycotted by the negroes. The colored people of Tulsa have accumulated property, have established stores and business organizations and have also made money in oil. They feel their independent position and have boasted that in their community there have been no cases of lynching. With such a state of affairs, it took only a spark to start a dangerous fire.[91]

The white community did not like the words of Du Bois. The fact that he spoke boldly for the Black community, wrote for *The Crisis* magazine, and advocated against lynching made him dangerous in their eyes. Following

---

88. See Appendix for tent picture.
89. Ross, *A Century of African-American*, 31.
90. Johnson, *Black Wall Street*, 50.
91. Johnson, *Black Wall Street*, 51.

the massacre, the governor wrote a letter to an insurance manager named D. P. Bailey stating that he believed Du Bois may have been an agitator for the people during his visit. He reported his name to the attorney general for investigation and, if they found any possibility of his involvement, they would have him indicted.[92]

Du Bois did not live in Tulsa; he had only come to speak. As a result, Du Bois was accused of being a possible instigator among the Negro race. On the other hand, no white people were seen as threats to the Black community or responsible for the massacre. The law offered no protection for the African-American community, nor did it provide justice for this marginalized race of innocent people. The white community did, however, like Booker T. Washington, who had also recently visited Tulsa. The sermon preached after the massacre by a white bishop of the Methodist Church speaks positively about Washington while criticizing Du Bois and further illuminates the racial division and inequality.

CONCLUSION

This chapter fully outlines the 1921 Tulsa Massacre beginning with the ethos in Tulsa and racial climate around the nation toward the Negro race. I highlight the details of the alleged elevator incident, which is always referenced as igniting the massacre on May 31 and June 1 in 1921. I explain the white supremacy and hegemonic practices that existed in Tulsa. I also explore from various perspectives what happened to cause the worst racial tragedy in American history and who was actually fighting or defending the Greenwood District. I use the womanist literary tradition from several women to gain insight into the Black community's life and values before, during, and after the massacre. The aftermath reflects the magnitude of devastation through terror and torture that existed in the attempted annihilation of the Negro race in Tulsa. I further record the statistics as revealed by various sources regarding the losses of life and property.

---

92. See Appendix for letter that expresses his intent.

CHAPTER 9

Following the Massacre
Black Resilience

Unshouted courage as a virtue is the often unacknowledged inner conviction that keeps one's appetite whet for freedom. The ethical speculation is that courage is the staying power of the Black community wherein individuals act, affirming their humanity, in spite of continued fear of institutionalized aggression.

—KATIE CANNON
Black Womanist Ethics

THE CHURCH AND THE COURTS

BISHOP E. D. MOUZON preached a sermon at the Boston Avenue Methodist Church following the massacre; I found the sermon printed in the *Tulsa World*. The headlines of the article included these statements: "Black Agitators Blamed for Riot," "Bishop Cites Radical Negro as One Cause of Battle," and finally another headline—"Allowing Little Africa To Become a Festering Sore and Wonder at Results." The journalist cites these opening words from Mouzon's sermon:

> That the visit of Doctor Dubois, editor of a magazine for negroes, "The Crisis," to Tulsa some time ago may have had a

bearing upon the trouble of the past week was intimated by Bishop E. D. Mouzon in his sermon last night at the Boston Avenue Methodist church on the subject, "The Tulsa Race Riot and the Teachings of Jesus Christ." The magazine was termed by the Bishop "dangerous" and Dubois himself characterized as the most vicious negro man in the country.[1]

Mouzon continued by stating he did not know who was responsible, but he said that Little Africa was the "blackest spot in Oklahoma" and something needed to be done regarding all the terrible things that took place in that area. People often referenced the "choc" joints (places that sold Choctaw beer, made from a tree root), clubs, and prostitution in the Greenwood District but not the positive aspects of the district. Mouzon continued with his sermon by saying we must raise the standards of the Colored race. One section in the sermon article is entitled, "No Racial Equality." In this portion of his sermon, Mouzon is explicit on how he understands race relations:

> There is one thing said the Bishop upon which I would like to make myself perfectly clear. That is racial equality. There never has been and never will be such a thing. It is divinely ordained. This is something that should be told to the Negroes very plainly. Steps toward social equality are the worst possible thing for the Negro... There should be separate hotels, schools, and churches for the Negro.[2]

The bishop of this Methodist church expressed that separation was divinely ordained. Mouzon's recapitulates Hughes's argument in *Myths America Lives By* and Nell Painter's theory of "whiteness as beauty" through early science, which historically established the deeply embedded racial bias and ostracism of Black ontology. This sermon should have been a critical moment of moral and ethical consciousness for white Tulsans to critique and recognize their sins of social injustice. Instead, Bishop Mouzon demonstrated the "lived praxis" thinking of white superiority, represented in religious belief, and the extreme discriminatory behavior perpetuated in and through American history against the African-American race. As a result of this socialization and practice, whiteness and racial inequality was absolutized, reiterating that whites saw themselves as a "chosen people by God," separate from and elevated above the other races, particularly the Black race.[3]

1. "Black Agitators Blamed for Riot."
2. "Black Agitators Blamed for Riot."
3. See Appendix for the full sermon.

The grand jury indicted Dick Rowland on June 6, 1921. They used and changed the very word of "assault" to "rape," as I discussed earlier. When Black men were accused of assaulting a white woman, assault meant rape as presented in this indictment. In *State of Oklahoma vs. Dick Rowland*, the indictment for the assault and attempted rape of Sarah Page, the grand jury concluded:

> [We] find that in said Tulsa Country and State of Oklahoma, on the 30th day of May in the year of our Lord One Thousand . . . and prior to the finding of this indictment one Dick Rowland did then and there, unlawfully, willfully, wrongfully, forcibly, violently, and feloniously make an assault upon one Sarah Page, a female . . . and of previous chaste and virtuous character, and not the wife of him, the said Dick Rowland and did, then and there, and thereby unlawfully, violently, forcibly, and feloniously, and against her will, attempt to ravish, rape, and carnally know her, the said Sarah Page, but was intercepted and failed in the perpetration thereof.[4]

What had been a simple trip into an elevator by a Black man, or an innocent stumble into a white woman operator, had now turned into rape in the indictment. The court attorney did not file the charges until September 15, 1921. In the meantime, Rowland's two court appointed attorneys, one of whom was Washington Hudson—a KKK member—tried to have the case dismissed but the judge overruled on September 16, 1921.[5]

Important to highlight is that Dick Rowland was never prosecuted because Page refused to assist the prosecuting attorney; as a result, Rowland was exonerated.[6] Shortly before Rowland's mother died at the age of eighty-seven, she gave an interview with Ruth Avery, commenting on her last encounter with her son following his disappearance. According to Damie, Dick was saddened by the massacre and interested in going to the shores of Oregon.[7] She also indicated "Sarah Page had followed her son to Kansas City."[8] When I interviewed people regarding this event, the oral tradition said Page and Rowland were still together years later. Everyone agrees neither of them were ever seen in Tulsa again. Steve Gerkin, author of *Hidden History of Tulsa*, tried to find Rowland, stating he disappeared from Kansas City's public records in 1926. He also searched in Portland

4. Johnson, *Black Wall Street*, 61.
5. Johnson, *Black Wall Street*, 61.
6. Johnson, *Black Wall Street*, 67.
7. Gerkin, *Hidden History of Tulsa*, 41–42.
8. Gerkin, *Hidden History of Tulsa*, 67.

but encountered only dead ends. One of the men in Special Collections at the Tulsa University Library said he also searched for Page and Rowland during his research regarding the riot; however, he could not find either one of them.

In addition to Rowland's case, the grand jury also filed a final report by an all-white jury blaming "colored men" for the riot. The wording of the jury is critical because Blackness appears always guilty when in contradiction to whiteness:

> We find that the recent race riot was the direct result of an effort on the part of a certain group of colored men who appeared at the courthouse on the night of May 31, 1921, for the purpose of protecting one Dick Rowland then and now in the custody of the sheriff of Tulsa county for an alleged assault upon a young white woman. We have not been able to find any evidence either from white or colored citizens that any organized attempt was made or planned to take from the sheriff's custody any prisoner; the crowd assembled about the courthouse being purely spectators and curiosity seekers resulting from rumors circulated about the city. There was no mob spirit among the whites, no talk of lynching and no arms. The assembly was quiet until the arrival of the armed negroes, which precipitated and was the direct cause of the entire affair.[9]

The verdict here emphasizes several critical points. First, although 1,500 to 2,000 whites gathered at the court house to lynch Rowland, this grand jury report states "no mob spirit" existed and "no talk of lynching" occurred. African-Americans were not only blamed but used as the scapegoats surrounding all the activities and destruction of their own community. I believe most would find this blame absurd and incomprehensible.

Second, the statement reads, "all was quiet until the armed Negroes came." I argue that the power of white supremacy and racism operates through this extreme assumed purity of whiteness and innocence in a social order constructed by white, hegemonic superiority and power with the results of injustice, which always finds the opposing Blackness as less than and guilty. Finally, the law operates and functions based on this ideology. "Historically white supremacy has been premised upon various political, scientific, and religious theories, each of which relies on racial characterizations and stereotypes about blacks which have coalesced into an extensive legitimating ideology."[10] Therefore, the law or legality was manipulated

---

9. Ellsworth, *Death in a Promised*, 95.
10. Crenshaw et al., *Critical Race Theory*, 112.

through white hegemony. Many of the key positions in the city government of Tulsa and in the court systems in Tulsa were held by Klan members. As a result, the whites who committed the massacre were innocent and the Black community, which was destroyed, was found guilty. No whites were ever convicted or punished for the terror and crimes committed on May 31 and June 1, 1921.

THE MONTHS AND YEARS FOLLOWING THE MASSACRE

In the months that followed the massacre, African-Americans exhibited a continuous unity for survival. Most in the Greenwood community had been displaced, without housing or their churches. "Traditional Communalism" has been one aspect of the womanist tenet theories that I have emphasized in this book. Whether we observe the various circumstances and perspectives for making the journey to Oklahoma, Black women's activism and contributions across the country during this same epoch, the lynching frenzy, or the biased racial social conditions that necessitated the building of Black Wall Street, we see a unifying presence among African-Americans that is ubiquitous.

In the 1921 July edition of *The Crisis*, Du Bois' writing further exemplifies how traditional communalism was continued in the African-American community, but this time the unity was visual and represented across the nation. Du Bois explains that a relief fund was immediately established by the NAACP for the Negro race. Communications for donations were made by telegrams. The funds raised for Tulsa residents were for support and legal defense, if required. Many of the NAACP branches across the United States participated in the movement by making donations. They also encouraged churches and fraternal organizations across the country to give.[11] The African-American race exhibited a phenomenal model of support to their own race. On a national and political level, the situation escalated even further.

The NAACP secretary sent a telegram to Governor Robertson of Oklahoma immediately after the massacre, urging him to end the violence and terror in Tulsa.[12] (See Appendix for the letter.) The NAACP secretary also sent a telegram to President Warren G. Harding in Washington: "The National Association for the Advancement of Colored People feels that an utterance from you at this time on the violence and reign of terror at Tulsa, Okla., would have an inestimable effect not only upon that situation but

11. Du Bois, "Oklahoma Riot Victims."
12. Du Bois, "The Tulsa Race Riots."

upon the whole country."[13] The President responded with a public regret and horror for the tragedy in Tulsa.[14]

As mentioned earlier, some individuals made it to New York to share the terror that was happening in Tulsa with the NAACP. They conveyed their stories to the press and they were published in all the prominent papers. The Tulsa Massacre appeared on the front page of the *New York World*. The other newspapers that carried the story included the *New York Times*, the *Tribune*, the *Herald*, the *Evening Post*, the *Globe*, and the *Evening World*.[15] The NAACP even sent out a representative to investigate the Tulsa Massacre. Although the resulting article did not mention the journalist's name, it was Walter White. He was the NAACP's secretary at the time. In addition to this assignment, White's job had also included the investigations of lynchings for the NAACP.

The details of White's report were outlined in "The Eruption of Tulsa." White was able to perform the Tulsa investigation undercover because his physical appearance allowed him to pass for white; however, he was a Black man. One aspect of the report revealed that Black economic success was a major concern for white Tulsans. Below is a small excerpt:

> First, the Negro in Oklahoma has shared in the sudden prosperity that has come to many of his white brothers, and there are some colored men there who are wealthy. This fact has caused a bitter resentment on the part of the lower order of whites, who feel that these colored men, members of an "inferior race," are exceedingly presumptuous in achieving greater economic prosperity than they who are members of a divinely ordered superior race. There are at least three colored persons in Oklahoma who are worth a million dollars each; J.W. Thompson of Clearview is worth $500,000; there are a number of men and women worth $100,000; and many whose possessions are valued at $25,000 and $50,000 each. This was particularly true of Tulsa, where there were two colored men worth $150,000 each; two worth $100,000; three $50,000; and four who were assessed at $25,000.[16]

The massacre was as much about racial hatred as it was about economic jealousy of Tulsa's Black Wall Street success; white hegemony was determined to eliminate the financial wealth and success of African-Americans

---

13. Du Bois, "The Tulsa Race Riots."
14. Du Bois, "The Tulsa Race Riots."
15. Du Bois, "The Tulsa Race Riots."
16. White, "The Eruption of Tulsa."

in Tulsa. Hundreds of pages at the Historical Society show that Black business owners filed insurance claims but all the insurance claims were denied to African-American business owners. This was another way that economic disparity was represented.

Black resilience and Black faith are other aspects this book has illuminated. In the years that followed the 1921 Tulsa Massacre, Black Wall Street was rebuilt. "By 1922, the rebuilding of Deep Greenwood was well under way. More than half of the destroyed churches began to hold worship services again. More than eighty business in the Greenwood District reopened."[17] The resilience of the African-American people was certainly demonstrated in their faith and commitment to the rebuilding of their churches. Vernon African Methodist Episcopal Church finished rebuilding in 1928 and it is still located in the same place today.

Mt. Zion Baptist Church struggled over the years, receiving several different pastors and instituting multiple fundraising campaigns; however, they were determined to pay off the original note from their newly built church, which was destroyed in less than a month of its completion. The process took twenty-one years but they finally paid the mortgage note in 1942. They built a new church and the dedication service for their church was in 1952, in the same place where it still stands today. The Black resilience and faith of the Greenwood community was exhibited as they thrived again in the 1930s and 1940s. Many African-Americans have worked to remember the legacy of outstanding accomplishments from Black Oklahomans' history and honor their resilience.

The Greenwood Cultural Center had its groundbreaking ceremonies in August of 1985, drawing prominent people such as Oklahoma Governor George Nigh, Oklahoma Congressman Jim Jones, Mayor Terry Young, Speaker of the House Jim Barker, and Oklahoma Senate President Rodger Randle.[18] The Cultural Center is committed to the African-American history, Tulsa's history, artists, scholars, the improvement of race relations, and promotes the historical Greenwood District.[19] The Center contains historical memorabilia and photos of Black Wall Street before and after the massacre. It is a multi-purpose building open to all races. "The City of Tulsa provided two and one-half acres of land and $275,000."[20]

Oklahoma State Senator Maxine C. Horner and Oklahoma State Representative Don Ross are primarily responsible for securing funds from the

---

17. Johnson, *Black Wall Street*, 96.
18. Johnson, *Black Wall Street*, 123.
19. Johnson, *Black Wall Street*, 123.
20. Johnson, *Black Wall Street*, 120.

State of Oklahoma. The center was developed in three phases. Phase one built the Cultural Center and restored the historic Mabel B. Little Heritage House in 1986. Phase two was the creation of the Goodwin-Chappelle Gallery in 1989, named after the publisher and attorney E. L. Goodwin and minister T. O. Chappelle. Phase three was the construction of the Oklahoma Jazz Hall of Fame and the Opal L. Dargan Renaissance Hall.[21] The Greenwood Cultural Center has become a major tourist site for the thousands who visit Tulsa each year.

The City of Tulsa was quiet about the massacre for over seventy-five years. Historian and Executive Director Bob Blackburn of Oklahoma's Historical Society defined the massacre as under a "conspiracy of silence." The history was not taught in the school curriculum. Even as I personally grew up in Tulsa, the massacre was not mentioned. Oklahoma House Representative Don Ross was instrumental in pushing to remember Black Wall Street with a memorial of the businesses, action from the city, and reparations. In 1996, Tulsa commemorated the "Tulsa holocaust," as Ross describes it, with the black granite monument located in front of the Greenwood Cultural Center. (See Appendix for a picture.) At that time, more than fifty Black survivors attended along with 2,500 other people.[22]

J. B. Stradford was another key figure and full-time attorney during the days of Black Wall Street. He departed Tulsa right after the massacre. On October 18, 1996, Stradford was pardoned by Oklahoma Governor Frank Keating.[23]

In 1997, Representative Ross and Senator Maxine Horner were able to establish the Oklahoma Commission to Study the 1921 race riot. "The two lawmakers secured $5 million for a museum and memorial, and $2 million in scholarships."[24] The Race Riot Commission was established to research the history for several reasons. First, they wanted to explore many of the details that had never been resolved, such as how many hidden bodies were dumped into unmarked graves. Second, they hoped to provide reparations for survivors or their legacies. Third, they wanted to give scholarships to survivors. Important information had never been clarified, such as just how many lives were lost during the massacre. A team of eleven people worked on this project for approximately one year. Many advocated over the years to make the teaching of the 1921 Massacre mandatory in the Tulsa public school system, but they were not able to accomplish that task.

21. Johnson, *Black Wall Street*, 125.
22. Ross, *A Century of African-American*, 9.
23. Johnson, *Black Wall Street*, 66.
24. Ross, *A Century of African-American*, 29.

I interviewed former Senator Judy Eason McIntyre, an African-American woman representative from Tulsa and member of Vernon African Methodist Episcopal Church, about the bill that would require mandatory teaching of the race riot. Senator McIntyre explained that the history regarding the massacre and politics in Tulsa were difficult to maneuver. She also stated that many politicians did not see the relevance of making the teaching mandatory.[25]

Senator McIntyre introduced Bill 1381, which stated, "School districts shall ensure that information concerning the *Tulsa Race Riot of 1921* is presented in high school courses in U.S. history or Oklahoma history."[26] This would have made the teaching of the "1921 Race Riot" mandatory by law. In March of 2012, the bill was passed in the Senate with a 33–6 vote and moved to the House, where it did not pass. The author of an article regarding the bill, Barbara Hoberock, writes, "The state has required the topic in Oklahoma history classes since 2000 and in U.S. history classes since 2004. It has been in Oklahoma history books since 2009, according to the agency."[27] Senator Eason McIntyre introduced the bill to legislation because the teaching regarding the 1921 Race Riot was often omitted or seen as optional and many do not teach on the topic. Now retired, Senator Eason McIntyre stated getting this bill passed continues to be a political issue and confronting the hatred of racism and the repercussions that resulted from the massacre are still relevant today.

Senator Maxine Horner was another African-American woman in Tulsa that I interviewed regarding her work in the state senate and the history of Black Wall Street. She served in the senate from 1986 to 2004; the laws regarding length of service have now changed. As a native of Tulsa, Senator Horner remembered Black Wall Street as a young girl growing up and stated all of the communities' needs were met by the services supplied from those Black Wall Street businesses. She reflected that even her father was a business owner on Greenwood. She admitted that most of the survivors over the years rarely talked about the tragedy; many others have echoed this observation.

Senator Horner elaborated that it was the lifework of House Representative Don Ross to push for the recognition and remembrance of Black Wall Street, including trying to get reparations for the survivors. She worked closely with Representative Ross and together they were able to pass a

---

25. Former Senator Judy Eason McIntyre, interview by author, December 4, 2016.
26. Hoberock, "Senate passes bill."
27. Hoberock, "Senate passes bill."

resolution in 1997, which created the Commission to Study the 1921 Race Riot.[28]

Some of the challenges in getting the approval for the Commission included the question from other Senators, "why?" In other words, "this is in the past and we have moved on." Horner and Ross argued that this is our history and people need to know this information. Senator Horner reflected on the comments of a Republican senator who prided himself as a historian, but he had never heard of the massacre; as a result, he supported them. She explained long debates occurred on the Senate floor to push this through. At the time, Democrats were in the majority and that was helpful.

Scholarships were also a part of their bill recommendations; however, they were not able to include reparations and, rather than lose the entire bill, they dropped the reparations. Others continued to advocate for reparations. Horner personally believed the inability to determine how to apply a particular dollar amount for reparations was a major obstacle. Horner further explained they also had the support of Oklahoma's Historical Society, located in Oklahoma City. The executive director of the society, Bob Blackburn, was part of the Study Commission. The Historical Society worked closely with them in performing a large majority of the research for the Commission.[29]

College education was a commitment that Senate Horner took seriously. She introduced the "Oklahoma Higher Learning Access Bill" in 1991, now called the "Oklahoma Promise." This bill gives any student in Oklahoma an opportunity to attend college in Oklahoma with free tuition. The required grade point average is 2.5, although the state fought her on this grade point. She argued two points. First, all youth do not have the same access to educational tools to prepare them for college. Second, the students who have a 3.0 or better have other available means to secure scholarships. The student must enroll during high school and a have clean record; they heavily promote the opportunity because many students are not aware of these benefits.

Senator Horner shared other important accomplishments. She was very excited and pleased that they were able to honor all the survivors from the Tulsa Massacre in Oklahoma City with the Black Caucus, and obtain their individual stories, which are now displayed on the walls of the Greenwood Cultural Center, along with their pictures. Senator Horner was also responsible for establishing the Oklahoma Jazz Hall of Fame in 1998. Oklahoma has a long history of jazz musicians.[30]

---

28. Former Senator Maxine Horner, interview by author, December 5, 2016.

29. Former Senator Maxine Horner, interview by author, December 5, 2016.

30. Former Senator Maxine Horner, interview by author, December 5, 2016.

Eddie Faye Gates's contributions played a key role in preserving the historical memories of Black Tulsans, the massacre, and speaking truth to power. She was inducted into Oklahoma's Historians Hall of Fame on April 19, 2013. Gates was born in Preston, Oklahoma, attended Tuskegee Institute, and graduated magna cum laude from the University of North Dakota. She is an oral historian, author, and was a high school teacher in Tulsa for twenty-two years. Gates spent time focusing on multicultural curricula and is an education consultant and Holocaust consultant.[31]

Gates performed outstanding work associated with the Tulsa Massacre. She served on the Oklahoma Commission to Study the Tulsa Race Riot of 1921. She was a strong advocate for reparations regarding Tulsa's survivors. Gates was also the chair of the Survivor Committee of the 1921 Tulsa Race Riot Commission, interviewing and obtaining the narratives of more than 200 survivors and more than 300 descendants.[32] Gates's research was significant in understanding some internal details related to the massacre and the Commissions' findings. She was a liaison for the reparations' lawsuit:

> In February of 2003 a legal team led by Johnnie Cochran and Harvard law professor Charles Ogletree Jr. filed a reparation lawsuit on behalf of the survivors and descendants of victims and survivors of the Race Riot, based on the 2001 Tulsa Race Riot Commissions report. The pro-bono legal team accused the city of Tulsa, the Tulsa Police Department, and the state of Oklahoma of not protecting its citizens and deputizing the white mob by supplying weapons. The lawsuit claims that officials failed to take action and further abused their power to propagate the riot and empower the rioting white mob.[33]

Eddie Faye Gates also wrote two books, *They Came Searching: How Blacks Sought the Promised Land in Tulsa*, and *Riot on Greenwood: The Total Destruction of Black Wall Street*. Gates's research is an excellent examples of Katie Cannon's "Black Woman's literary tradition," which uses both the oral narrative devices from the survivors and capsulizes the insularity or hidden uniqueness of the Black community.

In the years following the massacre, another important development occurred concerning Black freedmen and freedwomen from the Indian Nation, when the Cherokee Nation attempted to remove their status and benefits from the Nation. "On March 3, 2007, a small fraction of

---

31. Uncrowned Community Builders, "Gates," lines 6–15.
32. Uncrowned Community Builders, "Gates," lines 17–23.
33. *Archaeology*, "The Tulsa Race Riot;" Gates, *Riot on Greenwood*.

the voting-eligible Cherokee Nation of Oklahoma population approved an amendment to the Cherokee Constitution."[34] This amendment would disenfranchise twenty-eight hundred Cherokee Black freedmen and freedwomen. This meant losing voting rights, health care, housing, and school scholarships.[35] On January 2011, the decision was reversed by Judge John Cripps of the District Court of the Cherokee Nation. A few days later, it was appealed. In August 2011, the Supreme Court of the Cherokee Nation reversed the January 2011 decision terminating the tribal citizen tribal rights of twenty-eight hundred freedmen and freedwomen.[36]

When I interviewed Hannibal Johnson in the fall of 2016, the decision on this debate was still pending. A final settlement was reached in September 2017 in favor of Black freedmen and freedwomen. This victory is another demonstration of Black resilience in the Cherokee Nation and represents years of fighting for their equal rights, property, and benefits. The Cherokee Nation was not the only nation that sought to change the 1866 Treaty. (See Appendix for the full newspaper article.)

The John Hope Franklin Center (JHF) was established in 2007 and the John Hope Reconciliation Park was completed in 2009, opening in 2010; both are named after the historian John Hope Franklin. Buck Franklin, John's father, was an attorney in Tulsa during the massacre and helped many to fight within the legal system in order to rebuild Black Wall Street. The purpose of the Center is to promote reconciliation between the races in Tulsa. Their vision, according to their website, is "to transform the bitterness and mistrust caused by years of racial division, even violence, into a hopeful future of reconciliation and cooperation for Tulsa and the nation."[37] The Reconciliation Park was derived from the work of the 2001 Oklahoma Commission to Study the Race Riot. The park is owned by the City of Tulsa.

I interviewed the current chairman of the JHF Center, Julius Pegues; he explained that it took millions of dollars to make this park possible. Two monuments are in the park. At the entry of Hope Plaza is a sixteen-foot granite structure with three bronze sculptures depicting Hostility (a white man armed with a gun), Humiliation (a Black man with his hands raised), and Hope (a white Red Cross director holding an African-American baby).[38] The figures represent people from the massacre. The second display

34. Johnson, *Apartheid in Indian Country*, 170.
35. Johnson, *Apartheid in Indian Country*, 170.
36. Johnson, *Apartheid in Indian Country*, 200–201.
37. John Hope Franklin Center for Reconciliation,"John Hope Franklin Reconciliation Park."
38. John Hope Franklin Center for Reconciliation,"John Hope Franklin Reconciliation Park."

is the Tower of Reconciliation, a twenty-five-foot tower that uses images to highlight the history of African-Americans, from Africa to the Tulsa massacre and reconstruction after the massacre.[39] The sculptures were made by "Ed Dwight, the nation's first African-American astronaut, and internationally known sculptor."[40]

Finally, after all these years have passed, "the curriculum of the *1921 Race Riot* will be taught statewide"[41] read a newspaper headline. The announcement was made on February 20, 2018 by Oklahoma Republican Senator James Lankford and Oklahoma Democrat Kevin Matthews, when they visited Douglass High School in Oklahoma City, which is the capital of Oklahoma. According to the above article, the education curriculum is now complete and will be taught statewide. The education also provides an online tool kit, one of the goals of the 1921 Race Riot Centennial Commission.[42]

The Oklahoma History Center assisted the Commission with designing the curriculum. The materials will teach about Black Wall Street, the massacre, and the aftermath. The teaching of the curriculum was a part of the training for teachers the summer of 2018 by the Oklahoma Department of Education. During the press conference, "Senator Matthews pointed out that the National Museum of African-American History and Culture in Washington, DC tells the history of the Race Riot, but that it is not taught in Oklahoma."[43] They were both pleased to be a part of the process. Matthew was glad to know Lankford shared the information on the Senate floor because he wants more people to know about the history.[44]

The Yoruba faith community has been celebrating the remembrance of Black Wall Street for at least the last twenty years in Tulsa. They are the only religious group that I found that has consistently remembered the 1921 Tulsa Massacre and their ancestors, with annual community marches down Greenwood, guest speakers, and worship services. All these activities are held toward the end of May each year. For the last several years, they have held their celebrations at Vernon African Methodist Episcopal Church. Two years ago, I was able to attend one of their annual worship and remembrance services. I interviewed Chief Ifalade F. Amusan, who explained

---

39. John Hope Franklin Center for Reconciliation, "John Hope Franklin Reconciliation Park."
40. Ross, *A Century of African-American*, 29.
41. Jones, "1921 Tulsa Race Riot curriculum."
42. Jones, "1921 Tulsa Race Riot curriculum."
43. Jones, "1921 Tulsa Race Riot curriculum."
44. Jones, "1921 Tulsa Race Riot curriculum."

their community is committed to remembering their ancestors and fighting against current injustices.

Chief Amusan, his faith community, and others have been instrumental in fighting to make the Greenwood District part of the historical district in Tulsa. Another challenge the chief and other Black Tulsa residents have fought against during the last several years included trying to keep a new entertainment development called the "Brady District," located just one street over from Greenwood, from using the Brady name. The Tulsa historical tie to the Brady name is connected with Tate Brady, an old KKK member and prominent businessman in Tulsa; albeit they convinced the city to use another person instead of Tate Brady. The artist they chose to represent the street still had the same last name Brady and thus the entertainment district has still been named the Brady District. According to the chief, the city claimed the businesses had already made their business cards and the area could not be renamed.

During the last three or four years, the Yoruba community has been challenged by trying to plan and celebrate Juneteenth and the Black Wall Street remembrance. Recently a white organization, whose name I do not know, has started appropriating the Juneteenth celebrations for Tulsa with their planning and activities. This Tulsa organization evidently has a large financial budget and brings in artists and music during the same time that the Yoruba community celebrates the remembrance of Black Wall Street, but they do not celebrate in conjunction with them. Again, white hegemony and financial power will rewrite Black Tulsans' history and the remembrance, if the Black community is not careful.

The following are some final comments through the womanist lens from Eddie Faye Gates and Vivian Clark-Adams. Gates wrote extensively in *Riot on Greenwood: The Total Destruction of Black Wall Street* about the events surrounding the massacre, including testimonies from Black survivors, white accounts of the massacre, and several reasons for what happened on May 31 and June 1 in 1921. She highlights these points: (1) The climate of American culture operated from a white privilege perspective and Blacks were considered second-class citizens. (2) On a national and local level there was a limited concern for Black peoples' issues. (3) A collective indifference existed for political, social, and economic inequities and injustices. (4) Race relations had little focus, and no real efforts were initiated to end lynching, racism, or the injustices around the nation. (5) The presidents that served during this era—Grover Cleveland, Woodrow Wilson, and Warren G. Harding—did not use moral leadership or ethical values to end injustice in America. Even after the massacre, Harding was not a proponent for racial grievances. (6) With more than 3,000 lynchings in America, Congress did not pass the Dyer Anti-Lynching Bill.[45]

The truth of the situation is that America did not regard Black lives as valuable and Tulsa was no different. Gates further writes, "There was an order by the City of Tulsa, prior to the Tulsa Race Riot of 1921, for merchants to sell munitions to whites only. They were specifically ordered not to sell munitions to blacks."[46] The culpability seems to fall directly on the police department and government of the city. According to Gates, the evidence in the preliminary report in February 2001 included that warnings to Blacks were posted on their doors to leave town by June 1, 1921 or suffer the consequences. The "whistle" theory is that the massacre was a systematic takeover from all areas of the city. The firefighters did not respond, and the list continues.[47]

Vivian Clark-Adams was another woman who served on the Race Riot Commission. Her background is important to understand the perspective she brought to the Commission. She was a long-time activist with a master's degree in history and a doctorate in education administration. Clark-Adams's background included moving to Tulsa at age eleven from Washington, DC in 1961. Clark-Adams was raised by her mother and father, Major Clark, who was a heavily decorated and experienced military officer, who began serving in 1940. She had great respect and appreciation for veterans because of her father.

Major Clark fought in Italy and received the Bronze Star. He was also decorated by the South Korean Army and the US Army for his service in Korea. He was considered the "godfather" of African-American soldiers and he believed the army mistreated Black soldiers. He spent time trying to correct the war records because he believed Black soldiers never received just recognition for their contributions because their lives were not valued the same as whites. Clark-Adams adored her father; she also valued the Black veterans who came to protect Dick Rowland on the Tulsa courthouse steps the day of the massacre.[48]

Clark-Adams brought a unique approach to the Commission's work. When the historian Ellsworth constructed a team of scholars such as law professors, anthropologists, and historians for the Commission, Clark-Adams brought an "Afrocentric view of the massacre, emphasizing the primacy of Black sources—old black newspapers and journals, the NAACP files at

---

45. Gates, *Riot on Greenwood*, 32.
46. Gates, *Riot on Greenwood*, 32.
47. Gates, *Riot on Greenwood*, 33.
48. Gates, *Riot on Greenwood*, 258.

the Library of Congress, interviews with elderly blacks in Tulsa, Muskogee, and elsewhere."[49] Clark-Adams believed, as other African-Americans did, that the massacre in Tulsa was intentional and not an innocent explosion ignited by the elevator incident and newspaper articles.

The final theory that Clark-Adams argues surrounding the massacre suggested the KKK was involved. This is a probable theory because many of the prominent positions in the city were held by Klan members. In the book *Hidden History of Tulsa*, Gerkin explains the Tulsa Benevolent Association was the holding company for the knights of the KKK. "On January 5, 1922, they signed the articles of incorporation for the Tulsa Benevolent Association which officially established the Ku Klux Klan as a legal organization in the state of Oklahoma. The Tulsa KKK was born a mere six months after the Tulsa race riot."[50] The articles may have made the KKK official, but I believe they had committed and active people long before they signed the articles.

All five of the trustees of the Tulsa Benevolent Association were distinguished pillars within the city. Wash Hudson was the chairman and Rowland's attorney; he also served as a state legislator and founder of the Tulsa Law School. John Rogers was the secretary, a future dean of the University of Tulsa College of Law, and served as general counsel for McMan Oil company. Alf G. Heggem was a trustee, a well-respected mechanical engineer. C. W. Benedict was also a trustee, a banker. Shelley Rogers was another trustee, a private attorney.[51] This short list of officers demonstrates the powerful positions Klan members held in Tulsa. "A Tulsa Klan registry from 1928 to 1931, discovered in the mid-1990s, revealed that the secret order had attracted Tulsa's top officials."[52] The hegemony of white supremacy dominated African-Americans in Tulsa but the corruption that would have existed by KKK in these positions of power all over Tulsa made the injustice insurmountable.[53]

Unfortunately, neither Clark-Adams nor the other commissioners ever found any of the evidence to prove the massacre was planned. No whites were ever convicted for the terror and crimes committed in the Tulsa Massacre on May 31 and June 1, 1921.

I interviewed Ms. Hazel Smith Jones, the last Tulsa Massacre survivor who remained in Tulsa. Jones recalled she was very young when all the violence happened but said that growing up they all knew about the massacre.

49. Gates, *Riot on Greenwood*, 258.
50. Gerkin, *Hidden History of Tulsa*, 23.
51. Gerkin, *Hidden History of Tulsa*, 23.
52. Gerkin, *Hidden History of Tulsa*, 26.
53. See Appendix for KKK seals, brochures, etc.

Yet, it was something they never really talked about. She said people were afraid it might happen again and the KKK was always around so they never discussed it; they just went on with life.[54] Ms. Jones died on March 4, 2018.

I end this chapter with a tribute to the last survivor of the 1921 Tulsa Race Massacre, Dr. Olivia J. Hooker. She was a native of Tulsa, but living in White Plains, New York. Dr. Hooker was the first African American woman to enlist in the United States Coast Guard. She also had a Coast Guard facility named after her for distinguished service. Hooker received her PhD in psychology from the University of Rochester and taught at Fordham University in New York for twenty-three years. Over the years, she gave many interviews regarding the 1921 Tulsa Massacre.[55] Dr. Hooker transitioned on November 21, 2018 at the age of 103. The historical Vernon African Methodist Episcopal Church in Tulsa celebrated and remembered her roots at the church with a memorial on November 23, 2018. May Dr. Olivia J. Hooker rest in peace; we are thankful for her service and all the contributions she made to American society.

CHAPTER CONCLUSION

In this final chapter I presented the perspective of many white Tulsans through a sermon preached the following Sunday at Boston Avenue Methodist Church by their bishop. This sermon reveals great insight of white religious praxis regarding race relations in general and in Tulsa in particular. I also showed who was blamed for the massive destruction through the grand jury's report. In the remaining portion of the chapter, I highlighted the months and years that followed. African-Americans in Tulsa demonstrated extraordinary Black resilience, unexplainable except through their faith in God.

They united in traditional communalism to rebuild their churches, businesses, and community, which existed for many years following the massacre. Many of the churches still live today. Many years later, the John Hope Franklin Center built a reconciliation park. The Race Riot Commission pushed for the curriculum regarding the massacre to be taught in public schools. The Yoruba faith community has continued with annual events to remember their ancestors and history. After being silenced for almost eighty years, the history and pictures of Black Wall Street and the

---

54. Hazel Smith Jones, interview by author, November, 2016.

55. *AME Christian Recorder* is the oldest existing periodical published by African Americans in the United States, established in 1848 under the name of *Christian Herald*, and later changing the name to the *Christian Recorder* in 1852.

1921 Tulsa Massacre are on display at the Greenwood Cultural Center in Tulsa, and the National Museum of African American History and Culture in Washington, DC. In September of 2021, a new museum will open in Tulsa called Greenwood Rising. The centennial year will begin in January of 2021 celebrating Black Wall Street and commemorating the 1921 Tulsa Race Massacre all year.

CONCLUSION

This book discussed the historical sources of concrete racial division of this American nation, which is racism and the function of white supremacy, giving rise to white privilege. The American social, economic, and political ethos in this country was established by creating racial bias based upon the lie of Black inferiority and the elevation of whiteness as pure and good. This ideology is deeply embedded into the woven fabric of America's existence, cementing structural racism and oppressive interlocking systems, which are supported by the early precedence of laws, while recent legal and legislative claims suggest that race issues or racial bias no longer hold relevance in the present day. To the contrary, today white supremacy and its powers still reign. Within these social constructs Black bodies and lives are terrorized daily.

When Black Americans are being publicly lynched in the street by police and quasi-police brutality producing "violence to death" from Trayvon Martin to George Floyd and beyond, but legislative houses of government will not change the laws, Black people continue to experience racial terror sanctioned by the state apparatus. When one out of every three African Americans are disproportionately incarcerated or connected with the criminal justice system, Black people experience slavery, just by another name. When the coronavirus is killing the Black race at five to seven times the rate of white people because of pre-existing health issues, lack of access to medical intervention and insurance, limited income availability, and living conditions, African Americans are not living in an America with equality and justice for all.

It is my hope that critical review of this tragic event in American history might spawn innovative ways to combat structural racism. As a reader of this text, what contributions are you making to help dismantle racism? What organizations do you belong to that are working on racial and gender equality? As a preacher, do your sermons create a consciousness for racial, gender, sexual orientation, and economic equality? As a scholar, how does your scholarship, lectures, syllabi, books used in the classroom, preaching, and teaching advocate for a more just society? My prayer is that our unjust history will move us to a just society where all God's creation can be included.

Appendix

Tulsa's Black Businesses 1907–1923

Table D-1 Black Business Establishments and Business Persons in Tulsa as Listed in City Directories, 1907, 1909-1914, and 1916-1923

ESTABLISHMENTS	'07	'09	'10	'11	'12	'13	'14	'16	'17	'18	'19	'20	'21	'22	'23
Bath Parlors									1						
Billiard Halls			2	1	3	3	3	6	5	4	5	6	9	4	6
Cigars and tobacco						1	2					2			
Clothing, dry goods, racket, second-hand, music, furniture, paints and oils, shoes				1	1	3	1		2	2	2	1	2	2	2
Confectionary, soft drinks				1	2	1		1	3	4	5	7	16	2	4	6	6
Feed and grain											1	1	1	1	1
Furnished rooms, boarding and rooming houses	3		2	3	2	1	4	3	1	6	5	9	11		3
Garages, auto repair and filling stations							1	1	1			1	2		3
Grocers, meat markets	3	3	2	5	8	10	9	7	18	11	21	23	41	34	31
Hotels			1	1	2	1	1	1	1	2	2	4	5	4	9
Restaurants	1	1		5	3	13	17	16	11	17	21	20	30	29	19
Theaters						1			1	1	1	1	2	1	
Undertakers' parlors								1	2	2	2	2	1	2	1
Total	7	4	9	18	22	31	39	42	47	52	76	72	108	83	81

PROFESSIONALS	'07	'09	'10	'11	'12	'13	'14	'16	'17	'18	'19	'20	'21	'22	'23
Dentists				1	1	1	1	1	1	1	1	3	2	2	2
Druggists and medicine manufacturers		1			1	2	1	1	4	3	3		4	3	3
Jewelers											1	1	1	1	
Lawyers	1	1	3	4	2	1	5	6	4	4	5	4	3	4	6
Nurses												2		1	

APPENDIX

PROFESSIONALS	'07	'09	'10	'11	'12	'13	'14	'16	'17	'18	'19	'20	'21	'22	'23
Photographers											1	1	2	1	2
Physicians and surgeons	2	2	2	3	4	7	5	3	4	10	12	13	15	10	10
Real estate, loans, and insurance agents	2						1	2	4	4	3	6	6	4	5
Private detectives															1
Total	5	4	5	8	8	11	13	13	17	23	26	30	33	25	29

SKILLED CRAFTS PERSONS	'07	'09	'10	'11	'12	'13	'14	'16	'17	'18	'19	'20	'21	'22	'23
Bakers												1			
Blacksmiths		1					1	1	1	1	1	1		3	2
Contractors, carpenters, builders, house and sign painters								1		2	7	3	5	6	2
Dressmakers					1			1	1	3	4		2	1	1
Milliners															1
Plumbers										2			1^1		
Printers							1			1	1	1	1	1	
Shoemakers and shoe repairers			2	2		1	2	1	1	1	3	2	4	6	3
Tailors				1		1	2	3	2	5	6	7	10	6	9
Upholsterers													1	1	
Total		1	2	3	1	3	6	7	5	15	22	14	24	24	18

SERVICE WORKERS	'07	'09	'10	'11	'12	'13	'14	'16	'17	'18	'19	'20	'21	'22	'23
Barbers	1	2	2	4	3	3	5	7	6	10	11	9	12	11	13
Cleaners, hatters, dyers, and pressers			2	2	1	6	4	4	7	10	7	5	5	5	6
Hairdressers								1		3	3		3		1
Launderers							1		1			1		2	1
Shoe shiners							2	2	5	4	6	4	6	6	1
Total	1	2	4	6	4	9	12	14	19	27	27	19	26	24	22

Source: Data from Hannibal B. Johnson, *Black Wall Street: From Riot to Renaissance in Tulsa's Historic Greenwood District* (Fort Worth, TX: Eakin Press, 1998), 251–52.

Mabel Little House
Greenwood Cultural Center
Tulsa, Oklahoma

Source: Author's photograph taken in Tulsa, Oklahoma.

Vernon African Methodist Episcopal Church
(1 of 3 Historical Black Churches in Tulsa)

Source: Author's photograph taken in Tulsa, Oklahoma.

Mt. Zion Baptist Church
(2 of 3 Historical Black Churches in Tulsa)

Source: Author's photograph taken in Tulsa, Oklahoma.

Mt. Zion Baptist Church
(2 of 3 Historical Black Churches in Tulsa)

Source: Photograph taken in Tulsa, Oklahoma by author's granddaughter, Shatia Stephens.

First Baptist Church
(3 of 3 Historical Black Churches in Tulsa)

Source: Photograph is from the church's website. This is not the original church structure from 1921.

Mary Jones Parrish
The Events of the Tulsa Disaster: An Eye-witness Account of the 1921 Tulsa Race Riot

Source: Picture from *Events of the Tulsa Disaster*.

Mabel Little
Fire on Mount Zion

Source: Picture is from the cover *Fire On Mount Zion*.

Contrast of Black Tragedy and White Women

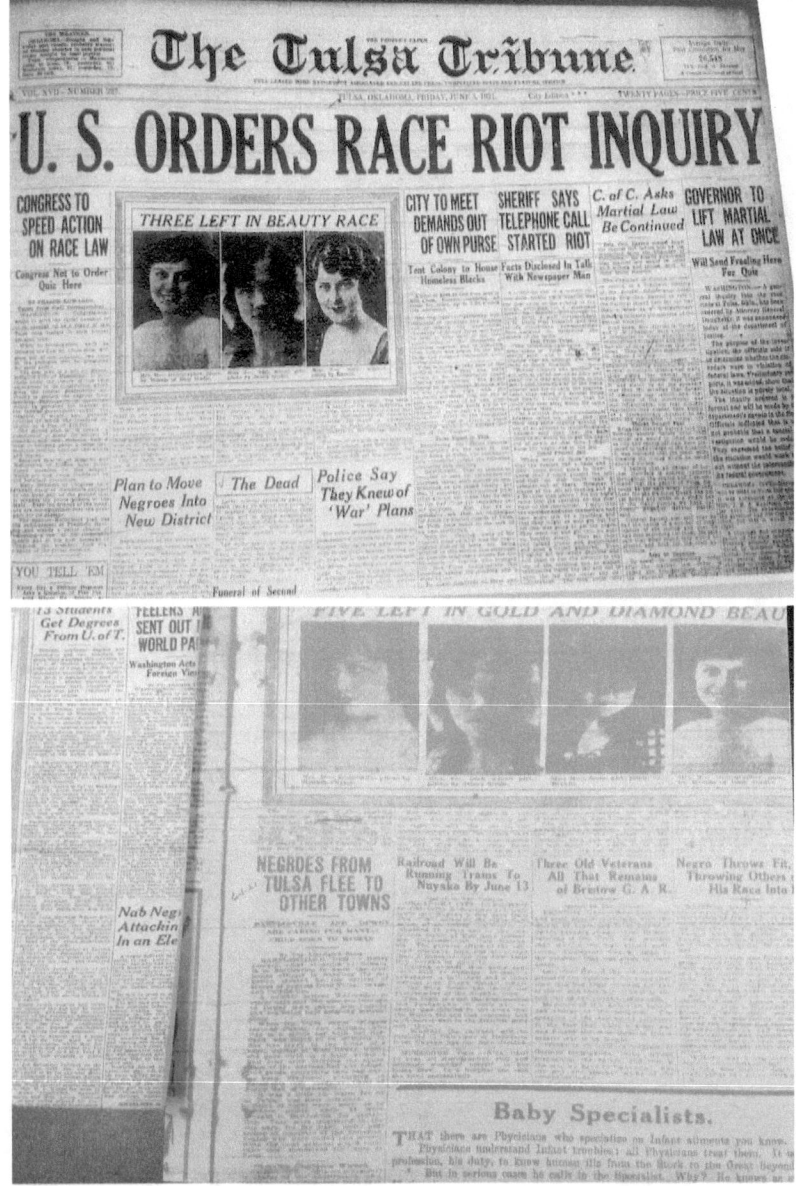

Source: Ruth Sigler Avery, Tulsa Race Riot archive. Oklahoma State University Library, Tulsa Campus.

KKK Brochures and Coin

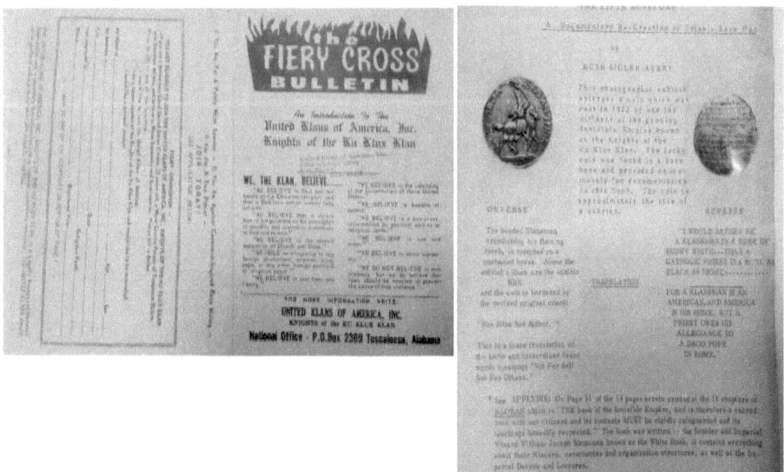

Source: Ruth Sigler Avery, Tulsa Race Riot archive. Oklahoma State University Library, Tulsa Campus.

Article on Tulsa Bombing

MARCH 13, 1983

Significa

By Irving Wallace, David Wallechinsky and Amy Wallace

Tulsa's "Negro Wall Street" after police broke up riot—and the neighborhood

First U.S. City To Be Bombed from the Air

In 1921, during one of the worst race riots in American history, Tulsa, Okla., became the first U.S. city to be bombed from the air. More than 75 persons—mostly blacks—were killed.

Before the riot, Tulsa blacks were so successful that their business district was called "The Negro's Wall Street." Envy bred hatred of the blacks, who accounted for a tenth of the segregated city's population of 100,000.

Then on May 30, 1921, a white female elevator operator accused Dick Rowland, a 19-year-old black who worked at a shoeshine stand, of attacking her. Though he denied the charge, Rowland was jailed. The Tulsa *Tribune* ran a sensational account of the incident the next day, and a white lynch mob soon gathered at the jail. Armed blacks, seeking to protect Rowland, also showed up. Someone fired a gun, and the riot was on.

Whites invaded the black district, burning, looting and killing. To break up the riot, the police commandeered private planes and dropped dynamite. Eventually, the National Guard was called in and martial law declared.

The police arrested more than 4000 blacks and interned them in three camps. All blacks were forced to carry green ID cards. And when Tulsa was zoned for a new railroad station, the tracks were routed through the black business district, thus destroying it.

Source: Ruth Sigler Avery, Tulsa Race Riot archive. Oklahoma State University Library, Tulsa Campus.

Aftermath Pictures

Source: Photographs from the Oklahoma Historical Society, Oklahoma City, Oklahoma.

Famous Historical Picture of Black Men Being Guarded After Massacre

Source: Danney Goble, *Tulsa! Biography of the American City*
(Tulsa, Oklahoma: Tulsa's Future, Inc., 1997), 122.

Historical Picture of Black Men Being Marched to Internment Camp

Tents African-Americans Lived in After the Massacre

Source: Oklahoma Historical Society, Oklahoma City, Oklahoma.

APPENDIX

Telegram from National Organization on Behalf of Black Tulsans

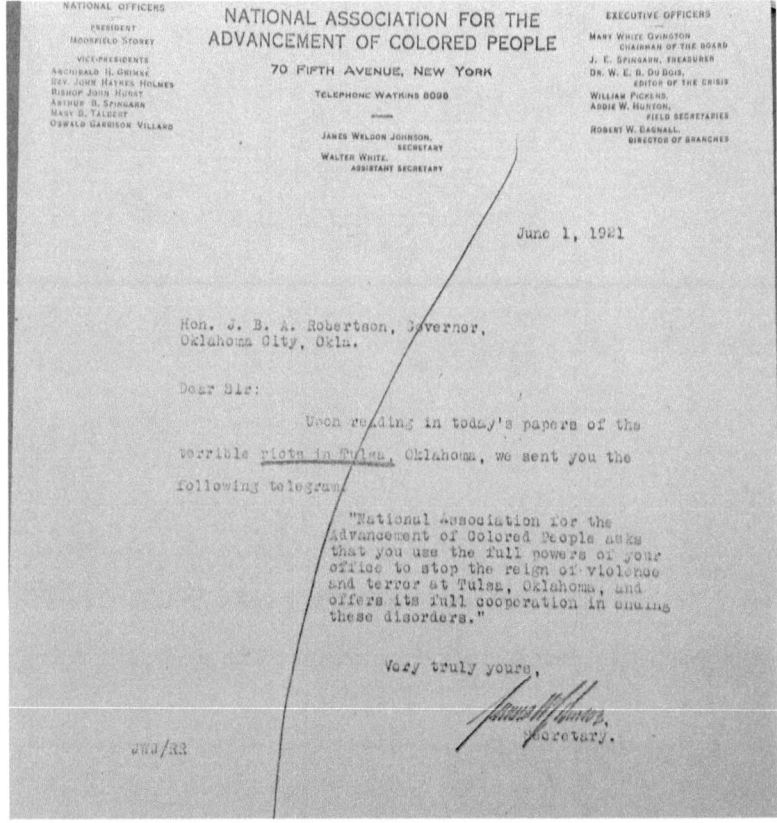

Source: Ruth Sigler Avery, Tulsa Race Riot archive. Oklahoma State University Library, Tulsa Campus.

APPENDIX

Telegram from National Organization on Behalf of Black Tulsans

> COLUMBUS KANS 10 AM JUNE 2 1921
>
> GOVERNOR J B A ROBERTSON
> STATE HOUSE OKLAHOMACITY OKLA
>
> HAVE YOU ANY CONTINGENT FUND YOU COULD USE TO AID INNOCENT COLORED MOTHERS AND BABIES OF THE COLORED PEOPLE OF TULSA SUFFERING ON ACCOUNT OF RIOT WHITE RUFFIANS IN ALL SECTIONS OF THE COUNTRY HAVE RESOLVED TO THIS SINCE THE EMANCIPATION PROCLAMATION NOT UNTIL THE OFFICERS OF THE LAW COMPEL ALL CLASSES TO OBEY SUCH AFFAIRS WILL CONTINUE WHITE PEOPLE COMMIT CRIMES COURT TRY THEM COLORED PEOPLES CHARGED CHARGED WITH CRIME MOB TRY THEM WE REGRET SUCH AFFAIRS SUCH REFLECT ON CHRISTIANITY
>
> NICK CHILES EDITOR TOPEKA PLAINSDEALERS PRESIDENT KANSAS OF THE DEFENCE SOCIETY TOPEKA KANSAS

Source: Ruth Sigler Avery, Tulsa Race Riot archive. Oklahoma State University Library, Tulsa Campus.

Letter Written by the Governor Blaming W. E. B. Du Bois

June 7, 1921.

Mr. D. F. Bailey,
Care Bailey & Collier,
Insurance Managers,
Dallas, Texas.

Dear Mr. Bailey:

I thank you for your letter, written from New York, relative to the Tulsa riot. I concur in your observations and conclusions. These riots are unfortunate affairs at all times and the less said about them the better for all concerned.

I have no sympathy with the so-called friends of the negro who live in the North and are always so anxious to give us advice on this and kindred subjects.

I appreciate what you have to say with reference to Mr. Du Bois. He is an agitator of the worst type and I have directed the Attorney General, who has charge of the investigation now under way at Tulsa, to inquire about his activities and if he is in any way responsible for this outrage, I am going to have him indicted and tried as any other criminal should be.

Again thanking you for the interest manifested, I remain

Respectfully,

Governor.

Source: Ruth Sigler Avery, Tulsa Race Riot archive. Oklahoma State University Library, Tulsa Campus.

APPENDIX

Monday, June 6, 1921—Sunday Sermon Referenced in Newspaper

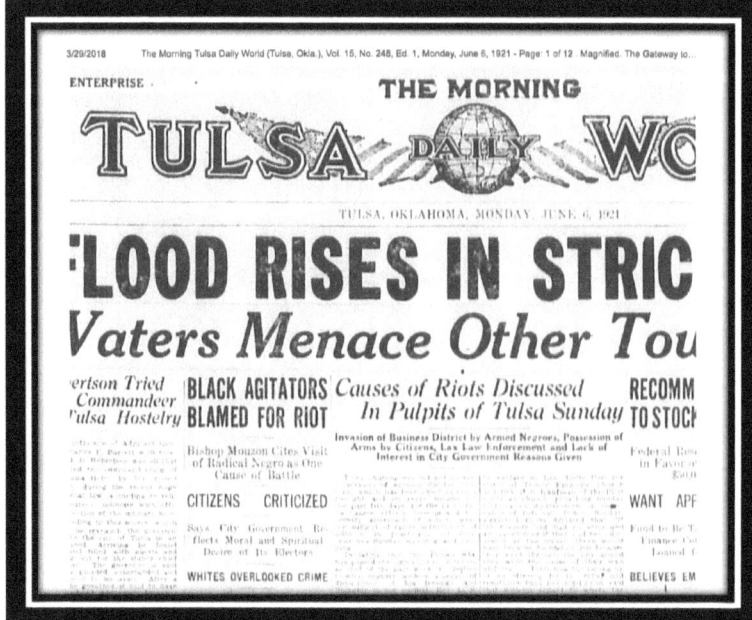

Source: University of Tulsa, McFarlin Library, Special Collections.

Actual Sermon by Bishop Mouzon
Tulsa World Newspaper

BLACK AGITATORS BLAMED FOR RIOT

Bishop Mouzon Cites Visit of Radical Negro as One Cause of Battle

CITIZENS CRITICIZED

Says City Government Reflects Moral and Spiritual Desire of Its Electors

WHITES OVERLOOKED CRIME

Allowed 'Little Africa' to Become Festering Sore and Wonder at Results

That the visit of Doctor DuBois, editor of a magazine for negroes, "The Crisis," to Tulsa some time ago may have had a bearing upon the trouble of the past week was intimated by Bishop Ed D. Mouzon in his sermon last night at the Boston Avenue Methodist church upon the subject, "The Tulsa Race Riot and the Teachings of Jesus Christ." The magazine published by DuBois was termed by the Bishop "dangerous," and DuBois himself characterized as the most vicious negro man in the country.

"I knew at the time that DuBois was here," declared the Bishop, "and I very keenly regret now, in view of the events of the past week, that I did not take advantage of that knowledge, and inquire into the purpose of his visit."

It was reported to him, stated the Bishop, that on the night of the riot the negroes went to the office of the Tulsa Star and there secured guns and ammunition.

"Where," asked the speaker, "did they get those guns and that ammunition? What business had they with them? Agitators, be they black or white, can accomplish nothing but serious harm, and social problems of city, state or country are never settled in that way."

Whites in Defense of Home.

"The mob," declared the Bishop, "is always wrong. It is never to be apologized for, never defended; it is ruinous to civilization. It is barbarous. As to what happened after the streets were filled with armed negroes, I do not know. I do not know who is to blame for what happened, but if it is true, that the city and county officials were powerless to stop that which threatened, if it is true that there was nothing done at a time when it was imperative that something be done, if it is true that our wives, our children and the people of Tulsa were threatened with being at the mercy of armed negroes, then the white man who got his gun and went out in defense with it did the only thing that is decent white man could have done. It is true that somebody blundered. Civilization broke down in Tulsa. I do not attempt to place the blame, the mob spirit broke and hell was let loose. Then things happened that were on a footing with what the Germans did in Belgium, what the Turks did in Armenia, what the Bolsheviks did in Russia. Tulsa has been disgraced. I am ashamed. It will take Tulsa a long, long time to get over that which has been done here. Papers the country over have carried in big headlines the happenings of that night.

Citizenship Blamed.

"I repeat," said the bishop, who was frequently interrupted by spontaneous bursts of applause, "that I make no attempt to place the blame for the disgraceful happenings of that night. It is easy to say, 'the city officials are to blame. The administration broke down.' But let me tell you, that if the blunder was made by the city officials, if the fault was the administration's, then you are equally to blame, for you yourselves are your city government; your city government is the exponent of your moral and civic life. Don't blame your city officials. Blame yourself.

"Little Africa," continued the Bishop, "was one of the blackest spots in Oklahoma. I am amazed at the open violation of law practiced there, that there were all sorts of 'joints' operating there. Of course the officers of the law knew all about it—but that was Little Africa! Certainly everything bad was going on there—but that was Little Africa! We must raise the standard of the colored race if we would solve the problem that is not only the problem of Tulsa just now, but of other cities as well, and you can't do that until we raise our own standards. A great many of us have not done that.

Paid No Attention to Crime.

"There has been petty pilfering going on in the kitchens of some of you women, and you have allowed it for fear of losing your servants. There has been immorality in your servants' quarters, and you have ignored it. You have known what is going on in Little Africa, and you didn't care. That is not the Christian attitude, and it is harmful to the world going to help uplift the negro race. You women should take an interest in negro women, their children and their problems; business men should confer with negro business men from time to time—a kind of clearing house, and the white ministers of this city ought to hold conferences with the negro ministers. Are we Christians or are we not? The dare to do the Christian thing for the betterment of the colored race.

No Racial Equality.

"There is one thing," said the Bishop, "upon which I should like to make myself perfectly clear. That is racial equality. There never has been and there never will be such a thing. It is divine ordained. This is something that the negroes should be told very plainly. Steps toward social equality are the worst possible thing for the negro man and the white thing. There should be separate hotels, schools, churches, for the negro. At the same time, we must have the Christian attitude toward the black man; he is made by the same creator, he is subject to the same Christian laws; he is our brother in Christ. I believe firmly in the right kind of education for the negroes, and I believe that the right kind of leader, such as Booker T. Washington, and not DuBois, can do more than anyone else for the

Source: University of Tulsa, McFarlin Library, Special Collections.

Law Office Set-up in Tent to Fight Legally after the Massacre

Source: Danney Goble, *Tulsa! Biography of the American City* (Tulsa, Oklahoma: Tulsa's Future, Inc., 1997), 128.

Freedmen and Freedwomen's Court Victory

TULSA WORLD

FRIDAY, SEPTEMBER 1, 2017 FORECAST: MOSTLY SUNNY, HIGH: 87, LOW 65. A12 | TULSAWOF

Cherokees won't appeal court ruling on freedmen

By Randy Krehbiel
Tulsa World

The Cherokee Nation of Oklahoma said Thursday it will not appeal a federal court decision that descendants of tribal freedmen must be granted tribal membership.

The court's decision, and the Cherokees' decision not to appeal it, settles a long-standing rift dating back to the recreation of Oklahoma tribal governments in the 1970s.

"While the U.S. District Court ruled against the Cherokee Nation, I do not see it as a defeat," Cherokee

» See Freedmen, page A3

Freedmen: Tribe won't appeal

» *From page A1*

Nation Attorney General Todd Hembree said in a written statement. "I see this as an opportunity to resolve the freedmen citizenship issue and allow the Cherokee Nation to move beyond this dispute."

On Wednesday, Senior Judge Thomas Hogan of the U.S. District Court for the District of Columbia ruled the Cherokee freedmen have the same rights to tribal citizenship as "native Cherokees" under an 1866 treaty.

"When Chief (Bill John) Baker ran in 2011, and again when he was re-elected, he said he wanted to bring closure to this issue," said Marilyn Vann, president of the Descendants of Freedmen Association and one of the litigants in the case.

"An appeal would not have brought closure."

It was not immediately clear how many people may be affected by the ruling, but Vann noted that about 12 percent of tribe members were freedmen in 1890. A similar percentage applied to the Cherokee Nation's 350,000 current members would yield around

Hembree

40,000 freedmen descendants.

In his 78-page opinion, Hogan determined that the 1866 treaty preempted the Cherokee constitution and the tribe's absolute right to determine its membership.

In the 1970s, when the current Cherokee Nation government was organized after nearly 70 years of dormancy, freedmen were included as full citizens. In the 1980s, however, tribal membership was restricted to descendants of "Cherokees by blood" listed on the 1890s Dawes Rolls.

In 2007, after tribal courts readmitted freedmen descendants, a constitutional amendment was adopted to restrict citizenship.

Vann said she believes the freedmen descendants were originally squeezed out because they wanted to "vote for somebody other than the chief" at that time. Thursday's news that the Cherokee Nation would not appeal, she said, filled her with "Ela-

tion. Gratitude to God. Thankfulness to those who helped get us to this point. It took a lot of teamwork."

The court's decision may also have implications for the Choctaw, Chickasaw, Creek and Seminole tribal governments, all of whom, like the Cherokees, owned slaves who became freedmen after the Civil War.

The Creeks and Seminoles signed treaties similar to the Cherokees' in 1866, but the Choctawa did not recognize their freedmen as citizens until 1883, and the Chickasaws never have.

Hembree said his overarching goal in the litigation had been to clarify the freedmen descendants' status, and that Hogan's ruling did that.

"My office will work tirelessly to thoroughly review this decision and its legal ramifications," Hembree said, "and will move forward in a way that best serves the interests of the Cherokee Nation and its citizens, including Freedmen descendants."

Randy Krehbiel
918-581-8365
randy.krehbiel
@tulsaworld.com
Twitter: @rkrehbiel

Source: *Tulsa World* newspaper.

APPENDIX

Yoruba Memorial and March
Sample Flyer Advertisement for Remembrance

17th Annual

BLACK WALL STREET MEMORIAL MARCH

Join us on Memorial Day Weekend to honor the legacy, remember the tragedy and continue to promote justice for the ancestors of Tulsa's Historic Greenwood District.

SATURDAY MAY 24, 2014
CONFERENCE SCHEDULE

- **10:30** Keynote Speaker Dr. Umar Ifatunde Johnson
- **12:30** Youth Power Lunch/Book Signing for Dr. Umar Johnson
- **2:00** The State of Black Tulsa Panel Discussion
  Moderated discussion wtih Community Elders

SUNDAY MAY 25, 2014
MEMORIAL MARCH

Keynote Speaker Dr. Umar Ifatunde Johnson
Vernon Chapel A.M.E. Church
311 N Greenwood Ave, Tulsa, OK
Starts at 5:00p.m.

FOR MORE INFORMATION

Facebook: Black Wall Street Memorial March
Phone: 918-716-6170
Email: blackwallstreetmemorial@gmail.com

Hosted By
EGBE EGUN FE WA & THE BLACK WALL STREET MEMORIAL COMMITTEE

Source: Chief Egunwale Amusan, organizer of the annual Black Wall Street Remembrance events.

APPENDIX

1921 Black Wall Street Memorial
(Located at the Greenwood Cultural Society)

Source: Author's photograph taken at the Greenwood Cultural Center, Tulsa, Oklahoma.

Unpaid Financial Claims

Source: Author's photograph taken at the Greenwood Cultural Center, Tulsa, Oklahoma.

Tulsa's Greenwood Street Today
(OSU and Langston University's Tulsa Campus)

Source: Author's photograph, Tulsa, Oklahoma.

Front Campus Entrance

Source: Author's photograph, OSU and Langston University campus, Tulsa, Oklahoma.

Bibliography

Archaeology. "The Tulsa Race Riot." https://archive.archaeology.org/online/features/massacre/tulsa.html.

Associated Press. "Senate Apologizes for Not Passing Anti-Lynching Bill." Fox News. https://www.foxnews.com/story/senate-apologizes-for-not-passing-anti-lynching-laws.

Berger, Peter L., and Thomas Luckmann. *Social Construction of Reality: A Treatise in the Sociology of Knowledge*. New York: DoubleDay, 1966.

"Black Agitators Blamed for Riot." *Tulsa Daily World*, June 6, 1921 (morning ed.).

Butler, Lee H., Jr. *Liberating Our Dignity, Saving Our Souls*. St. Louis: Chalice, 2006.

———. "Lynching: A Post Traumatic Stressor in a Protracted Traumatic World." *Sacred Spaces: The E-Journal of the American Association of Pastoral Counselors* 4 (2012) 8–34.

Callahan, Allen Dwight. *The Talking Book: African Americans and the Bible*. New Haven, CT: Yale University Press, 2006.

Cannon, Katie Geneva. *Katie's Canon: Womanism and the Soul of the Black Community*. New York: Continuum, 1995.

———. *Black Womanist Ethics*. Atlanta: Scholars, 1988.

Cannon, Katie G., Emile M. Townes, and Angela D. Sims, eds. *Womanist Theological Ethics: A Reader*. 1st ed. Louisville, KY: Westminster John Knox, 2011.

Chang, David A. *The Color of Land: Race, Nation, and the Politics of Landownership in Oklahoma 1832–1929*. Chapel Hill, NC: The University of North Carolina Press, 2010.

Clio. https://theclio.com/web/entry?id=11051.

Cleage, Albert B., Jr. *Black Christian Nationalism: New Direction for the Black Church*. New York: William Morrow & Company, 1972.

Collier-Thomas, Bettye. *Jesus, Jobs, and Justice: African American Women and Religion*. New York: Alfred A. Knopf, 2010.

Cone, James H. *The Cross and the Lynching Tree*. Maryknoll, NY: Orbis, 2011.

———. *Martin & Malcolm & America: A Dream or a Nightmare*. Maryknoll, NY: Orbis, 1991.

Cormack, Mike. *Ideology*. London: B T Batford Ltd, 1992.

Crenshaw, Kimberle, Neil Gotanda, Gary Peller, and Kendall Thomas. *Critical Race Theory: The Key Writings that Formed the Movement*. New York: The New Press, 1995.

DeWitty, Dorothy Moses. *Tulsa: Tale of Two Cities*. Langston, OK: Langston University, 1989.

Dodson, Jualynne E. *Engendering Church: Women, Power, and the AME Church*. Lanham, MD: Rowman & Littlefield, 2002.

Du Bois, W. E. B. *The Souls of Black Folk*. New York: Penguin, 1989.

———. "Oklahoma Riot Victims' Relief and Defense Fund." *The Crisis*, July 2, 1921, 114.

———. "The Tulsa Race Riots." *The Crisis*, July 2, 1921, 114–16.

Ellsworth, Scott. *Death in a Promised Land: The Tulsa Race Riot of 1921*. Baton Rouge, LA: Louisiana State University Press, 1982.

Epstein, Dena J. *Sinful Tunes and Spirituals: Black Folk Music to the Civil War*. Urbana, IL: University of Illinois Press, 1977.

Equal Justice Initiative. *Lynching in America: Confronting the Legacy of Racial Terror*. Montgomery, AL: Equal Justice Initiative, 2015.

Fanon, Frantz. *The Wretched of The Earth*. New York: Grove, 2004.

Floyd-Thomas, Stacey M. *Mining the Motherlode: Methods in Womanist Ethics*. Cleveland, OH: Pilgrim, 2006.

Forty-ninth General Conference. *The Doctrine and Discipline of the African Methodist Episcopal Church*. Nashville: AMEC House, 2012.

Frazier, E. Franklin. *Negro Church in America*. New York: Schocken, 1974.

Gates, Eddie Faye. *Riot on Greenwood: The Total Destruction of Black Wall Street, 1921*. Fort Worth, TX: Eakin, 2003.

Gerkin, Steve. *Hidden History of Tulsa*. Charleston, SC: The History, 2014.

Giddings, Paula J. *IDA: A Sword Among Lions*. New York: Amistad, 2008.

Glaude, Eddie S., Jr. *African American Religion: A Very Short Introduction*. New York: Oxford University Press, 2014.

Goble, Danney. *Tulsa! Biography of the American City*. Tulsa: Tulsa's Future, 1997.

Grant, Jacquelyn. *White Women's Christ And Black Women's Jesus: Feminist Christology and Womanist Response*. Atlanta: Scholars, 1989.

"Greenwood Cultural Center." http://www.greenwoodculturalcenter.com/mabel-b-little-heritage-house.

Epstein, Dena J. *Sinful Tunes and Spirituals: Black Folk Music to the Civil War*. Chicago: University of Illinois Press, 1977.

Higginbotham, Evelyn Brooks. *Righteous Discontent: The Women's Movement in the Black Baptist Church 1880–1920*. Cambridge, MA: Harvard University Press, 1993.

Higginbotham, A. Leon, Jr. *In the Matter of Color: Race and The American Legal Process*. New York: Oxford University Press, 1978.

Hirsch, James S. *Riot and Remembrance: The Tulsa Race War and Its Legacy*. New York: Houghton Mifflin Company, 2002.

Hoberock, Barbara. "Senate passes bill requiring teaching of Tulsa Race Riot history." *Tulsa World*, March 16, 2012. http://www.tulsaworld.com/news/government/senate-passes-bill-requiring-teaching-of-tulsa-race-riot-history/article_a50233b4-64b8-5520-ab81-6472c493a2c1.html.

Hopkins, Dwight N. *Being Human: Race, Culture, and Religion*. Minneapolis: Fortress, 2005.

Horan, Marian. "How Did Black Women in the NAACP Promote the Dyer Anti-Lynching Bill, 1918–1923?" Women and Social Movements in United States, 1600–2000. http://womhist.alexanderstreet.com/index.html.

Hughes, Richard. *Myths America Lives By.* Chicago: University of Illinois Press, 2003.
Jacques, Michele. "Testimony as Embodiment: Telling the Truth and Shaming the Devil." *Journal of the Interdenominational Theological Center* 22.2 (Spring 1995) 129–45.
Jager, Steven J. "Dyer Anti-Lynching Bill (1922)." BlackPast. http://www.blackpast.org/aah/dyer-anti-lynching-bill-1922.
John Hope Franklin Center for Reconciliation. "John Hope Franklin Reconciliation Park." https://www.jhfcenter.org/reconciliation-park.
Jones, F. "1921 Tulsa Race Riot curriculum to be taught statewide." *The Oklahoma Eagle Newswire*, February 21, 2018. http://www.theoklahomaeagle.net/home/2018/02/21/senator-kevin-matthews-unveils-tulsa-1921-race-riot-statewide-curriculum/.
Johnson, Hannibal B. *Apartheid in Indian Country? Seeing Red Over Black Disenfranchisement.* Fort Worth, TX: Eakin, 2012.
———. *Black Wall Street: From Riot to Renaissance in Tulsa's Historic Greenwood District.* Fort Worth, TX: Eakin, 1998.
Jones Parrish, Mary E. *Events of the Tulsa Disaster.* Tulsa: John Hope Franklin Center for Reconciliation, 2009.
Katz, William Loren. *The Black West.* Seattle, WA: Open Hand, 1987.
———. *Black Women of The Old West.* New York: Atheneum Books for Young Readers, 1995.
Kelsey, George D. *Racism and the Christian Understanding of Man.* New York: Charles Scribner's Sons, 1965.
Kovel, Joel. *White Racism: A Psychohistory.* New York: Columbia University Press, 1970.
Krehbiel, Randy. "Cherokees won't appeal court ruling on freedmen." *Tulsa World*, September 1, 2017 (morning ed.).
Lincoln, C. Eric, and Lawrence H. Mamiya. *The Black Church in the African American Experience.* Durham, NC: Duke University Press, 1990.
Little, Mabel B., Nathan Hare, and Julia Hare. *Fire on Mount Zion: My Life and History as a Black Woman in America.* Langston, OK: Melvin B. Tolson Black Heritage Center, 1990.
Loden, Abby. "Carrollton Courthouse Massacre." Approach History. Accessed November 7, 2017. https://approachhistory.wordpress.com/2013/07/22/carrollton-courthouse-massacre.
Mays, Benjamin Elijah. *The Negro's God: As Reflected in His Literature.* Boston: Chapman & Grimes, 1938.
Mays, Benjamin Elijah, and Joseph Williamson Nicholson. *Negro's Church.* New York: Arno, 1969.
Martin, Clarice J. "Biblical Theodicy and Black Women's Spiritual Autobiography." In *A Troubling in My Soul: Womanist Perspectives on Evil & Suffering*, edited by Emilie M. Townes, 13–36. Maryknoll, NY: Orbis, 1993.
National Association for the Advancement of Colored People. *Thirty Years of Lynching in the United States 1889–1918.* New York: Arno, 1969.
Nevels, Cynthia Skove. *Lynching to Belong: Claiming Whiteness Through Racial Violence.* College Station, TX: Texas A&M University Press, 2007.
Painter, Nell Irvin. *History of White People.* New York: W. W. Norton & Company, 2010.
Patterson, Orlando. *Rituals of Blood: Consequences of Slavery in Two American Centuries.* New York: Basic Civitas, 1998.

Perdue, Theda, and Michael D. Green. *North American Indians: A Very Short Introduction*. New York: Oxford, 2010.
Raboteau, Albert J. *African-American Religion*. New York: Oxford University Press, 1999.
———. *Slave Religion: The "Invisible Institution" in the Antebellum South*. New York: Oxford University Press, 2004.
Riley, Peggy. "Women of Great Falls African Methodist Episcopal Church, 1870–1910." In *African-American Women Confront the West, 1600–2000*, edited by Quintard Taylor and Shirley Ann Wilson Moore, 122–39. Norman, OK: University of Oklahoma Press, 2008.
Ross, Don. *A Century of African-American Experience; Greenwood: Ruins, Resilience and Renaissance*. Unpublished, 2003.
Stafford, Roy E. "Jim Crow Laws." *Daily Oklahoman*, 1907. http://www.dougloudenback.com/maps/jimcrowhistory.htm.
Taylor, Quintard. *In Search of the Racial Frontier: African Americans in the American West 1528–1990*. New York: W. W. Norton & Company, 1998.
Taylor, Quintard, and Shirley Ann Wilson Moore, eds. *African-American Women Confront the West 1600–2000*. Norman, OK: University of Oklahoma Press, 2003.
Terrell, JoAnne Marie. *Power in the Blood? The Cross in the African-American Experience*. Eugene, OR: Wipf and Stock, 2005.
Tolnay, Stewart E., and E. M. Beck. *A Festival of Violence: An Analysis of Southern Lynchings, 1882–1930*. Chicago: University of Illinois Press, 1995.
Tolson, Arthur L. *Black Oklahomans, a History: 1541–1972*. New Orleans: Edwards Printing, 1966.
Townes, Emilie M. *In a Blaze of Glory: Womanist Spirituality as Social Witness*. Nashville: Abingdon, 1995.
———. *Womanist Ethics and the Cultural Production of Evil*. New York: Palgrave MacMillan, 2006.
———. *Womanist Justice, Womanist Hope*. Atlanta: Scholars, 1993.
———. "Joy Came in the Morning Risking Death for Resurrection: Confronting the Evil of Social Sin and Socially Sinful Structures." In *A Troubling in My Soul: Womanist Perspectives on Evil and Suffering*, edited by Emilie M. Townes, 48–64. Maryknoll, NY: Orbis, 2002.
Uncrowned Community Builders. "Judith Horton." http://www.uncrownedcommunitybuilders.com/person/judith-horton.
———. "Eddie Faye Gates." Accessed August 27, 2018. http://www.uncrownedcommunitybuilders.com/person/eddie-faye-gates.
Walker, Alice. *In Search of Our Mothers' Gardens: Womanist Prose*. San Diego: Harcourt Brace Jovanovich, 1983.
Ward, Rick. "The Carroll County Courthouse Massacre, 1886: A Cold Case File." Mississippi History Now. http://mshistorynow.mdah.state.ms.us/articles/381/the-carroll-county-courthouse-massacre-1886-a-cold-case-file&gt.
Wells, Ida B. *Crusade for Justice: The Autobiography of Ida B. Wells*. Edited by Alfreda M. Duster. Chicago: The University of Chicago Press, 1970.
Wells-Barnett, Ida B. *Southern Horrors: Lynch Law in All Its Phases*. New York: The New York Age Print, 1892.
Wesley, Charles Harris. *History of the National Association of Colored Women's Club: A Legacy of Service*. Washington, DC: Mercury, 1984.

White, Deborah Gray. *Too Heavy a Load: Black Women in Defense of Themselves 1894–1994*. New York: W. W. Norton & Company, 1999.

White, Walter. *Rope and Faggot: A Biography of Judge Lynch*. Notre Dame, IN: University of Notre Dame Press, 2001.

White, Walter F. "The Eruption of Tulsa." AMDOCS: Documents for the Study of American History. http://www.vlib.us/amdocs/texts/tulsa.html.

Williams, Delores S. *Sisters in the Wilderness: The Challenge of Womanist God-Talk*. Maryknoll, NY: Orbis, 1993.

Wilmore, Gayraud S. *Black Religion and Black Radicalism*. Maryknoll, NY: Orbis, 1983.

Wilson, Linda D. "Guthrie." Oklahoma Historical Society. http://www.okhistory.org/publications/enc/entry.php?entry=GU003.

www.ingramcontent.com/pod-product-compliance
Lightning Source LLC
Chambersburg PA
CBHW022007220426
43663CB00007B/994